Hurting Kids

Hurting Kids

What Incarcerated Youth Are Teaching Me about
Whiteness, Compassion, Accountability, and Healing

MICHELLE MARY LELWICA

CASCADE *Books* • Eugene, Oregon

HURTING KIDS
What Incarcerated Youth Are Teaching Me about Whiteness, Compassion, Accountability, and Healing

Copyright © 2024 Michelle Mary Lelwica. All rights reserved. Except for brief quotations in critical publications or reviews, no part of this book may be reproduced in any manner without prior written permission from the publisher. Write: Permissions, Wipf and Stock Publishers, 199 W. 8th Ave., Suite 3, Eugene, OR 97401.

Cascade Books
An Imprint of Wipf and Stock Publishers
199 W. 8th Ave., Suite 3
Eugene, OR 97401

www.wipfandstock.com

PAPERBACK ISBN: 978-1-6667-3553-6
HARDCOVER ISBN: 978-1-6667-9270-6
EBOOK ISBN: 978-1-6667-9271-3

Cataloguing-in-Publication data:

Names: Lelwica, Michelle Mary, author.

Title: Hurting kids : what incarcerated youth are teaching me about whiteness, compassion, accountability, and healing / Michelle Mary Lelwica.

Description: Eugene, OR: Cascade Books, 2024 | Includes bibliographical references.

Identifiers: ISBN 978-1-6667-3553-6 (paperback) | ISBN 978-1-6667-9270-6 (hardcover) | ISBN 978-1-6667-9271-3 (ebook)

Subjects: LCSH: Restorative justice—United States. | Criminal justice, Administration of—United States. | Family violence—Religious aspects—Christianity. | Post-traumatic stress disorder in children—Treatment.

Classification: HV8688 L45 2024 (paperback) | HV8688 (ebook)

VERSION NUMBER 080924

To the youth who have participated in the mindfulness group

Each of us is more than the worst thing we've ever done.
—Bryan Stevenson

Contents

Preface | xi
Acknowledgments | xv

    Introduction | 1
1. The Seventh Angel | 11
2. Divine Humanity | 16
3. "People with Privilege Need to Hear Our Stories" | 18

Part I: Whiteness

4. "Don't You Think White People Need to Learn about Race?" | 25
5. What Is "Whiteness"? | 27
6. What Does Whiteness Look Like? | 30
7. "It's *Weird* to Stare into Someone's Eyes" | 32
8. "How Come You're Not Afraid of Us?" | 34
9. "Hey, No Disrespect to Your Silver Spoon" | 38
10. "If There's a God, He's an Asshole" | 41
11. "I Was Born a Criminal" | 43
12. "Because I'm a *Bad* Kid" | 46
13. "I Want to Know What Really Happened" | 48
14. "I Did Not Know How to Feel" | 52
15. "Same Old, Same Old" | 55
16. "Not All Black Kids Are the Same" | 59
17. "A Shitty Hand of Cards" | 62
18. "I'd Give Anything to Be Able to Decide What to Have for Breakfast" | 64

19 "I Have All the Time in the World" | 66
20 "My Bad, My Bad" | 69
21 "Showing Your True Feelings Made You Look Weak" | 73
22 "I Hope My Daughter Grows Up to Be a Lesbian" | 77
23 "I Come from Violence" | 79
24 "Hood Dreaming" | 81
25 "I Want to Be Sure People Understand Me" | 84

Part II: Compassion

26 The Creative Power of Life | 89
27 What Is Compassion? | 91
28 "Dead or in Jail" | 93
29 "Deep Streets" | 95
30 "Bro" | 100
31 "When Kids Don't Have a Chance to Be Kids When They're Kids" | 103
32 "The Reason Kids Like Us Do Drugs . . ." | 107
33 "Houses of Refuge" | 109
34 "Does Punishment Work?" | 112
35 "What Keeps Me up at Night" | 115
36 "You Have to Believe in Jesus or You're Going to Hell" | 118
37 "I'm Afraid of God" | 121
38 "I Would Talk about . . ." | 124
39 "I Already Died Once" | 126
40 "All the Love in My Heart Went Out of Me That Day" | 128
41 "Grievid" | 131
42 "We Were Not Violent Girls. We Were Girls Who Were Hurting" | 134
43 "When Someone Is Beating up Your Mom" | 138
44 "That's When I Knew That My Brother Was Dead Too" | 141
45 "I Want to Give Him, Just Like the Rest of My Family, the World" | 143

Part III: Accountability

46 "A Cold-Blooded Killer" | 147

47 What Does It Mean to Be Accountable? | 149

48 "The Wages of Sin Is Death" | 152

49 "That's Two Years of My Life Down the Drain" | 155

50 "J'ai Dû M'Fuir de Chez Moi" | 158

51 "I Wasn't Even Holding the Gun" | 161

52 "Monster" | 164

53 "My Brother Is Six Feet in the Ground" | 166

54 "Bless Me, Father, for I Have Sinned" | 168

55 "Sleeping Bags of Self-Pity" | 172

56 "Nobody Asked Me *Why* I Did What I Did" | 174

57 "When I Was in the Sixth Grade, I Got into a Fight at School" | 176

58 "I'm Not Going to Apologize for Things I'm Not Sorry For" | 181

59 "Out There, It's 'Live by the Gun, Die by the Gun'" | 184

60 "I Only Have Myself to Blame" | 187

61 "We Are All Criminals" | 191

62 "The Belief That I Won't Get Caught" | 194

Part IV: Healing

63 "I Don't Know Why I Keep Ending Up in Jail" | 201

64 What Does Healing Mean? | 203

65 "The Kinship of Heaven" | 206

66 "He Was Really Thirsty!" | 208

67 "Being on the Run" | 211

68 "It's Been a Hard Week" | 214

69 "You Go to the Margins" | 217

70 The Hula Dance | 220

71 "Because It Calms Our Amygdala" | 223

72 "What Have You Been Struggling with Lately?" | 226

73 "If I Can't Learn to Control My Temper . . ." | 229

74 "I Was Thinking That I Probably Need Forgiveness from You" | 233

75 "I'm Thankful to Be Here and Not under the Ground in the Cemetery" | 237

76 "Those Who Cannot Be Redeemed" | 240

77 "All of Them Have Some Type of Involvement with the Juvenile Justice System" | 242

78 "You Can't Be Happy If You Have PTSD" | 245

79 "Which Wolf Will You Feed?" | 247

80 "No One Ever Taught Me How to Love Myself" | 250

81 "When We Were Dancing" | 252

82 "It's a Huge Slap in the Face to Enjoy the Little Things" | 255

83 "I'd Create a Program for Kids like Me" | 257

84 "You Can't Trust Anyone until You Trust Yourself" | 260

85 "I Am Enough. This Is Enough" | 263

Conclusion: "LOVE ME" | 266

Bibliography | 269

Preface

FOR MORE THAN THIRTY years, I've been researching, writing, and talking about the religious underpinnings and spiritual dimensions of women's conflicted relationships with their bodies. In different ways, my first three books expose the patriarchal religious norms and narratives that echo in the beliefs, rituals, images, and moral codes that encourage women to find "salvation" by punishing and perfecting our supposedly shameful, wayward flesh.

This previous work may seem far removed from the experiences of incarcerated youth. And yet, my studies in both areas are connected by the insight that secular culture is never purely secular. If you look closely, you can see the "afterlife" of religion,[1] Christianity in particular, on virtually every institution and ideology in America. *Hurting Kids* examines the ambiguous, often hidden, yet powerful influence of certain Christian theologies on our youth justice system, the lives of teens caught up in that system, Americans' conflicting beliefs about teenage wrongdoing, and the presumed innocence of those of us with privilege.

My advocacy for a compassionate approach to juvenile justice stems from my conversations with incarcerated youth, whom I've been visiting since January 2018. By sharing snippets of these conversations, I encourage readers who may never set foot in a juvenile prison or detention center to understand and care about the complicated humanity of a population of teenagers who are often deemed not only "delinquent," but dispensable. I want you to see that whatever harm they've inflicted on others is rooted in the unmetabolized hurt they have somehow managed to survive. Invariably, such hurt happened to them *before* they ever picked up a gun, stole a car, sold or used drugs, assaulted someone, attempted murder, or worse. Their suffering is rooted in the historical traumas and systemic injustices from which nonincarcerated people with privilege—people like me—still

---

1. Jakobsen and Pellegrini, *Love the Sin*, 21.

benefit. I hope this book prompts readers to consider how the lives of youth in confinement relate to our own, reflect on what we owe them, and act accordingly.

As much as I want you, the reader, to hear from the youth I've met, I need to protect their identities. To this end, I never use their real names and have changed some details of their stories to enhance confidentiality.

Though *Hurting Kids* incorporates scholarship on the youth justice system, historical perspectives, and theological analysis, my research is a classic case of "me-search." My desire to better understand my subject doubles as an effort to better understand myself. Thus, this book is as much about me—and my own journey of ignorance seeking understanding—as it is about the kids I visit. By personalizing my analysis, I'm interested in engaging a more than academic audience, especially White Christians, in the hopes that the book prompts them to examine their assumptions about the nature of divine power and justice, as well as sin, penance, and salvation, and to consider the implications of those beliefs for the lives of incarcerated teens.

By identifying White people as my intended audience, I'm not saying that people of color can't or shouldn't read this book. But I doubt they need to. The vast majority already know about the catastrophic consequences of systemic oppression, including the disproportionate number of teenagers of color entangled in America's youth justice system. In 2019, compared to Whites under age eighteen,

- Black youth were 4.4 more times as likely to be incarcerated
- Tribal youth were 3.2 times as likely
- Latinx youth were 27 percent more likely[2]

Youth of Asian descent had the lowest rates of incarceration. Because these numbers closely reflect the overrepresentation of youth of color among the kids I visit, I've opted not to explicitly identify individuals by what I believe to be their racial or ethnic identity. Usually, however, I've chosen aliases that reflect the racial group from which I perceive them to come.

In her trenchant critique of the juvenile justice system, *Burning Down the House*, award-winning journalist Nell Bernstein concludes that there's no good way to lock up a child. I don't disagree. But I do believe some ways are better than others. And in the interim between now and the dream of abolishing youth incarceration, we must find ways to reduce the suffering of hurting kids. For this to happen, privileged people—by which I mean

---

2. See https://www.ojjdp.gov/ojstatbb/ezacjrp/ for current statistics (cited statistics accessed July 30, 2023).

Whites who are economically comfortable—must bear witness to the pain that permeates the lives of the youth we incarcerate in this country and ask ourselves how our religiously, culturally conditioned beliefs and habits tacitly contribute to their situations. When we understand the roots of teenagers' harmful behavior, we'll advocate for a kind of justice that challenges systemic oppression and promotes compassion, accountability, and healing, and we'll strive to build a world where no child feels inclined to manage their suffering by passing it on to another.

Acknowledgments

EASILY ONE OF MY favorite parts of writing a book is being able to publicly thank people who have directly supported my work. With deep gratitude, I'd like to acknowledge:

- My community partners at the detention center—James O'Donnell, Josh Swanson, Ryan Sandven, and especially Dustin Berg—for being open to collaborating with me to create an opportunity that I hope benefits the youth they serve at least as much as it enriches my students and me

- Students in my Religion, Race, and Social Justice course, especially Maggie Pfeffer and Heather Ukaonu, for co-facilitating the writing workshop we did with youth as part of our research on compassionate justice, and Hailey Puppe and Derreck Christianson, for assisting me with summer visits

- Marilyn and Gordon Eid, for funding my student assistants, and Michelle Brislin for connecting me with Marilyn and Gordon

- Darlene Ross, for supporting the writing of this book during my sabbatical

- Christopher Crutchfield, Sherisse Truesdale, and Emily Baxter for having valuable conversations with me about *Hurting Kids* in its early stages

- Abdur-Rauf Ahmed, for his brilliant feedback on the manuscript after it was submitted (I regret not being able to incorporate this feedback into the final version!)

- Dr. Jacqueline Bussie, executive director of the Collegeville Institute during my writer's residency there, for her friendship and our conversations about what it means to be a person with privilege; and staff at the Collegeville Institute, especially Karla Durand and Connor Kockler, for their kindness, intelligence, and hospitality

- Members of my mom's book club (Rose, Judy, Barb, Karen, Pat, Dianne, Cathy, Bea, and Maryjude), for graciously reading a too-long draft of *Hurting Kids* and offering insightful questions and suggestions; Tom Backen, dear friend and former English teacher, for reading the same too-long draft and offering precisely the encouragement I needed to persevere with this project; and Kevin LaNave, director of Social Justice at Christ Church Newman Center in St. Cloud, Minnesota, for sharing both enthusiasm and resources that benefitted this project

- Colleagues at Concordia College, especially Dr. Susan Larson (provost); Dr. Ken Foster (director of community engagement); Jillain Veil-Ehnert (director of grants); Dr. Elna Solvang (my department chair) and other members of the religion department (Drs. Ahmed Afzaal, Michael Johnson, Anne Mocko, and Jan Pranger), for supporting my outside-the-box teaching proclivities

- Carol Kapaun Ratchenski, poet, writer, and therapist extraordinaire, for teaching me about self-compassion, for encouraging me to trust myself and open to the wholeness of Life, and for facilitating the mindfulness group during my sabbatical; and Paul Perez, for recently joining me to co-facilitate the mindfulness group and for sharing his peaceful, authentic, and compassionate presence with the youth

- Dr. Margaret Miles, for continuing to be a wise mentor and becoming a dear friend through decades of thinking, feeling, and wondering together

- Dr. Cindy Larson-Cassleton, Dr. Ellen Aho, Katy Stelzer Anderson, Ann Laue Welshons, and Anne McGeary Snowdon for being the kind of friends with whom you can tell the truth, appreciate beauty, and have a therapeutic laugh

- Roy Hammerling, for being another truth-telling friend and for reading an almost-done draft of *Hurting Kids* and offering insightful feedback

- Theresa Traynor, for weathering the joys and pains of life with me through forty-some years of laugh-out-loud and grieve-till-you-weep friendship—including the labor of birthing this book by reading a near-final draft, offering expert feedback, and encouraging me to trust my Knowing

- My siblings—John, Jim, Sue, and Mark Lelwica—for having faith in me and my work
- Giulio, Anthony, and Robert Angotti, for picking up the slack and tolerating my moods when my commitment to writing this book made me less than fun to be around
- My parents—Marge and Ted Lelwica—for showing me in a gazillion ways what it means to be loved

Most of all, I want to thank all the youth who have attended the mindfulness group since it started in January 2018. Some of you I got to know well, others only briefly. But every one of you has challenged me to grow beyond my current assumptions, risk the discomfort of confronting my privileges, and recognize our shared need for compassion, accountability, and healing.

Introduction

I DIDN'T KNOW MUCH about the youth justice system when I decided to make weekly visits to a local detention center integral to a new course I was designing called Religion, Race, and Social Justice.[1] It was 2017, and I'd just read Michelle Alexander's *The New Jim Crow*, which examines mass incarceration in the US as the moral equivalent of Jim Crow. The book made me want to do something to help my students and me grow our capacity to not just academically grasp but care about the cruel consequences of systemic racism. One of the biggest challenges I face as a White professor, teaching mostly White students to recognize and challenge racial oppression, is our comfortable distance from racism's dehumanizing effects. This chasm makes it difficult to develop the intellectual understanding, emotional habits, and moral sensibilities we need to practice anti-racism. As civil rights lawyer Bryan Stevenson's grandmother told him, "You can't understand most of the important things from a distance . . . You have to get close."[2]

Getting Close: The Mindfulness Group

The detention center that my students and I visit serves up to eighty youth, generally ages eleven to nineteen of different genders (female, male, nonbinary, and trans). It has a nonsecure and transitional program, but the youth we meet are in the locked unit—usually because they've been arrested, some for violent crimes. These residents are not behind bars, but their freedoms are strictly limited—doors between rooms, pods, and hallways are locked; they wear the same-colored pants and T-shirts, eat the same food, have limited minutes for showers. Despite such carceral conditions, the facility's administrators are committed to moving away from the punitive culture that permeates the broader justice system by providing educational and

1. My description of this course draws on Lelwica, "Power of Proximity."
2. Stevenson, *Just Mercy*, 14.

therapeutic programming that aims to foster learning, accountability, and healing.

The kids I currently visit participate in the facility's residential treatment program, which provides resources like trauma therapy and chemical dependency groups to help the youth turn their lives around. While many experience "being locked up" as punishing, some express gratitude for, in the words of one resident, "the opportunity to learn from my mistakes." More than a few residents have told me that if they weren't in detention, they'd likely be dead. "When I joined that gang," a boy recounted, "I agreed that the only way to un-join was death. It's pretty simple: I try to leave, they kill me." It's easy to critique the current system; but the situations and needs of youth in confinement are often more complicated than we realize.

I don't think of our detention center visits as "community service." I tell the youth (and by proxy, my students[3]) that we're not there to *serve* or even to *help* them and that we can't fix anything about their situation. After naming the elephant in the room—the enormous opportunity gaps that have created our drastically different life situations—I explain that our primary aim is to *learn* and to use what we learn to help us close those gaps. The quote at the top of my syllabus captures the ethos that grounds our visits. Attributed to Lilla Watson, an aboriginal activist, it reads: "If you have come here to help me, you are wasting your time. But if you have come here because your liberation and freedom are bound up in mine, then let us work together."

The residents we visit are disproportionately youth of color, and there are more boys than girls. Every week, depending on the time of year, anywhere from four to twelve youth voluntarily participate in what's come to be known as the mindfulness group. Sometimes we meet in the facility's gym and sometimes in a large, carpeted classroom. Students and I bring navy-blue meditation cushions (called *zafus*) for everyone to sit on.

The circle of cushions creates a sense that the mindfulness group is a space and time apart from our ordinary routines. The group starts with some short (two-to-three minute) meditation practices—for example, conscious breathing (feeling the sensation of inhaling/exhaling), checking (and accepting) our "internal/emotional weather," watching our "mind movies" (without judgment), silently reciting a mantra, relaxing the body ("strong back, soft front"). When we have time, the group concludes with some mindful listening to music.

---

3. Throughout this book I refer to my students as "students" to distinguish them from the youth we visit, even though the detention center residents are also students (they attend school at the facility).

My decision to make mindfulness practice central to our visits was influenced by trauma therapist Resmaa Menakem and Buddhist teacher Ruth King, both of whom suggest that anti-racism must include strategies for calming the fight, flight, or freeze tendencies of our "lizard brain."[4] As a mental health resource, mindfulness practice has other advantages: it doesn't require or promote specific beliefs, and the practice can be accessed for free any time or place. Especially if it's trauma informed,[5] mindfulness practice can help those of us who have survived hard or even horrendous experiences develop our capacity to pay attention to what's happening inside us, stay present to difficult emotions, cultivate a state of calm, and feel safe in our bodies.

At the start of every semester, I ask the youth if they know why I'm sharing mindfulness practice with them. Once, one of the boys responded loudly: "Because we're a bunch of angry kids." The other residents and my students laughed, and so did I.

"Not exactly," I replied. I briefly explained the benefits of learning to pay attention to our internal experience, without judgment. Then I told them the truth: "I'm teaching you how to practice mindfulness because it's something I need to learn."

Most of our time together is spent in small groups discussions. I invite everyone to continue practicing mindfulness by paying attention, not interrupting, and listening deeply to what others have to say. To spark our conversations, I either prepare quotes and questions in advance, or we use the prompts on discussion cards I bought online. Topics range from favorite foods, films, and music, to current events and social issues, to mental health challenges and childhood adversity. Many of the stories the youth share expose the violence that structural oppression—especially racism, poverty, and sexism—has inflicted on their lives. These stories compel us to consider the humanity of kids who are invisible to most people with privilege and to reflect on our unwitting complicity with the injustices they have survived.

Hurting Kids invites all Americans to witness and care about the humanity of youth in confinement by asking us to reconsider the meaning of justice in light of these kids' backstories. Drawing on Stevenson's grandmother's wisdom, I aim to make these teenagers' humanity more *proximate* to readers who will never have a chance to spend time with them and thus never get to witness both the worlds of pain from which they come and the creative potential they possess. In this book, I share what I've learned not just *about* but *from* incarcerated teens—about my own privileges and

---

4. R. King, *Mindful of Race*; Menakem, *My Grandmother's Hands*.
5. See Treleavan, *Trauma-Sensitive Mindfulness*.

complicities and about their need for compassion as they struggle to acknowledge the harm they've caused while coming to terms with the wounds they carry. Ultimately, the stories and perspectives these condemned kids have shared with me affirm the truth of the adage: *Hurt people hurt people.*

Compassion Complicates the Meaning of Justice

Recognizing the hurt that precedes and propels the harm youth offenders have inflicted on others raises questions about the meaning of justice. Consciously or not, many of us believe that punishment—inflicting painful consequences for wrongdoing—is necessary, appropriate, and fair. T. Richard Snyder argues that this belief contributes to the "spirit of punishment" that's evident in American culture's addiction to "getting even."[6] The more I listened to the stories of kids in confinement, the more I began to wonder what "justice" even means. Is punishment an effective way to get traumatized teenagers to take responsibility for their destructive actions? Is it the most ethical? How can we move beyond mentalities that implicitly or explicitly reduce *justice* to retribution—the idea that appears in certain theological narratives that you must *pay* for your crime (your "sin") through sacrificial suffering? As a religion scholar, I'm interested in how these and other religious narratives have shaped how Americans think about youth justice and about the kids caught up in the system—for better and for worse.

Centering social justice, compassion, accountability, and healing as guiding values for rethinking youth justice doesn't give us a clear recipe for fixing the current system. This is more of an idea book than a solution book. Yet, as Ibram X. Kendi has shown, *policies matter.*[7] Whether kids who have harmed others accept responsibility for their actions and heal depends on the kinds of laws and strategies politicians and administrators create *based on what they believe the public supports*. And while solutions must come from people closest to the problem, my assumption is that all of us have a moral responsibility to actively care about our nation's most marginalized children.

In the end, we can't legislate our way out of the habits of thought and feeling that fuel our society's vindictive tendencies. Punitive policies depend on the beliefs, attitudes, and sensibilities of people who support them—and on the indifference of those who don't care. Experts and political leaders can tweak or change laws, but until we reevaluate some of our most basic assumptions about "justice" and about those who get caught up in the

---

6. Snyder, *Protestant Ethic*, 1.
7. See Kendi, *Stamped from the Beginning* and *How to Be Anti-Racist*.

system—until we transform the habits of our hearts—the US will continue to be the most punitive developed nation on earth.

Americans' Conflicting Beliefs about Criminal Justice

America incarcerates more youth than any other industrialized country.[8] In 2020, some twenty-five thousand kids were held in juvenile facilities, most of them in confinement. That's a lot! But it represents a 77 percent decrease since 2000.[9] This decrease parallels a general drop in teen crime and arrests during the same period, and some experts say those parallel declines are not coincidental.[10] Yet, as of 2022, twenty-two states had no minimum age for prosecuting children in the youth system.[11] In 2023, about one in sixteen justice-involved juveniles (under age eighteen) was locked up in an adult facility.[12] Overall, America's reputation as an incarceration-prone nation is hard to deny. With 5 percent of the global population, we have between 20 and 25 percent of world's prisoners, many of whom are serving long, punitive sentences for nonviolent crimes.[13]

This may be a crucible moment regarding this system. Despite many Americans' ongoing support for "tough on crime" legislation, a 2018 poll found that among registered voters:

- Seventy-six percent thought America's criminal [adult] justice system needed major renovations.
- Eighty-five percent believed the criminal justice system's primary goal should be "rehabilitation," not punishment.
- Eighty-seven percent strongly supported "replacing mandatory minimum sentences for non-violent offenders with a system that allows judges more discretion."

These beliefs were *widely shared across party lines*, suggesting, as the study concludes, that "criminal justice reform is NOT a partisan issue."[14]

---

8. Human Rights Watch, "Children behind Bars," para. 10; Saxon, "U.S. Has World's Highest."
9. Rovner, "Youth Justice by Numbers," para. 1.
10. Pilnik and Mistrett, *If Not the Adult System*, 8–9.
11. National Juvenile Justice Network, "Raising the Minimum Age," para. 1.
12. Sawyer and Wagner, "Mass Incarceration," para. 41.
13. Dressinger, *Incarceration Nations*, 8; Wagner and Bertram, "What Percent of U.S.," para. 5; Minton et al., "Correctional Populations."
14. Blizzard, "National Poll Results," 2. See also T. Walker, "New Poll Shows," 1.

Even more relevant for this book, a growing number of us appear to prefer nonpunitive and effective responses to juvenile wrongdoing.[15] Three quarters strongly support "getting juvenile offenders the treatment, counseling, and supervision they need to make it less likely that they will commit another crime, even if that means they spend no time in a juvenile corrections facility." Only 21 percent firmly advocate "making sure juvenile offenders receive a serious punishment and not just a slap on the wrist, even if that means they spend time in a juvenile corrections facility." Significantly, Americans of *all* political, regional, age, gender, and racial-ethnical backgrounds want a youth justice system that prioritizes providing services and supervision over punitive responses.[16]

Historically, Christians have had the most power to shape Americans' beliefs, which is why my analysis focuses primarily on the norms and narratives within this tradition that have influenced how we think about justice. Certain Christian ideas (the necessity of divine punishment for sinful behavior) have provided the conceptual template for the largely punitive justice system that operates in America today. But other teachings within this tradition (God's mercy and forgiveness) have encouraged more compassionate responses to crime. Even Americans who don't identify as "Christian" or "religious" are invariably impacted by these competing storylines. Both are part of our cultural DNA.

"Not Even Paper Clips": Punishment and Protection

Despite strong public support for remedial responses to teenage crime, much of our youth justice system still embodies a punitive concept of justice—though perhaps less by *intent* than by *impact*. Across America, most kids living in detention centers and prisons experience "carceral conditions" similar to those described above (locked doors, etc.).[17] While the individual rooms of the youth I visit are brighter than the dreary jail cells you see in the movies, their size is about the same and their contents are similar (low-standing metal toilet, small bed with a thin mattress, narrow window overlooking a parking lot). You might think such an inhospitable environment was intentionally designed to punish its occupants. But these barren conditions have another purpose: preventing the youth from hurting themselves.

---

15. National Juvenile Justice Network, "Polling on Public Attitudes," 1–2; cf. Belden and Russonello, "Existing Survey Research"; Bolin et al., "Americans' Opinions."

16. Pew Charitable Trusts, *Public Opinion*.

17. Sawyer, "Youth Confinement," para. 9.

During my first visit to the detention center to set up the plan for my class's weekly visits, the director of programming stressed the importance of confidentiality and keeping everyone safe. "Please tell your students not to bring their phones into the facility," he said. "Actually, just tell them not to bring anything," he continued. "Not even paper clips." This last instruction surprised me, but I quickly assumed that we shouldn't bring paper clips because the residents could weaponize them by unbending the wire to poke each other. As if reading my mind, the director clarified that the main concern was not that kids would use paper clips to injure their peers, but that they would use them to harm themselves. I didn't fully understand the importance of the paper clips ban until I saw the scars on some of the residents' forearms—scars they had brought with them that were visual reminders of their painful histories.

Both my research and my proximity to incarcerated youth have made me critical of punitive approaches to juvenile justice. Yet, from what I've observed, in practice the lines between punishment and protection are not always clear. (Here I'm not talking about the public's need for safety and protection from the actions of violent offenders, which I address in Part III). A number of teens are placed in residential confinement not simply as a disciplinary sanction for delinquency, but as a way of shielding them from abuse at home, connecting them to therapeutic services, and/or preventing them from hurting themselves and/or others.

Challenges in Writing *Hurting Kids*

The tension between punishment and protection is one of several challenges I encountered while writing this book. Discussing the experiences and perspectives of a population of kids whose backstories differ so drastically from my own presented multiple difficulties that I have not resolved. Among the biggest:

- Centering whiteness. For more than a century, Black, Brown, and Indigenous people have been asking Whites who seek to understand racism to stop focusing all their attention on "the other" and start examining the ways whiteness has impacted *our* lives.[18] Throughout this book, I incorporate memoir and self-examination as strategies for identifying and interrogating my own racist conditioning. But these strategies are prone to "centering whiteness"—a common habit among White people to make our own privileged experiences both the default

18. DiAngelo, *What Does It Mean*, 148.

setting for humanity and the center of attention. Even as I aim to model the kind of critical self-scrutiny Whites need to do to recognize and challenge our racist indoctrination, attempting to do this without reinforcing my own unwittingly racist habit of making Whites/myself the protagonist of every drama has been a challenge. Additionally, my soul-searching efforts mean little if they don't tangibly benefit people of color.

- The "savior" complex. White saviorism has been a crucial concern for me since I first set foot in the detention center. Intellectually, I understand the problems with "White benevolence" and the colonial violence it perpetuates.[19] The idea that middle- and upper-class Whites know what's best for racially and/or economically oppressed people, or that we're doing them a favor by condemning the dehumanizing ideologies and institutions that our own racial/economic group created and still benefits from, is condescending at best. Regardless of their color, gender, or class, the youth I visit need to be empowered, not rescued. *I know this*. Still, my conscious critique of this complex doesn't inoculate me from succumbing to it. Additionally, there's no denying that, despite my *intentions*, the very *structure* of the visits looks like saviorism.

- The "White vampire" syndrome. I created this term to describe the potential for aspiring anti-racist Whites like me to feed off the racialized trauma of others as an unconscious strategy for affirming our sense of virtue, for reassuring us that "things could always be worse," and/or for meeting our need for "inspiration." In *Mindful of Race* Ruth King provides a glaring example of these tendencies. A White man who facilitated a prison support group comprised mostly of men of color told her that he "felt more alive when he heard [these men's] stories—I needed my weekly fix!" This example exposes White do-gooders' penchant for "feeding on the energy of black lives and other POC."[20] King asks Whites to relinquish our sense of entitlement to other people's suffering. Rather than feed off the pain of others to make us feel better, we must develop the capacity to identify, feel, and transform our own distress and grief. If we don't learn to compost our own suffering, we'll be prone to passing it on to others, just as our ancestors did. As Resmaa Menakem points out, Europeans tortured and terrorized each

---

19. See Gebhard et al., eds., *White Benevolence*.
20. R. King, *Mindful of Race*, 195–96.

other long before they committed genocide against Indigenous people and enslaved and brutalized African Americans.[21]

- "Trauma porn." I've also wrestled with how to honor incarcerated teenagers' backstories of intense adversity in ways that rouse readers' empathy without further "otherizing" the youth. Young adult author Jason Reynolds cautions against engaging in "trauma porn," the unwitting objectification and sensationalizing of the traumatic stories of "others."[22] Many privileged Americans' long-standing perceptions of "juvenile delinquents" as "other people's children"[23] replicates the "not me" mentality that operates when members of a socially advantaged group voyeuristically observe the anguish of strangers as a form of entertainment and/or as an unconscious strategy for reassuring ourselves of our own (supposed) normalcy and superiority.[24]

- Unpaid labor. Writing this book is how I hold myself accountable for the incredible lessons the youth have taught me. Yet none of them have been compensated for this labor. The potential for exploitation here fits a familiar pattern. People in socially marginalized groups—for example, members of the disability and/or LGBTQ communities, religious minorities, Brown, Indigenous, and Black people—are regularly asked, if not required, to teach folks who don't share their minority status about the suffering that comes from not being considered the default human. This dynamic happens not just with the youth I visit, but also with minority students, staff, and professors back on campus, who find themselves having to educate people like me about things we'll never fully understand because of our privileged social locations.

Recently, I described these writing challenges to some colleagues. A White male professor remarked: "I wouldn't touch that project with a ten-foot pole." Though I disagree with his avoidance strategy, I understand the sentiment of his comment. As a White person, I'm bound to make mistakes in my efforts to understand racism. Moreover, the combination of my social privileges and lack of formal training in the field of youth justice virtually guarantees that I'll get some things wrong in my effort to communicate the humanity of incarcerated youth. I hope that five years from now I'll have

21. Menakem, *My Grandmother's Hands*, 61–66.
22. León, "Jason Reynolds." See also Reynolds, "Fortifying Imagination."
23. This is the title of ch. 3 of Bernstein's *Burning Down the House*, 52–70.
24. This challenge comes from the field of disability studies. In *Shameful Bodies*, I engage the insights of disability and feminist studies to critique this "not-me" mentality as a psychic strategy that produces cultural "others."

new insights and perspectives—and that I won't cringe too much at what I've written in the pages ahead. Meanwhile, I'm opting not to let fear prevent me from sharing with you the incredible lessons the youth in the mindfulness group have taught me about whiteness, compassion, accountability, and healing—and what these lessons reveal about the meaning of justice.

1

The Seventh Angel

During the summer months, I have only one or two students accompanying me on the weekly visits to the detention center. So, one August afternoon, when Norris, a staff member, asked me how many kids he should bring to the group, I suggested we limit it to six. Keeping the number small tends to raise the quality of our interactions, in part because the staff pick the most well-behaved kids to attend. Still, I don't like excluding anyone, so I told Norris: "If there's a seventh resident who really wants to come—and he's an angel—by all means send him." Understanding my humor, Norris smiled and said, "Will do."

The six boys who showed up helped move the desks and chairs to the side of the room to create space for the larger circle we sit in before breaking into smaller groups. We'd brought enough *zafus* for nine participants: my student, six boys, me, plus the possible seventh "angel."

Just as I was about to start the group, I heard Norris unlocking the classroom's door. Another resident walked in.

It was Bao.

I don't know what country Bao is from, but I suspect his family immigrated to the US relatively recently because he spoke English with a thick accent, and he mentioned that learning the language was difficult. Sometimes I had a hard time understanding him, not because of his accent but because he talked very fast.

Bao could be very sweet, but he wasn't exactly my definition of an "angel." During his first month attending the group, while everyone else sat cross-legged on the cushions, Bao would lie on his belly, head facing the center of a discussion circle, doing fast, effortless push-ups in between his contributions to the conversation.

One day, I asked Bao about the push-ups. "I have really bad ADHD," he said. "This [doing rapid-fire push-ups] is how I get my energy out."

"I see," I responded, both amused and envious of his athleticism. "Guess how many push-ups I can do," I playfully challenged, pulling up the sleeve of my T-shirt to brandish my right biceps. This got the attention of the other boys in my group, all of whom hesitated to respond to my question, apparently worried about hurting my feelings with their answer. "Just guess," I persisted, "How many push-ups do you think a muscle *this* big can do?"

"Ten!" one of the boys boldly offered.

"Five?" another sheepishly speculated.

"I'm going with three," a third boy guessed, sounding apologetic.

Still smiling, I turned to Bao: "And what do you think?"

"I don't know, man . . . maybe five?"

"I hate to disappoint you all," I said, "but I can do *exactly zero* push-ups!"

"Whoa," a few of them murmured, as if it were inconceivable to them that there are actually humans who can't do a single push-up.

"In fact, I've never done a push-up in my life. Never! *Not one*."

Their eyes were wide with astonishment.

"I know, right!?" I continued to humor them. "I mean," adding with a smile, "Don't you think muscles that look this strong should be able to do *at least one*?"

In all seriousness, Bao responded, "Yeah, but that muscle definition you have in your arm . . . It's just 'cause you're old. I mean, you still have that saggy part underneath your bicep. No offense."

In the silent pause following Bao's comment, the other boys looked at me to see if my feelings were hurt.

Then we all burst out laughing.

It wasn't Bao's hilarious comment about my aging arms that, in my mind, made him less than angelic. It was his strong tendency to be mentally elsewhere. His distractibility made it hard for his peers, many of whom also struggle with ADHD, to stay focused for even a few seconds.

But the afternoon that he showed up late to the mindfulness group, Bao was unusually attentive. He volunteered to read the first quote on the handouts I'd distributed—a passage from Stevenson's *Just Mercy*: "Each of us is more than the worst thing we've ever done."

"What does that mean?" Booker asked, looking at me.

I turned the question back to the group: "What do you all think it means?"—adding, "I doubt there's just one answer."

"I think it means we all make mistakes," Nikan commented.

"Yeah," Bao added, "like, no one's perfect."

Before we had a chance to explore Stevenson's wisdom more deeply, I heard the classroom door being unlocked and turned to see another resident being let in.

It was Phil.

I'm not sure how an eighth resident was allowed to attend the group that day. Probably some miscommunication. But it didn't matter. I motioned for Phil to join our group, realizing that the likelihood of distraction in our discussion just tripled. Like Bao, Phil struggled significantly with paying attention.

Phil had been to the mindfulness group several times before, but not for a few weeks. As he sat down, I asked how he'd been. Grinning, he explained that he'd been sent to the third floor, which means he'd gotten into some kind of trouble. The facility's third floor used to be where the highest-level offenders resided. The youth in the residential treatment program (on the second floor) got transferred there when their behavior became harmful to others, the staff, or themselves. Knowing this, the other boys smiled as well, while Phil appeared to enjoy his devious reputation.

Attempting to redirect everyone's attention back to our discussion, I asked Phil if he'd be willing to read the second quote—this one a two-sentence passage from Stevenson's book. "Sure," he said, cheerfully. But as soon as he started reading, it became apparent that Phil struggled with a reading disability. He could decipher only one word at a time. I felt horrible for asking him to read the quote—I should have known better. Over the years, I've met several youth who couldn't read. Yet Phil had seemed perfectly willing to do so. Was I projecting the shame I would have felt in his predicament?

With no visible sign of embarrassment, Phil soldiered on as the other boys patiently waited, occasionally pitching in to help with the longer words.

When he'd finally finished, Phil looked up at the rest of us. Smiling, he said, "Sorry. I can't read too well."

"That's okay," I rushed to assure him.

"The reason is," he said, ignoring my silly attempt to affirm his effort, "I stopped going to school in ninth grade."

"Why's that?" I asked, suppressing my thought that most kids in the US learn to read in grade school.

"I got in trouble the first day of school that year," Phil said, "so I just stopped going. I hated school anyway."

Phil elaborated that once he started skipping school, he found a way to make a lot of money: selling crack. "I had to get cash fast because my girlfriend had a bun in the oven," he explained, as if this were the most logical thing any ninth grade boy in his predicament would do.

"Well," Booker interjected, "selling that stuff is better than using it."

"Yeah," Phil agreed. "I ain't that stupid . . . But I sure do wish I could read."

By then, the energy of the group had mellowed, and we started discussing another one of the prompts I'd prepared. But as we did, Bao intermittently interrupted whoever was talking to ask me if I wanted him to pray for me. The first time he asked, I had a hard time registering his question, which seemed to come from out of the blue. The second and third time, I started to wonder if he was serious. But each time, I responded by putting my index finger on my closed mouth to indicate that someone else was talking and to encourage him to pay attention.

As the discussion wrapped up, Bao asked me again whether I'd like him to pray for me. I quickly surveyed the other boys' faces. None of them seemed the slightest bit phased by Bao's question. Still not knowing if he was serious, I said, "Sure. I need all the prayers I can get."

Looking pleased with my response, Bao assumed a posture of prayer. Hands folded. Head bowed. Eyes closed. The other three boys followed suit, as if on cue they knew what to do. Following their lead, I took the same prayerful posture.

After a silent pause, I heard Bao clear his throat and ask in an apologetic tone: "Um, sorry, but what's your name again?"

I realized he was talking to me and stifled an urge to laugh. His query felt utterly comical, given the solemnity of the moment. Over the years, I've learned not to take this question personally. It makes total sense that the residents aren't as invested in me as I am in them and that they don't put a lot of stock in our relationship, which is inevitably temporary.

"Dude," Phil intervened before I had a chance to respond, "her name's Michelle," adding, "you should know that."

"It's totally fine," I assured them both.

"Okay, Michelle," Bao said as he and the other boys resumed their devotional postures. Then, in the sweetest, clearest, gentlest voice, I heard him pray: "Heavenly Father . . ."

For an instant, I involuntarily cringed at the patriarchal God language, which I haven't used for several decades. But the kindness and sincerity of Bao's voice cracked open my heart.

"Bless this fine lady Michelle," he continued in a prayerful voice. I felt my entire body soften to receive the grace of his holy benediction.

"She has a good heart," Bao went on to say. "She comes here to be with us. She's like a Wonder Woman who is doing her best to help us." I resisted the cognitive urge to clarify that I don't see myself as "helping" anyone, and instead just absorbed the beauty of Bao's blessing. I wish my memory were sharp enough to recall the entire prayer, which lasted at least another minute, during which the other boys remained silently bowed, eyes closed, hands folded. Beyond the first few lines, which I vividly remember, there were lots of "thank yous" and "bless hers." Once he'd finished, Bao looked up at me, beaming. I was smiling, too, holding back tears, and marveling at the seventh angel before me.

You don't have to believe in angels to know that whatever harm incarcerated kids have inflicted, their inherent worth, dignity, and goodness—their divine humanity—cannot be destroyed.

2

Divine Humanity

In Sunday school, I learned about the incarnation—the Christian teaching that God became human in the person of Jesus.

Truth be told, this dogma made more sense to me as a child, when my mind naturally gravitated toward myths and stories. As I got older and learned about biology and history, the doctrine of the incarnation confused me. I asked my parents: How could something as big and almighty as God, who created *everything*, become a single person? (At the time, I didn't have the critical thinking skills to ask why God would opt to become a *man*). I also wondered why God decided to show up only once in human history—some two thousand years ago in a place most people will never even visit.

My parents' explanation—"It's a mystery"—was unconvincing. I suspected that *mystery* was a word they used to hide the fact that the teaching didn't make sense to them either.

After four decades of studying religion, I've come full circle to my childhood understanding of the incarnation as a myth, but not in the sense of being untrue. Rather, the story that God became human in the person of Jesus is a mythical way of reminding Christians of the divinity that dwells in *everybody* and *everything*. For me, the incarnation is a metaphor for the indelible goodness and creative power—the divinity—in all earthly beings, including humans.

Divine humanity is a way of naming the indestructible dignity, beauty, and worth of every person, including the young people society has condemned. Stevenson alludes to this intrinsic goodness: "*Each of us is more than the worst thing we've ever done.*"[1] The phrase "divine humanity" also affirms justice-involved kids' tremendous capacity for transformation. It's common to refer to this population as "at-risk" or "vulnerable" youth, which, of course, they are. But that vocabulary doesn't illuminate incarcerated teenagers' *creative potential*, including their inherent capacities for love, empathy, wisdom, courage, resilience, accountability, and healing.

Diverse spiritual traditions name humans' intrinsic worth and creative potential differently. Christians share the Jewish affirmation that we are created "in God's image" (Gen 1:27). This idea resembles the Hindu concept of Atman: the universal divinity/God that inhabits everyone and represents our truest self. Without reference to God, Buddhists refer to Bodhicitta, or "Buddha nature"—our capacity to awaken, evolve, and heal—to talk about humans' indelible goodness. In Islam, especially among Sufi mystics, belief in God's oneness (*tawhid*) is felt through an experience of union between the divine and human spirit. The Christian idea that "Christ" lives in each of us is another way of affirming our divine humanity.

You don't need to be religious to perceive the innate dignity, worth, and capacity for growth in every person. Some of the most influential human rights leaders were (and are) agnostics and atheists. What matters is not *what* you call humans' intrinsic goodness and creative potential, but *that* you recognize, validate, and tend to this sacred presence in yourself and in others, including those our society has failed to nurture.

---

1. Stevenson, *Just Mercy*, 17–18; emphasis original.

3

"People with Privilege Need to Hear Our Stories"

Discussing the prompt "What are you most afraid of?," Jordon responded immediately: "That I won't be able to go to college." Hector said he worried that his little brother would grow up like him and "end up in juvie." Phil shared that he was afraid of spending the rest of his life locked up. Then Phil turned to Jordon and said, "I went to college, but I dropped out." He explained that he had stopped going to classes, did some "bad stuff," and gotten arrested. "I've been in juvie six times in the past two years," he said matter-of-factly. "I'm impulsive."

You may wonder how—or whether—this boy who struggled earnestly to read two sentences really went to college.

The truth is, I don't know. Was he admitted and then dropped out when the reading requirements became overwhelming? Did he fabricate the story to claim status by suggesting that he'd already achieved Jordon's dream? Regardless, these questions point to a tangle of thorny issues that academics describe as "methodological": 1) How trustworthy are my "data"—including what the youth have told me; 2) How reliable are my recollections and interpretations of that data? 3) What principle guides those interpretations?

Basically, I don't know if everything the youth tell me is true. I don't have access to their records, so I can't confirm the accuracy of the backstories they share with me. Moreover, they're not supposed to talk with each other, my students, or me about what they did that got them locked up. Sometimes they tell me anyway. Usually, however, I don't know why they're in detention. Nor do I necessarily want or need to know. Once a resident told me that what he most liked about coming to the mindfulness group was that he got to talk to people who don't know about the things he's done that he regrets. "You and the students get to see the side of me that's not just a criminal. That feels good."

Though I usually don't know why the youth I visit are being detained, national statistics point to a continuum of harm that leads to teenage confinement:

- 43.8 are held for "person offenses" (simple, aggravated, or sexual assault; robbery; homicide)
- 20.8 percent for "property" crimes (auto theft, burglary)
- 14.2 percent for "public order" offenses (gang activity, disorderly conduct, illegal weapons)
- 14.2 percent for "technical" violations (failing to meet probation requirements)
- 4.4 percent for drug-related charges (drug trafficking and other drug offenses)
- 3.8 percent for "status offenses" (actions that get kids in trouble because of their age, such as underage smoking or drinking, or truancy)[1]

Activist and educator Miriame Kaba distinguishes between "harm" and "crime" because not all behavior that's criminalized is harmful, and not all harmful behavior is criminalized.[2] The terms I use to describe actions that lead to youth confinement—"harmful," "hurtful," "destructive," and so on—are imprecise. Were it not so stylistically clunky, I'd nuance them each time I use them.

Other terms and phrases I use are similarly inexact and potentially misleading. For example, youth "offenders" are also *victims*. Moreover, not all justice-involved kids are incarcerated, and not all juveniles in locked facilities are there because of delinquency charges. (The plight of youth in immigration detention centers is beyond the scope of this book). Some end up in confinement because their family is unable to care for them, and/or they have run away from home and are homeless, and/or they are experiencing a mental health crisis. While a few of the youth you'll meet in this book are in detention because they have nowhere else to go, most are locked up because of some kind of delinquency or harm they have caused others.

---

1. Sawyer and Wagner, "Mass Incarceration," slideshow 5.
2. Kaba, *We Do This*, 3.

Ultimately, I don't need to know the magnitude or details of whatever mistakes these kids made to know that they need to feel seen, safe, supported, and cared for if they are to accept responsibility and heal. Nor do I need to know that everything they share with me is true. And since doubting their veracity risks invalidating their experiences, I choose to err on the side of saying, "I believe you"—even if it means that by conventional scholarly standards, my methodology is messy.

Related to this potential messiness is the conundrum of what gets lost with time and translation. In some instances, I'm confident I've quoted a youth either verbatim or almost verbatim because their words were so poignant, they were easy to remember. Mostly, however, I've reconstructed conversations to the best of my memory. The residents whose writings I directly quote have given their permission for me to do so. Most of this writing is from a cohort of youth who participated in a summer creative writing workshop that two students and I facilitated.[3] I haven't sanitized the occasional use of profanity in this writing, though I've edited some sentences for clarity.

Residents in the mindfulness group have expressed excitement about this book. Still, by sharing stories and perspectives they've entrusted to me, I risk engaging in "the indignity of speaking for others."[4] I've sought to mitigate this danger by telling you what *I'm* learning from my conversations with them, rather than assuming to know (or trying to interpret) *their* thoughts and feelings. Whenever something a youth said or wrote seemed to require analysis, I've sought to nuance my interpretation with words like "perhaps," "maybe," "seems like," and so on. More broadly, I've relied on the principle of compassion and my perception of the youths' divine humanity to guide my interpretations. I'm aware that not everyone shares my basic assumption that people with privilege ought to care about and nurture the well-being of incarcerated kids.

Ultimately, there's no getting around the fact that I'm curating the stories and perspectives of youth whose life experiences I don't share. The world I've inhabited for nearly my entire life is the "other world" Ta-Nehisi Coates describes in *Between the World and Me*. Though I wasn't raised in the suburbs, my childhood environment included many of the makings of what Coates refers to as "the Dream": pot roasts and blueberry pies, green lawns and wooded backyards, fireworks, ice cream, and, importantly, the "lie of innocence." I don't have a clue about what it's like growing up in "the

---

3. This workshop was part of a research project that explored the benefits of "compassionate justice" through writing, yoga, meditation, and small group discussion. This project received approval from my college's institutional review board.

4. Halperin, *Saint Foucault*, 50.

hood" or having "fully one third of my brain" preoccupied with surviving the violence of the streets.[5]

Given my lack of firsthand experience with poverty or being on the receiving end of racism, is it even ethical for me to attempt to recount the stories and perspectives of the youth I've met at the detention center and through my research? My intentions are good, but humans are masters of self-deception. Indeed, Coates warns his fifteen-year-old son about "White educators" like me: "Forget about intentions," he says, because for Whites, "good intention" has functioned as "a hall pass through history, a sleeping pill that ensures the Dream."[6]

Knowing that my best intentions may well be meaningless, I remain motivated to write this book because every incarcerated youth I've met says they wish the outside world understood where they came from, why they did what they did, and what they hope to do with their lives.

One day, I asked a cohort of residents in the mindfulness group, "What would you like people in the free world to know about you and your lives?" One of the girls responded in a loud, unsteady voice that sounded simultaneously anguished and angry: "People with privilege need to hear our stories."

---

5. Coates, *Between the World and Me*, 20–29, 102.
6. Coates, *Between the World and Me*, 33. See also Alcoff, "Speaking for Others."

PART I

Whiteness

4

"Don't You Think White People Need to Learn about Race?"

D*URING THE SUMMER OF* 2017, my colleague Amena Chaudhry and I were sitting in her office. Amena was the inaugural diversity coordinator at the college where I teach and is now a diversity, equity, inclusion, and belonging coach and consultant. As a woman of color and strong advocate for racial justice, I was excited to tell her about the new course I was designing called Religion, Race, and Social Justice. "It's going to be interfaithy," I said. "Students will learn about religion's ambiguous potential as a tool for justifying—or challenging—White supremacy in America," I explained. "And I'm going to use mostly Black authors—not just MLK, but Malcolm X, W. E. B. du Bois, Michelle Alexander, James Cone, Audre Lorde, Alice Walker, Mariame Kaba, Ta-Nehisi Coates, Ruth King, and others." I went on, enthusiastically, "I really hope I get a lot of students of color in the course."

Amena gave me a puzzled look. "Why do you hope students of color take the course?" Her tone was curious and ever-so-slightly amused. I realized that I'd just said something stupid, but I wasn't sure what. Sensing my confusion, Amena offered another question: "Don't you think White people need to learn about race?" Then she pulled Robin DiAngelo's *What Does It Mean to Be White* off her shelf and read the following passage to me: "Often in multicultural education endeavors, we learn about the experiences of people who are in marginalized groups, but seldom are we asked to consider what it means to be in a dominant group."[1]

---

1. DiAngelo, *What Does It Mean*, 39.

So began my journey to explore how my own racial identity has shaped every facet of my life—from my emotional, intellectual, and spiritual habits to the relationships I've cultivated, professional goals I've been able to pursue, forms of entertainment I enjoy, and even the "personal" issues with which I've struggled. The more I've explored DiAngelo's question—"What does it mean to be White?"—the more mind-boggling it is that this query never occurred to me until Amena brought it to my attention.

Yet the absence of this question in my life isn't surprising. After all, one of the daily advantages of being White is that you don't have to think about race. This is a signature feature of social privileges: you don't realize you have them—unless you're fortunate enough to be around minoritized people who are willing to risk reminding you. But many Whites operate in worlds where we have minimal meaningful interactions with people of color and virtually no encouragement to reflect on our own racial identity.[2] This was certainly the case for me prior to spending time with incarcerated youth.

---

2. DiAngelo, *What Does It Mean*, 69.

5

What Is "Whiteness"?

THE FIRST TIME I heard the term "whiteness," I assumed it referred to the color of White people's skin. After reading the works of scholars who study race, I now understand "whiteness" as referring to *White privilege*: the unearned advantages and perks light-skinned people of European descent enjoy, knowingly or not, in a White supremacy society like the US.

Let's pause. How do you feel about the term "White supremacy"? If this phrase triggers discomfort, that may be because you associate White supremacy with hate groups like the Ku Klux Klan or with head-shaven men in army fatigues who proudly and sometimes violently profess their hatred. Without question, these groups represent extreme examples of White supremacy. But I'm using the term more broadly to name the historical, ideological, and institutional dominance of Whites—and the corresponding devaluing of people of color—that structures American society. In this sense, White supremacy is synonymous with racism: a social system that elevates Whites as a group by making us the default, most valued, and authoritative human beings.[1] This system benefits White progressives just as much as White conservatives.[2]

To conceptualize racism as *systemic* is to say that racial oppression is not reducible to isolated events, individuals, or a conscious belief that people of color are inferior. White supremacy is so deeply embedded in America's culture that none of us are immune to its influence. The structure of racism reaches back to the era of slavery and genocide of Native people and

---

1. DiAngelo, *What Does It Mean*, 61–79, 145–46.
2. Menakem, *My Grandmother's Hands*, 167.

is maintained through laws and institutions, cultural and religious norms, popular images and stories that condition us to see White supremacy as *normal*. To describe racism as systemic is to acknowledge that although most Whites don't *intentionally* try to oppress people of color, our society has evolved to grant us advantages we didn't earn, whether we know, want, or intend it.

Systemic racism is also sustained by psychological and spiritual habits that perpetuate America's history of slavery. Psychologically, this legacy echoes in Whites' tendencies to feel entitled, seek status, and desire control. These mental/emotional habits quietly recycle the master/slave paradigm of superiority/inferiority. I'm still learning to identify how this paradigm unconsciously operates in my own past and present habits of whiteness—for example, in how I used to torture my body by treating it like a "slave"; in my workaholic pursuit of "success"; in my need to be "right." As these examples suggest, racism manifests itself in psychological patterns that may not seem to be directly connected to White supremacy but that nonetheless reflect our social conditioning in a country indelibly marked by its origins in slavery.

The status-seeking, entitlement-driven, controlling psychology of White supremacy is supported by hierarchical theologies that personify divine power. "God" is envisioned as a supreme being who rules over everything and demands obedience through the threat of punishment. In Christianity, this almighty power is often portrayed as an omnipotent White man—the invisible patriarch in the sky who lords over "His" subjects and uses fear to keep them in line. This familiar image is revealing if you consider anthropologists' observation that human models *of* God function as models *for* our relationships with each other.[3] When we reduce the creative power of the universe to a mighty slave master, we get a theology that sanctions dominant/subordinate relationships. This toxic theology generates spiritual habits like self-judgment and judgment of others, sacrificial suffering, control, powerlessness, and shame.

To sum up: *White supremacy* refers to a racially stratified system that's sustained by a network of social policies, ideologies, institutions, and everyday psychological and spiritual habits that recycle the legacy of slavery. *Whiteness* names the myriad benefits to which Whites generally have greater access in a racist society—for example, mental and physical health care, educational opportunities, psychic ease, social respect, financial security, housing, safe neighborhoods—and our tendencies to claim those benefits as our own.

---

3. Geertz, *Interpretation of Cultures*, 87–125.

How Whites experience whiteness and white supremacy depends on variables such as gender, class, ethnicity, sexuality, (non)religious orientation, (dis)ability, not to mention family histories, hereditary dispositions, political leanings, where we live, and so on. My experiences are far from universal. By sharing them, I aim to encourage you to reflect on the ways whiteness has shaped your own life journey, how this journey relates to the youth offenders you'll meet in this book, and whether the promises of whiteness have delivered the happiness you seek.

Much of what I'm learning is not just that the social advantages I've taken for granted are far from universal, but that my own efforts to claim the benefits of whiteness have not served me well. Nearly all the "personal" issues with which I've struggled—stress, workaholism, catastrophic thinking, self-doubt, defensiveness, perfectionism—are rooted in my unwitting pursuit of the status, control, and happiness associated with whiteness. Perhaps this is true for many people with privilege: *what we struggle with is a symptom of what we've bought into*, including the dominant expectations and empty promises that alienate us from the deeper truths of our lives. Truths like our shared divine humanity.

6

What Does Whiteness Look Like?

THEORETICAL DESCRIPTIONS OF "WHITENESS" can sound abstract. Let me try to put more flesh on this concept.

I drafted this book during a writer's residency program at the Collegeville Institute, located on the tree-lined banks of Stumpf Lake on the campus of St. John's University in Minnesota. The campus is surrounded by lakes, forests, and wetlands—a literal bounty of natural beauty. The irony of writing a book that challenges Whites to examine our privileges as I enjoyed the tranquility of such a lovely setting is not lost on me. Spending time with incarcerated kids is teaching me not to take for granted privileges that used to feel normal.

As a teenager, one of those privileges was the chance to attend a summer leadership camp on St. John's campus from age thirteen to fifteen. The next year, the priest who directed the camp invited me to work as a counselor. I was only a year older than some of the campers, but he encouraged me to embrace my leadership role.

My mind swarmed with memories of those camp counseling years as I walked across campus to Lake Sagatagan, where I used to take campers canoeing. The beach hadn't changed much since the days I spent baking my body in the sun after the campers went home, soaking up some much-needed rest and some not-so-much-needed ultraviolet rays.

Recollecting my teenage tanning days reminded me of an observation Malcolm X made to a crowd of Black supporters in Harlem. He was encouraging them to appreciate the dark beauty of their skin, which he told them "looks like gold" compared to White people's blanched tone. "You find that old pale thing ['the White man'] laying out in the sun trying to get to look like you."[1]

Earlier in my life, I might have taken offense at such remarks. But now I see them as both amusing and true. There's something ironically absurd about my teenage pursuit of darker skin—the "look" of White affluence associated with having enough leisure time to sunbathe—given that I was utterly oblivious to the struggles of people of color and totally ignorant about the ways my own racial identity implicated me in those struggles.

The sentiment behind X's observation reminds me of the day a cohort of youth of color at the detention center educated me on the meaning of "mild." Booker used this word in a context I didn't comprehend. I asked him to clarify.

"'Mild' means *boring*," he explained.

Juan added, "White people are mild."

"No offense," Booker inserted.

"None taken," I replied.

That comment made me think about just how differently the Brown, Black, and Native residents at the detention center must see White people, compared to how I've been socialized to see my own racial identity, which, first and foremost, is to *not* see it! Whereas they actually *see* the racially segregated social system that privileges Whites, especially those who are economically secure, for most of my life, my whiteness was invisible to me. Perhaps White people are "boring" to Booker and Juan because we so regularly get to be the norm.

In *White Women*, Regina Jackson and Saira Rao use the term "mild" in a different context. They suggest that the very term "White privilege" is euphemistically "mild"—not strong enough—if you consider the oppressive consequences of whiteness for people of color.[2]

I've heard White people who proudly proclaim that they "don't see race." The trouble with this "colorblind" approach is that if you "don't see race"—including your own racial identity as a White person—you can't see racism.[3] And if you can't see racism, you won't notice one of the most consequential aspects of American society, not to mention your own life.

---

1. Hampton, "Time Has Come," 14:26.
2. Jackson and Rao, *White Women*, 63–64.
3. DiAngelo, *What Does It Mean*, 130.

7

"It's *Weird* to Stare into Someone's Eyes"

Daunte kept coming to the mindfulness group, though I wasn't sure why. He seemed disengaged. During small group discussions, he sat slouched, looking at the floor, ceiling, or walls—basically anywhere *except* at the person who was speaking. He also avoided eye contact with the rest of us when he spoke. It was my first semester visiting the detention center, and though I knew that many of the youth struggle with attention deficit, I foolishly took such apparent inattention personally. (BTW: My response was a perfect example of White centering.)

One day, I was in a group with Daunte and two other boys. All of them seemed distracted during our discussion. Though they contributed to the conversation, none appeared to be listening to what others were saying, which struck me as not just inattentive, but possibly rude. I finally decided to say something.

"Hey guys, one way to practice mindfulness is to give your full attention to whoever's talking, and you do that in part through your body language, like making eye contact." I explained that looking someone in the eye—whether you're listening or talking to them—lets them know you're present and demonstrates respect. By the time I'd finished what I thought was a pretty good sermon on the nonverbal aspects of healthy interpersonal communication, Daunte looked utterly perplexed.

"It's *weird* to stare into someone's eyes," he said.

Ade agreed. "Yeah, in my culture, you don't look people in the eye, especially an adult. You bow your head and listen to your elders, which shows respect."

George agreed that looking folks in the eye "just isn't cool."

You don't need a PhD in communication studies to know that I'd just flunked Intercultural Communication 101. I'd assumed the habits specific to my socialization as a middle-class White woman represent the default for proper communication, as if these habits ought to be the standard for everyone—including kids who come from racial, religious, and socioeconomic cultures that are foreign to me. Not only did I assume I knew what paying attention looks like, but my annoyance with these boys' apparent distraction suggests that I felt entitled to their attention.

Ugh!

After apologizing for my assumptions, I asked the boys to tell me more about the communication habits that are most familiar and comfortable to them.

I'm grateful that none of the youth with whom I've interacted over the years has ever shamed me for my ignorance. Which is pretty amazing if you consider how much the world has shamed them.

8

"How Come You're Not Afraid of Us?"

NOT ALL THE RESIDENTS avoid eye contact. One afternoon, as I was about to start the mindfulness group, Hakeem, a tough-looking, tattooed boy sitting next to me, looked directly at me and asked: "How come you're not afraid of us?" I noticed a low wave of anxiety involuntarily washing through me. Why was Hakeem asking me this?

I should clarify: there was nothing threatening in the tone of Hakeem's question. And luckily, the anxiety it activated in my nervous system dissipated almost as soon as it came. Still, that uninvited flash of fear is evidence that I'd absorbed stereotypes of young Black males as threatening.

As Menakem says, "Only a fraction of [racism] exists in our cognitive brains. For the most part, white supremacy lives in our bodies."[1] Similarly, Coates asserts that racism is not just a structural reality, but a "visceral experience."[2] Religion scholar Eddie Glaude also alludes to the more-than-cognitive dimensions of racism when he talks about "racial habits," including *White fear*: the common (and sometimes lethal) perception that Black people are dangerous.[3] Glaude notes that White fear is "bigger than any one person."[4] Sometimes it even shows up in Blacks because the omnipresence of racist stereotypes makes them easy to internalize. There doesn't need to

---

1. Menakem, *My Grandmother's Hands*, ix, xx.
2. Coates, *Between the World and Me*, 10.
3. Glaude Jr., *Democracy in Black*, 52–65.
4. Glaude Jr., *Democracy in Black*, 74.

be any actual threat of harm for White fear to be activated; just the *idea* that Blacks are prone to violence is enough to trigger it.[5]

Stereotypical associations between criminality and people of color played a pivotal role in the development of punitive policies that fueled mass incarceration. Beginning in the mid-1960s, in the wake of significant civil rights victories, politicians developed laws that disproportionately criminalized people of color.[6] By the 1970s, the "war on drugs" and "tough on crime" movements led to more severe sentencing and harsher punishments for convicted criminals, particularly people of color.

During the "law and order" era (roughly the 1960s through the 1990s), politicians were rewarded for devising laws that assured their constituents that convicted criminals, including juveniles, would pay severely for their mistakes. These laws tended to target people of color. A few states even competed to see who could punish juvenile delinquency most harshly. By the 1990s, every state had passed laws designed to make the youth system more punitive.[7]

In the mid-1990s, some Ivy League scholars exacerbated White fear by concocting the myth of "superpredators." These scholars warned the public that a growing number of severely troubled youth, mostly Black males, lacked any moral sensibilities and endangered Americans' safety with their extremely violent tendencies.[8] Fears of these "menaces to society" prompted forty-seven states to tighten their grip on justice-involved youth by placing more kids in the adult system. Meanwhile, the superpredator narrative made Black boys even more susceptible to hyper-criminalization.[9] This phenomenon is brilliantly depicted in the TV miniseries *When They See Us*, which tells the story of "the Central Park Five"—the Black and Brown youth who, after being falsely accused of beating and raping a White woman, spent between six and thirteen years in prison. During the "tough on crime" decades, a punitive approach to youth justice intensified and numbers of incarcerated youth skyrocketed, peaking at 109,000 in 1999.[10]

Glaude suggests that Whites' suspicion that Black people are dangerous is rooted in their anxiety that at some point either Black people or God would seek revenge for the sin of slavery. Whites' fear of vengeance is as old

---

5. Glaude Jr., *Democracy in Black*, 75–76.

6. Weaver, "Frontlash," 230-31.

7. Bernstein, *Burning Down the House*, 236, 71–80; McCarthy et al., "Future of Youth Justice," 4.

8. Stevenson, *Just Mercy*, 160; Equal Justice Initiative, "Superpredator Myth."

9. Bernstein, *Burning Down the House*, 75; DuVernay, dir., *When They See Us*. See also DuVernay, dir., *13th*; Gilliard, *Rethinking Incarceration*, 13–25.

10. McCarthy et al., "Future of Youth Justice," 4.

as our country. Thomas Jefferson, who owned six hundred slaves during his lifetime, worried about divine retribution for forcing fellow humans into bondage. Despite such worry, Jefferson played a leading role in creating the racial categories that he and other Whites used to justify the institution of slavery.[11]

Prior to the modern era, most Euro-Americans derived their sense of identity and belonging from their religious affiliation, geographic origin, and/or economic status. By the late eighteenth century, however, leaders like Jefferson needed a way to explain the glaring moral contradiction between the principles of freedom, equality, and justice that he professed, and the realities of slavery, genocide, and colonization that he supported. He posited that there were *intrinsic differences* between Whites and darker-skinned people and that Whites were naturally superior. This theory fit with the burgeoning "race science," which used pseudoscientific methods like measuring skulls to "prove" that Whites were biologically superior and which solidified the use of racial categories to identify people's status on the social hierarchy.[12]

There's no evidence whatsoever that "race" has a biological basis.[13] Rather, "race" is a category elite White men invented to explain and protect their privileges. Thus, Coates points out, "Race is the child of racism, not the father."[14] Even though race is essentially a fiction, this fiction has had enormous power to influence Americans' minds, hearts, and bodies, as is evident in White people's habitual perception of people of color as dangerous, and in our guilty anxiety that someday racism will yield some kind of karmic payback.

Today, White fear also includes many Whites' nervous hunch that a more equitable, inclusive, and just America implies a loss of status. This anxiety isn't necessarily conscious. Yet a significant portion of Whites knowingly worry that racial equality means losing (rather than sharing) power. Glaude cites a study that says, "Sixty percent of working-class white Americans believe that discrimination against whites is a bigger problem than discrimination against blacks."[15] This belief flies in the face of the reality that Whites enjoy *systemic* advantages in every sector of mainstream society—the media, health care, entertainment, education, politics, economics and business, religion, the military, scientific research, and so on.

11. Glaude Jr., *Democracy in Black*, 84–85.
12. DiAngelo, *What Does It Mean*, 98–99.
13. Harvard Library, "Scientific Racism," para. 5.
14. Coates, *Between the World and Me*, 7.
15. Glaude Jr., *Democracy in Black*, 87.

The irony of White fear is that the real danger is not people of color, but the pernicious harm of structural violence to which justice-involved youth are vulnerable in a racist society. If you honestly examine the history of this country and its social landscape today, it is abundantly clear which racial group wields the most power to inflict harm, and it's not people of color.

9

"Hey, No Disrespect to Your Silver Spoon"

When I introduce a new cohort of residents to the mindfulness group at the start of the semester, I share my belief that no one comes out of the womb destined to harm others or themselves. "If you grew up with enough financial and emotional support to concentrate on something other than survival, I doubt you'd be sitting here." The youth often nod their heads in agreement. They know the world isn't fair.

A conversation one of my students facilitated and wrote about in her paper illustrates some residents' understanding of the world's unfairness:

> We were talking about the cards we are dealt ... [Manuel] talked about the different hands we all get, some with the royal flush and others who get dealt just a couple random odd numbers. And then he said, "Ya know, some people were given a silver spoon when they were born. And other people, they were given a plastic spoon. Hey, no disrespect to your silver spoon though."

In her paper, my student said she knew what Manuel said was true. She wondered whether other kids in the group agreed with his analysis. Jayla chimed in:

> "Yea! I mean I don't know your life growin' up, but I know mine and ... I wouldn't trade my plastic spoon for the world." [Manuel] says, "Me either." [Steven] says, "Nope." And [Keesha] goes, "Yea same." Then there is some more quiet. And [Jayla] starts to

laugh and says, "Look at us over here just talking about spoons."
We all laughed.

What or who determines the kind of spoon we were handed at birth? There's a lot at stake in how we answer that question because what we believe about the origins of injustice shapes whether and how we see our responsibility for transforming it.

A common response to questions about the origins of injustice is some version of "God has a plan." This theory stops short of answering the question while affirming there *is* a reason, which God only knows. I hear this popular theology when students in my Christianity and Religious Diversity course study the Holocaust. While not the majority, some students say that though they don't know why the Holocaust happened, God must have had a reason.

It's not my job to talk students out of their faith convictions; but I do urge them to think critically about the assumptions and implications surrounding religious platitudes. Too often, the ideas that provide spiritual consolation to people with privilege unknowingly function to protect those benefits.

According to a 2018 survey, 78 percent of American Christians believe God is all-powerful, and 70 percent think God mostly or always dictates what happens in their lives.[1]

Conveniently, beliefs that God is almighty and has a "plan" allow us to avoid having to think too deeply about the hardships that kids growing up in poverty experience. If America's massive wealth inequality is part of God's mysterious plan, we don't have to ponder our responsibility for an economic system that distributes silver spoons to some children and plastic to others. Nor do we have to interrogate the morality of a system in which the top 10 percent of earners own 69 percent of America's total wealth, while the bottom 50 percent own 2.4 percent of that wealth.[2] Among the most dangerous consequences of the belief in God's omnipotence is human apathy, often expressed in some version of "nothing I do will make a difference."

God-has-a-plan theology also protects us from the possibility that life is intrinsically absurd. Assuming there's some divine power orchestrating everything enables us to ignore the random, nonsensical reality to which Manuel alludes in his observation that some people get dealt a "royal flush" while others get "just a couple of random odd numbers." Of course, you can believe God purposely distributes winning and losing hands for reasons we

---

1. Pew Research Center, "When Americans Say."
2. Data for Q1 2023, as had appeared at https://www.statista.com/statistics/203961/wealth-distribution-for-the-us/ (accessed July 17, 2023).

can't understand. But what kind of God would design a world that favors some children with opulent abundance while leaving others to subsist on crumbs?

Some of my students nuance their belief in God's almighty power with the notion of human freedom. Their thinking mirrors the 56 percent of those surveyed who say God *could*—but doesn't—stop human suffering because everything "is part of a larger plan," and God chooses not to interfere with our free will.[3] This latter notion has the advantage of increasing humans' responsibility for the world's cruelties. Still, we must wonder what kind of a God would sit back as people use their freedom to traumatize others. Doesn't this God understand that silence equals complicity? Minimally, this God needs some serious bystander training.

I can't speak for Jews, Muslims, or people of color, but White Christians' uncritical view of "God" as "almighty" has been dangerous, at best. If we insist that God either controls or allows everything that happens (for a reason), we not only create God in the image of a slave master, we avoid some difficult questions about the origins of injustice. Instead of asking why God causes or permits the unjust, dehumanizing circumstances into which some children are born, we should ask why humans create such circumstances and allow them to continue.

One afternoon, a small group of residents and I sat in a circle. Dario was slouching and looking tired. He perked up, however, when he saw the question on his discussion card. "Oh, wow," he said, "Can we discuss this one?"

He read the prompt: "Why is there still poverty in the twenty-first century?" The other boys shared Dario's enthusiasm for the topic. They had much to say about growing up in scarcity—so much that I don't remember the details of their conversation. I do, however, vividly recall the conclusion they unanimously arrived at in response to the question. Their answer wasn't God, but *greed*.

---

3. Pew Research Center, "In Their Own Words," para. 12.

10

"If There's a God, He's an Asshole"

THE KIDS I'VE MET at the detention center don't typically gravitate to questions about God or spirituality. So when these topics come up, I'm deeply curious about what they have to say. One day, a fellow resident asked George if he believed in God.

"If there's a God, he's an asshole," George bitterly replied.

Not all the youth who've shared snippets of their theology with me would agree with George's perspective. Linh not only believed in God but was afraid of "His" judgment. She was equally afraid of how the courts would adjudicate her case. It looked increasingly likely that she'd be tried as an adult, which would mean years in prison. Awash with anxiety, she wrote a poem/letter to God that she shared with me. In it, she begged God to forgive her for what she'd done and questioned why God was putting her through such an ordeal. She didn't accuse God of being cruel, but she believed "He" had a hand in her situation and could somehow spare her the pain of the worst-case scenario she feared.

In contrast to both George and Linh, Juan told me he doesn't believe in God, but he believes in angels, namely, his three dead brothers. "I pray to my brothers," he explained. "I know I'd be dead like them if they weren't looking out for me, and I know my angels are gonna help me when I get out of here." Juan's spiritual beliefs creatively draw on his Catholic/Latinx upbringing to address his excruciating experience of loss. I asked him if his family was religious. He responded, "Hell, yes! My grandma had statues of saints all over the house. Mostly of Mary. My grandma and my mom were always praying to Our Lady."

As a religion professor, it's hard not to appreciate the critical thinking in George's response to the question of God, the honesty of Linh's lament, and the ingenuity of Juan's spiritual connection to his dead brothers. I wish all of us felt the freedom to argue with God, express our despair, and create a spiritual connection that directly addresses our grief.

11

"I Was Born a Criminal"

Though I've yet to meet a teenager in confinement who doesn't recognize the world's unfairness, some appear to have internalized the view that their "delinquency" is rooted in an inherent moral deficiency, rather than oppressive and traumatic environments.

On one summer visit, I forgot to bring the discussion cards, and I hadn't prepared my own prompts. So, I asked a small group of residents what they wanted to discuss.

Denzel asked, "Can we talk about why we are the way we are and why we do the things we do?"

As Denzel spoke, I noticed that another boy, Dan, was holding his side, wincing with pain.

"You okay?" I asked.

Dan explained that sometimes he had painful flare-ups from a car accident that nearly killed him years ago. Still holding his side, he changed the topic back to Denzel's question. "The reason I'm the way I am is because I was born with fetal alcohol syndrome. I was already fucked up at birth because of my mom's addiction." His voice sounded resigned. "I think that's why I did the things I did. I was born bad."

Denzel spoke next: "I don't know, but maybe we do the things we do because of fate."

I wanted to ask him what he meant by "fate." But Darius, who struggled with PTSD so severe that he would sit in a small group discussion only if his back was positioned against the wall, quickly said, "I know why I'm bad. I'm a rape baby." Then he added, "That's why I'm retarded. That's what some therapist told me in grade school." Darius attributed not just his illiteracy but his schizophrenia to being a "rape baby."

Darius's "rape baby" comment left me dumbfounded and triggered my desire to fix. I wanted to say the right thing to convince both him and Dan that the circumstances of their birth need not become their destiny. But this urge to fix easily doubles as a desire to be in control. It's a variation on the theme of wanting to be a savior/hero—a classic habit of whiteness. Instead of fixing, the late Jewish Zen master/social activist Bernie Glassman recommends *bearing witness*. To bear witness is to be fully present to whatever life puts in front of you (or stirs within you) in any given moment, without fixed ideas, agenda, interpretations, or answers.[1] To bear witness is to relinquish the twin illusions of control and certainty. I'm trying to practice bearing witness to interrupt my White supremacy habits.

A small group of youth and I were discussing the question: "How do you understand the purpose of your life?"

Lucas responded: "I guess it's to get into trouble."

I couldn't tell if he was joking.

Following Lucas's lead, Corey said that his purpose is "to be a robber." His tone sounded simultaneously serious and humorous. Corey explained that although his family lived in "a rich people's town," they were very poor. "I've been stealing stuff since I was in first grade." Stealing was how he tried to keep up with the "rich kids."

I asked the boys whether they really thought they were *born* to be "troublemakers" and "robbers"—or whether they resorted to harmful behaviors because of the really challenging situations in which they grew up. Corey doubled down on his answer: "I know my family situation was rough, but I was *born* a criminal."

"But do you think you'd have resorted to stealing if your needs had been met as a child?" I asked. "Do you think seeing yourself as a criminal could become a self-fulfilling prophecy?"

Corey wasn't interested in my questions. He kept insisting that he was "*born* a criminal."

When I finally abandoned my fixaholic desire to rescue Corey from what seemed to me to be a hopelessly immovable mindset, I was left to confront my own arrogance and discomfort in the wake of my failure to "save" him from his self-perception. My urge to "enlighten" kids who have internalized our society's view of them as "bad" says more about my privileges than my virtue. Yes, I wanted Corey to see whatever mistakes he's made as rooted in the harsh circumstances he inherited at birth rather than some

---

1. Glassman, *Bearing Witness*, xvi, 16.

inborn malicious disposition that destines him for a life behind bars. But coupled with my failure to bear witness, this desire became just another expression of whiteness.

12

"Because I'm a *Bad* Kid"

We can't blame incarcerated youth for internalizing a view of themselves as natural-born "criminals." Many receive this message from parents, peers, teachers, siblings, coaches, and police officers who have absorbed stereotypes of teenage offenders as inherently immoral or predisposed to crime. Once, during a weekly check-in, a girl who chose the alias Rose Marie shared her disappointment that her family didn't answer her phone calls. I asked her why she thought they didn't answer. She replied in an isn't-it-obvious tone: "Because I'm a *bad* kid."

Even youth offenders who don't internalize a sense of themselves as "bad" must deal with dehumanizing public perceptions of them. Bernstein asked incarcerated teens how they thought the outside world perceived them. Their responses included: "'Dirtbag,' 'fuckup,' 'lazy,' 'worthless,' 'lower than the low.'"[1]

On his first day in the mindfulness group, Tyrell hesitated when it was his turn to share what he'd been struggling with lately, as if deliberating how truthful he wanted to be. Finally, he said, "Well, I'm just gonna be honest. My hard thing is being Black." He quickly added, "Not *being* Black, because I *like* being Black. What I mean is the way other people see me. They don't really see me. They just see a Black kid who's probably going to get in trouble, or already is in trouble. Which I am."

Black youth are especially prone to being perceived as "criminals," and this stereotype negatively impacts how they are adjudicated. In a study of pre-sentencing reports, Black teenagers' illegal behavior was more often

---

1. Bernstein, *Burning Down the House*, 67.

attributed to *internal* characteristics (for example, a "defiant personality") and given harsher penalties. By comparison, White juveniles' offenses were more often seen as stemming from external factors (like a "broken home") and meriting less severe sentencing.[2] Our culture's tendency to criminalize Black boys in particular—to see them as morally deficient and destined for a life of crime—also influences their self-perceptions. Listen to the self-descriptions that surfaced in a conversation among three Black males in the mindfulness group:

"I've got Black skin," Curtis said. "I'm a criminal. I'm a *felon*."

Apollo responded: "I'm a felon too."

Pointing to the others, then himself, Martin agreed, "Yeah, we're all felons here."

Conscious or not, our views contribute to a reservoir of public perceptions that impacts how teen offenders are judged and how they perceive themselves. Examining the origins of our assumptions about them is the least we can do. Ultimately, Denzel's questions—"Why are we the way we are?" and "Why do we do the things we do?"—are equally relevant for our own self-understanding. For if we honestly explore these queries, we'll invariably have to reflect on our privileges.

---

2. Kaplan et al., "Individual Differences."

13

"I Want to Know What Really Happened"

The first time I read about Malcolm X's depiction of White people as "the devil,"[1] I did what people with unacknowledged privilege often do when someone points out their group's power to harm: I assumed he was overreacting. I made the same assumption when I learned that X called Christianity "the white man's religion." Growing up Catholic and considering myself to be a "good person," these comments struck me as not just hyperbolic, but offensive. However, the more I studied America's racial and religious history, the more I understood why Malcolm X said these things about White people and Christianity.

Many White Christians don't realize that throughout US history, their religion functioned as a powerful tool of racial oppression. In *The Sin of White Supremacy*, Jeannine Hill Fletcher exposes how the racial and economic disparities that plague America today are rooted in historical injustices and traumas that White Christians inflicted on people of color. Her analysis documents how White superiority evolved in tandem with a theology of Christian supremacy, which held that Christianity is the one and only true religion and that it's God's plan for everybody to be Christian. These racial and religious superiority complexes were so intertwined that for much of US history, being White and being Christian were virtually synonymous.

During this history, federal policies associated being "American" with being both White and Christian, thus fusing these three identities ("American," "White," and "Christian"). The colonial narrative that God had chosen

1. Lomax, "Summing Up."

America to be a Christian nation served to justify slavery and genocide. Powerful White Christians claimed to be doing "heathens" and "savages" a favor by "civilizing" and "saving" them.[2] As Hill Fletcher points out, it wasn't the "ignorant masses" who produced the toxic theologies that claimed it was "God's plan" for European-American Christians to dominate non-White, non-Christian people. It was educated White men—celebrated politicians, philosophers, Christian preachers, college professors and presidents—who, with support from their White wives, laid the foundations for America's racial, religious, and economic injustices *in the name of the Christian God*.[3] As Ibram X. Kendi observes, conversations with Whites about racism can be difficult because most Whites have only rudimentary knowledge of America's history.[4]

One day I asked a cohort of six residents whether they were aware that politicians in dozens of states were trying to ban education about the unflattering side of American history, claiming that such knowledge would make young people "unpatriotic." The youth are usually pretty up to speed on current events, but only one had heard of this controversy. The others thought I was joking. When I explained that censoring learning about parts of our nation's history was really a thing, they were visibly upset.

"Don't they think we can handle the truth?" Antoine asked.

"You've got to wonder what they're trying to hide," Trina remarked.

"They can send us to fight wars overseas when we're eighteen," Carlos said in disbelief, "but they can't tell us what our government did to my people?"

Then Angelica, said something that reminded me of some of Malcolm X's statements: "White people are evil." She added, "They need to be punished."

Whites often respond to the despair of racial minorities with accusations that they are exaggerating the problem and/or being "overly sensitive." In so doing, we showcase our lack of knowledge of both the historical anguish that state-sanctioned forms of terrorism, theft, and torture created for racially and religiously marginalized communities, and the ongoing effects of that trauma for generations after the original wounds were inflicted.

The term "historical trauma" was initially used by First Nation and Aboriginal people in Canada to describe how the mass slaughter of Indigenous peoples, the cultural devastation, stolen land, family separations, and religious coercion wreaked havoc on Indigenous people for generations. A

---

2. Hill Fletcher, *Sin of White Supremacy*, 5, 13–16, 24.
3. Hill Fletcher, *Sin of White Supremacy*, 1–16.
4. Kendi, "How to Be an Antiracist," 20:50.

similar pattern impacts the lives of African Americans today, whose families and communities are forced to grapple with the devastating legacies of slavery, Jim Crow, lynching, and countless other ways Blacks have been terrorized throughout US history. As Ruth King reminds us, "What's unfinished is reborn." And, "When harm of such magnitude is deliberately inflicted, it makes the trauma more difficult to overcome psychologically, snowballing into communicable social disease that affects generational well-being for all humanity."[5]

King reminds us that while minoritized communities are most directly devastated by the consequences of historical trauma, members of privileged groups are not unaffected. To illustrate this point, she describes photographs of lynching rituals that were common in the South since the 1800s. Looking at the faces of White children standing next to their parents in the pictures, King wonders what they were feeling. Though these boys and girls didn't orchestrate the terror, they witnessed it. As Menakem points out, whatever was happening in those little White bodies as they watched Black bodies hanging or burning would someday be passed down to their children.[6] King also wonders what was going through the minds and hearts of the Black people as they helplessly watched family and community members being lynched. "What stopped them from going insane or erupting in a rampage?" King asks. "What behavior was required to survive? . . . How did they adjust their hearts to exist with such human hatred?"[7]

In a meticulously researched report, the Equal Justice Initiative chronicles the history of racial terror lynching in America. Organized and attended by Whites, often as festive family occasions, these horrifically violent acts were tolerated by government officials at both state and federal levels, especially in the South. Emboldened by theologies of White supremacy, such public spectacles of torture evolved in tandem with the criminal justice system, shaping *how* punishment was delivered—and *to whom* and *by whom* it was administered—in ways that continue to complicate and compromise the justice system we have today. "Mass incarceration, excessive penal punishment, disproportionate sentencing of racial minorities, and police abuse of people of color reveal problems in American society that were framed in the terror era" of lynching, particularly between 1880 and 1940.[8]

In *The Cross and the Lynching Tree*, theologian James Cone challenges White Christians to reflect on the connections between America's history

---

5. R. King, *Mindful of Race*, 28.
6. R. King, *Mindful of Race*, 29–30; Menakem, *My Grandmother's Hands*, 200–204.
7. R. King, *Mindful of Race*, 29.
8. Equal Justice Initiative, *Lynching in America*.

of racialized lynchings and the Roman Empire's crucifixion of Jesus, which he describes as "a first-century lynching."[9] Scholar and prison abolitionist Nikia Roberts takes this connection a step further: "Jesus' first century lynching as a despised Palestinian Jew was a deplorable criminal's death that conjoins the lynching of Africans to the scapegoating of Black bodies in the Carceral State."[10]

To the extent that Whites are unwilling to learn about, reflect on, and openly discuss the ugliest chapters of US history, we simply cannot understand the utter frustration expressed in Angelica's description of White people as "evil" and deserving of punishment. Interestingly, right after she made these remarks, Angelica said something else: "I want to go to college and study history. I want to know what really happened." She reasoned that if she could survive the things she's survived, she could handle the truth about America's history.

But can we handle the truth?

---

9. Cone, *Cross and the Lynching Tree*, 30–31.
10. Robert, "Penitence, Plantation and the Penitentiary," 49.

14

"I Did Not Know How to Feel"

DEEP LEARNING OFTEN INVOLVES discomfort. My students and I experience some degree of disequilibrium and unease every time we visit the detention center. These visits expose the systemic injustices that pervade our society, making explicit and proximate what's largely invisible or merely theoretical for Americans with racial and/or economic privilege.

Years ago, during our orientation visit, a group of youth on the third floor had just finished school and needed to transition from their locked classroom back to their locked pod. To make space in the hallway, my students and I were ushered into the control room, which is where staff persons monitor the screens showing footage from cameras located throughout the building. The upper walls of the control room are almost entirely windows, so my students and I could see the residents, whom we had not yet met, as they walked by. Some made funny faces at us. Others smiled and waved. A few looked at their feet.

There's no shortage of unscripted moments on our weekly visits to the detention center, but this one felt particularly awkward. One of my White students whispered to me in a troubled voice that she'd never seen so many people of color in one place. She'd grown up on a farm in rural North Dakota. The next week, this student wrote a paper about this incident. She was especially troubled by the question of whether she should have smiled at the residents who walked by when we were in the control room:

> I wanted to smile at them because . . . I wanted them to know I thought of them as fellow human beings with a simple smile, but I also knew a smile could indicate that I was happy, which I was not.

In the end, this student resolved to smile at the residents with whom she made eye contact because she "wanted to somehow acknowledge their humanness and greet them as equals." Later in her paper, however, she analyzed her uneasiness and the dilemma of whether to smile as possible evidence of her "internalized dominance":

> Maybe it was not my job to let the youth know that I wanted them to know they were equals. Maybe in doing so, I was asserting my privilege over them. At the same time, I did not want to look them in the eyes blank-faced because maybe that would give [them] the impression that I thought I was better than them. I did not know how to feel. I was very conflicted.

The uneasiness my students and I experience in proximity to some of our nation's most vulnerable youth is a symptom of just how normally disconnected our lives are from theirs. Our discomfort is a by-product of our privilege. It's also an invitation to learn.

A lot of Whites in America grow up in racially segregated environments, insulated from the realities of racial oppression. As DiAngelo points out, Whites' distance from these realities fosters "expectations for racial comfort" and diminishes our "ability to tolerate racial stress." The result is a condition she calls "white fragility"—"a state in which even a minimum amount of racial stress becomes intolerable, triggering a range of defensive moves," from emotional displays of anger, fear, and guilt, to behaviors like arguing, shutting down, or physically leaving a hard conversation.[1]

I recognize my own socialized tendencies in DiAngelo's definition of White fragility. Not only was my upbringing virtually void of people of color, but like a lot of girls from White, bourgeois families, I was taught to be *nice*, avoid conflict at all costs, and do whatever it took to make sure people liked me. These lessons were not communicated explicitly, and I had no idea they were preparing me to pursue the privileges of White, middle-class womanhood.

It's worth pausing to ponder the linguistic roots of this (supposedly) feminine virtue. "Nice" comes from the Latin, *nescius* (*ne*—not and *scire*—to know), which means "ignorant." Throughout Christian history, women have been expected to *be nice*, to cultivate deferential "feminine" qualities like sacrifice, meekness, obedience, and service to others, even if it meant ignoring our inner truths. Both the linguistic and the patriarchal religious roots of White women's socialization to be nice underscore the external and internalized oppression that compulsory niceness perpetuates.

---

1. DiAngelo, "White Fragility," 54.

White women's cultural conditioning to be nice preserves racism by preventing us from speaking out against injustice. Simultaneously, our training to please others limits our ability to be honest with ourselves, which erodes our integrity and preempts trustworthy relationships. In *White Women*, Jackson and Rao propose that the antidote to the toxicity of White women's niceness is *kindness*, which stems from authenticity rather than a desire to be liked.[2]

Developing racial literacy strengthens our stamina for racial discomfort, enables us admit when we don't know how to feel, and prepares us to risk speaking our truths in the face of injustice.

---

2. Jackson and Rao, *White Women*, 19–28.

15

"Same Old, Same Old"

Keesha enjoyed being the center of attention during our visits to the detention center. Once, while the rest of us chose spots in the circle of cushions in the middle of the gym, she did backflips (literally) beneath one of the basketball hoops. Her energy was usually playful and upbeat. But when someone in our small group brought up the recent killing of Daunte Wright—a twenty-year-old Black man who was shot by a White police officer—her mood became noticeably somber. I asked her how she felt about his death. Shaking her head, Keesha said in a tone of resignation mixed with disgust, "Same old, same old."

In a pattern that's become all too familiar, Wright was pulled over for a minor traffic violation. Minutes later, he was dead. The agent who killed him said she mistakenly grabbed her gun instead of her Taser as he appeared to be resisting arrest. The incident happened ten miles from where another White police officer, Derek Chauvin, was on trial for killing George Floyd. Reeling with grief over the death of her son, Daunte Wright's mother exclaimed: "'Justice' isn't even a word to me."[1] What could *justice* possibly mean to a mother whose child was carelessly killed by a system with a centuries-long track record of targeting Black males?

Roshuan said he was certain he'd been racially profiled by police. "Just like Daunte Wright," he added. I asked how he knew this. He replied, "The cops have a target on my back." He said the police "always" sat in their parked black-and-white SUVs in his neighborhood, "just watching and waiting for us to mess up." Roshuan is not alone in his suspicion. According

---

1. Katie Wright, quoted in Ruttenberg, *On Repentance and Repair*, 183.

to the NAACP, 65 percent of Black adults in this country have felt targeted because of their race.[2]

There's so much pain in America, especially among low-income communities of color, surrounding the issue of police violence. That pain is legitimate and needs to be addressed for healing to happen. But demonizing law enforcement won't create the kind of justice Wright's family, Roshuan, and others need and deserve. For one thing, many cops in this country risk their lives daily on behalf of the people they serve. While writing this chapter, I read about a deputy who tried to protect a woman from her violent partner. The woman survived. The officer didn't.[3] Moreover, as Atiba Goff reminds us, speculating about police officers' character or assuming racist motives isn't helpful since we don't have access to their inner thoughts, intentions, or feelings. What we do have access to is data on the differences between police interactions with White and non-White suspects. Having studied this evidence, Goff confirms that there are "massive disparities" in how police deal with suspects.[4]

In *The Rage of Innocence*, law professor Kristen Henning cites research showing that in heavily surveilled neighborhoods or areas where stop and frisk is routine, Black and Latinx kids experience a kind of perpetual psychological trauma, including high rates of fear, anxiety, depression, and distrust of authority figures. The trauma comes both from being the direct target of police surveillance and from watching police monitor their peers. Over-policing criminalizes normal adolescent behavior (like playing loud music or wearing saggy pants) and creates a cycle of mistrust and bias that flows both ways: "Police expect Black youth to be violent and aggressive; Black youth expect the police to be biased and antagonistic."[5] Henning says we need to "reduce the police footprint" in minority and low-income communities, in part by releasing them from the responsibility of doing work they're neither qualified to do nor interested in doing. This is not an abolitionist argument, she says, since the vast majority of cops don't want to be doing mental health work.[6]

Law enforcement's differential treatment of youth of color is also evident in the uneven rates at which minoritized kids and their White peers are arrested and imprisoned. Restorative justice expert Fania Davis reports that in some states, "Black boys are incarcerated at rates twenty to twenty-four

2. NAACP, "Criminal Justice Fact Sheet," para. 8.
3. Fox 9 Staff, "Pope County Deputy Killed."
4. Atiba Goff, "Changing Behavior."
5. Henning, *Rage of Innocence*, xvii–xviii.
6. Henning, *Rage of Innocence*, 204–35.

times higher than white boys," despite similar levels of illegal behavior.[7] More broadly, "41% of incarcerated young people are Black, despite making up only 15% of the adolescent population."[8] Residents in a juvenile facility Bernstein visited had a saying: "Your skin is your sin."[9]

Just over a week after George Floyd's murder, I visited my mother, a White woman in her eighties who leans strongly left on nearly all political issues and whose heart is soft as a pillow and big as the sky. Mom surprised me by expressing her discomfort with the "rioting" she'd seen on the news. "You know I support Black Lives Matter, but why do they have to destroy property?" she asked, genuinely concerned. While the vast majority of protesters were peaceful, my mom was referring to a few who had set fire to the Third Precinct police building in Minneapolis.

It's hard to understand the intensity of frustration—the sheer desperation—expressed in such violent protests without knowing something about the origins of policing in America, specifically its roots in the slave era. This is not a history lesson most Americans learn in school. Even college students studying criminal justice rarely encounter this history in their textbooks.[10] Yet knowing this history is essential for understanding the often-fraught relationship between the Black community and police today.

In the early 1700s, racial profiling was baked into the unwritten job descriptions of one of the earliest forms of policing in America: the Southern "slave patrols." These patrols included armed men who assumed responsibility for hunting down and returning runaway slaves. They used violence to suppress slave uprisings, instill fear in the minds of Blacks who might be plotting rebellion, and punish enslaved persons who disobeyed their enslavers.[11] After emancipation, slave patrols were replaced by militia-like groups of White men whose job it was to enforce the "Black Codes," a series of laws that criminalized Blacks for minor "offenses"—for example, talking too loud, spitting, drinking, missing work, being homeless or unable to show that you had a job. Designed to criminalize newly freed slaves, these laws led to the arrests of tens of thousands of Blacks, whom state officials rented out to owners of plantations, factories, and labor camps. As leased convicts, Blacks had even less protection than they'd had as slaves since those who rented their labor had no incentive to protect their bodies.

7. Davis, *Little Book of Race*, 64.
8. Leonard, "Racial and Ethnic Disparities," para. 3.
9. Bernstein, *Burning Down the House*, 59–60.
10. Turner et al., "Ignoring the Past."
11. Turner et al., "Ignoring the Past," 185–86. See also NAACP, "Modern Day Policing," para. 1.

Thanks to the Black Codes, there was a steady stream of other "criminals" to replace them. According to Davis, "One third of the inmates in labor camps were adolescent boys," foreshadowing the criminalization of young Black males today.[12]

Davis recounts that even after convict leasing was outlawed in the early 1900s, Black prisoners were forced to work in chain gangs. Beneath the shadow of an overseer's whip, they sweated and toiled to build the roads and other infrastructure in the South. Others were forced to work without compensation for White landowners who had paid the fines related to their arrests.[13] Many middle- and upper-class Euro-Americans today don't understand that *the gross wealth disparities between African Americans and us stem from centuries of free labor that Blacks were forced to provide for Whites*—forced with the help of White "law enforcement." Nor do we recognize that the often-tense relationship between the Black community and police today reflects the history of White supremacy as it infected the evolution of law enforcement in America. Most Whites don't realize that many people of color experience the state-authorized violence against members of their community as the "same old, same old."

I explained this history to my mother. She said it helped her feel more empathy for people who resorted to desperate measures in their struggle for racial justice, even though she still doesn't condone the violence.

---

12. Davis, *Little Book of Race*, 60–61.
13. Davis, *Little Book of Race*, 62.

16

"Not All Black Kids Are the Same"

THE INCARCERATED YOUTH OF color I've met are reliably insightful about the ways systemic racism has impacted their lives. Moira said she was having a hard time because she'd recently found out that her aunt had been murdered. Her face was sad, but there was anger in her voice as she asked me: "White people don't have to talk about their aunts getting murdered, do they?"

In another conversation, Roshuan commented: "What most of us in here did is minor compared to that White kid who killed two people. How come he gets to walk free?" Roshuan was referring to Kyle Rittenhouse, a White teenager who was acquitted on all five counts after fatally shooting two people and seriously injuring another during a night of racial upheaval and violent protest in Kenosha, Wisconsin. Rittenhouse, who was seventeen at the time and who came to the protest armed with an AR-15–style rifle, said he shot these men because he feared for his life.[1]

On a different visit, one of the Black residents, Shevon, said to my mostly White students, only half jokingly, "I'm locked up for doing something I *know* lots of you college kids do on weekends. And how come you don't get arrested?" Though fewer than 5 percent of youth in confinement are held for drug-related offenses,[2] Shevon's comment made me wonder how different the population of incarcerated young people would be if police surveilled college dorms, apartments, and off-campus housing as

---

1. Sullivan, "Kyle Rittenhouse."
2. Sawyer, "Youth Confinement," para. 22.

heavily as they monitor low-income neighborhoods whose residents are mostly people of color.

During the same visit, Shevon shared his perspective on "the difference between Black and White kids" (his words): "When White kids come home, their mom asks [using a sweet tone]: 'How was your day, honey?' When Black kids come home, their mom asks [using a stern, interrogating voice]: 'Why you home? You in trouble? Who's gonna pay the bills?'"

After he said this, Alison, who is also Black, responded, "Not all Black kids are the same. I'm adopted and my parents are White." To further illustrate her point about the diversity among Black youth, she shared that her Black friends tell her she "sounds White."

"Don't you think I sound White?" she asked the group. "Can't you tell the difference between the way Shevon and I talk?"

Looking intrigued, Shevon responded, "I swear, I've never noticed your White accent before, but now that you mention it, I definitely hear it."

Incarcerated or not, Black youth are not a monolith. While this point should be obvious, Whites are notorious for lumping people of color together. Even the phrase "people of color" effaces the infinite *diversity within* minoritized communities while feeding the delusion that we/Whites are without race. Whites' habit of viewing Indigenous, Brown, and Black people as first and foremost members of their racialized communities perpetuates overgeneralizations. Shevon called out this homogenizing habit of whiteness as he expressed pride for his own racial identity. "I'm proud of my skin. I'd *never* want to be White . . . White people all look the same—and I know you think the same about us."

If we don't think Black boys from low-income communities know we've been culturally programmed to see them as criminals, we're fooling ourselves. But we're not fooling them. One of these boys described this racist programming in his poem, "Do You?"

> Do you ever look at a colored man
> and think he's gonna sound "ghetto"?
> Then he speaks.
> He speaks properly,
> You know in your head it sounds weird.
> Do you think he grew up in a white family?
> Do you think he's putting on an act?
> Do you think he's embarrassed?
> No. That's just how he talks.
> But . . .
> If you didn't see his face and
> Just heard his voice

You would assume he's white.
I know you would.

The blanket presumptions Whites make about people of color are the flip side of our socialization to see ourselves as individuals (rather than members of a racial group) and to expect others to see and value our individuality. This self-perception leads us to believe that we're unaffected by the racist systems we inhabit. "I know some Whites who are racist," we say, "but I'm different." Yet this insistence that unlike most Whites, we've managed to transcend the ugliness of White supremacy only demonstrates our lack of understanding of racism's systemic quality. The more we fancy ourselves to be immune from this system's toxicity, the more vulnerable we are to being poisoned by its ubiquity.

17

"A Shitty Hand of Cards"

I ASKED A SMALL group of residents whether and how poverty had impacted their lives. One insisted that if his family could have afforded a "*real* lawyer," he would be home. Another responded that he didn't mind the flat mattress in his room because he hadn't had a bed growing up. Another said she wouldn't *want* to come from a rich family because then she would have become a snob ("like the girls at my school") and because she wouldn't know how to survive the way she does now.

Economic insecurity profoundly impacts the life trajectories of kids who engage in harmful or illegal behavior. Research points to strong correlations between childhood poverty, self-harm, and violent crimes later in life.[1] One study found homicide rates were *eighteen* times higher among poor youth compared to their wealthier peers.[2] Economic impoverishment is one of the main drivers of violent crime in America.[3] Poverty influences kids' delinquent behavior in multiple ways—for example, by depriving them (and their parents) of meaningful educational opportunities, adequate nutrition, health care and mental health services, employment opportunities, and creative/artistic venues to express themselves and develop their talents further.

America is the richest nation on the planet, yet one out of eight children here live in poverty, and "more than a million public schoolchildren are homeless (living in motels, cars, shelters, and abandoned buildings)."

---

1. Mok et al., "Family Income Inequalities"; Puzzanchera et al., *Youth and the Juvenile Justice System*.
2. Males, "Age, Poverty, Homicide," para. 2.
3. Sered, *Until We Reckon*, 3.

"A Shitty Hand of Cards"

Studying these realities, sociologist Matthew Desmond concludes that poverty persists "not for lack of resources. We lack something else."[4]

In another discussion about wealth inequality in America, Nick, who is White, commented, "Kids like us were dealt a shitty hand of cards from the start." I asked him to elaborate. He said that the "shitty hand of cards" represents the poverty into which he and kids like him were born. Nick said he used to dread the start of the start of school each year because that's when all the other kids would have new clothes, backpacks, and sneakers—"the things that make you 'cool' in the eyes of others." As he spoke, the other residents in the group nodded in solidarity, as if the pattern he described was painfully familiar.

Nick's comment got me thinking that the term "whiteness" needs more nuance. There are, after all, varying degrees to which White people get to enjoy the benefits of being White in a racist society. The myth of White supremacy includes a supporting narrative that some Whites are more valuable than others. I grew up in a rural area where references to "white trash" were common. Middle-class White kids used this dehumanizing term to describe poor Whites who lived in trailer courts or run-down houses surrounded by rusty car parts and other "junk."

For centuries, elite Whites have harbored disdain for impoverished Whites, even as they deployed the ideology of White supremacy to persuade poor Whites not to join forces with people of color, fearing that a coalition of society's underdogs would threaten their dominance. Still today, this racist solidarity provides psychic compensation to impoverished Whites: they may be poor, but at least they are White and thus supposedly better than someone.[5]

Affluent White people have a different relationship with whiteness than Whites who are economically insecure. The same could be said about the varying levels of privilege among Whites who experience physical or cognitive disabilities compared to those who are able bodied. Or Whites who identify as straight compared to those in the LGBTQIA community. *Whiteness is not a monolith.* Some of us benefit more from our racial advantages than others.

---

4. Desmond, *Poverty*, 6–7.
5. Menakem, *My Grandmother's Hands*, 70–71.

18

"I'd Give Anything to Be Able to Decide What to Have for Breakfast"

IT WAS MY TURN to share what I'd been struggling with lately. I told my small group that I'd been agonizing over a difficult decision. Without divulging details, I explained that I generally hate making decisions. Big or small. "I'm pathologically indecisive," I explained. The kids laughed, but I was only partially joking. "I don't even like having to decide what to eat for breakfast, so I have the same thing every morning."

Trina, who was characteristically cheerful despite the hellish sexual abuse she'd survived, responded with a smile: "I'd give *anything* to be able to decide what to have for breakfast." Her voice was full of longing. "Every morning it's the same thing: gluten-free Rice Krispies."

Trina's comment helped me realize that, like many of my "problems," my decision-making difficulty is a symptom of my privileges—the result of the abundance that I often take for granted. This difficulty is also tied to my lifelong struggle with perfectionism. My fear about making the "wrong" decision assumes that there's a "right" choice that will lead to the perfect, pain-free life I crave.

According to Jackson and Rao, my desire for things to be "perfect" is another oppressive habit of whiteness to which White women seem especially drawn. With the help of consumer culture, social media, and entertainment industries, the dream of "perfection" propels many of us to chase fantasies that are painfully elusive: perfect body, perfect home, perfect children, perfect job performance, etc. This same perfectionistic mindset prevents us from taking risks to challenge racism. Fearful that we'll "make a mistake" or that a person of color will call out our unintentionally racist assumptions or behavior, we remain silent.[1] The myth of perfection (falsely) promises to protect us from the shame we've been programmed to feel—that sense of never being "good enough." The painful consequences of my perfectionism remind me that my unwitting habit of chasing after the privileges of whiteness hasn't served me well.

---

1. Jackson and Rao, *White Women*, 1–17.

19

"I Have All the Time in the World"

SPENDING TIME WITH PEOPLE whose freedoms are severely restricted illuminates not just the privileges I take for granted, but the ways those advantages create more headaches than happiness when I pursue them to bolster my own sense of worthiness and importance. One of the ways I do this is by staying constantly busy. In the framework laid out by Tricia Hersey, a womanist theologian, artist, poet, and community activist, I have unknowingly "donated my body" to America's "grind culture." Hersey describes grind culture as "a collaboration between capitalism and white supremacy" that perpetuates the dehumanizing, exhausting, violent work ethic of the system of chattel slavery. This system, Hersey says, stamps out humans' divinity by turning our bodies into machines.[1] Clearly, I've bought into grind culture. Some days at work, I dehydrate myself because I'm not sure when I'll have time to pee.

On one of those days, I was late leaving campus for the detention center. My effort to make up time by exceeding the speed limit was stymied by one of the many trains that run through town. This unwelcome pause gave me a moment to notice the irony of breaking the law (speeding) to be on time for a visit with incarcerated teens, during which we would practice mindfulness! I anxiously waited for the train to pass, trying to calm myself with conscious breathing. But my effort was half hearted, and my stress continued to pulse like the flashing lights and dinging bells at the crossing. Cognitively I knew there was no point in stressing about something I couldn't control. But I've internalized grind culture to the point where its

---

1. Hersey, *Rest Is Resistance*, 38.

more-better-faster ethos is involuntary. By the time the caboose passed and crossing bars lifted, my car's steering wheel was moist from the stress of my sweaty hands.

Students who had left campus on time were waiting in the facility's lobby. Once everyone was accounted for, a staff person escorted us to the classroom upstairs where a cohort of youth awaited us. Entering the room was like walking into a force field of *un*hurried energy. The atmosphere could not have been more unlike the adrenaline that was still speeding through my body and the bodies of students who'd been caught behind the train. Like me, they'd all had busy days, and the train delay had only escalated our chronic war against time. During check-ins, several students shared about their stress and being "too busy." Lord knows, I could relate.

"Sometimes I think 'too busy' should be my middle name," I said, "because this seems to be my response whenever someone asks me how I am. Sometimes 'too busy' is not just *how* I am, but *who* I am. That feels oppressive."

Tauri, the youth sitting next to me, had been listening attentively. Slowly, in a soft, careful voice, he said: "I have the opposite problem. I have all the time in the world." He said that being in detention is boring. "When you're doing time, every day feels like it lasts forever. If I were busier, time would go quicker."

Together with Hersey's critique of grind culture, Tauri's perspective on the snail's pace of time in detention exposes my always-in-a-hurry habit as yet another product of my privileges. To be sure, many Americans are forced into overworking just to put food on the table, and some of my students work dozens of hours each week to pay for college. But those are not my situations. For me, feeling chronically time famished is a direct result of my social advantages, including meaningful work. My struggle against time is a symptom of *abundance*, not scarcity.

Which is ironic since I'm pretty sure that my sense of never having enough time is rooted in a deeper sense of "not enough." This sensibility fuels my pursuit of productivity and self-improvement. Being "too busy" is how I prove my worth. My painful allegiance to "grind culture" is also one of the ways I have unknowingly chased after the privileges of whiteness.

By sharing his struggle with the slowness of "doing time," the lesson that Tauri offered nonincarcerated people with privilege is not that we should be grateful because kids like him have it so much worse. Rather, his perspective invites us to examine the places where our privileges hide, including the habits that cause us considerable distress, like frantically rushing or chronically overworking. What if we learned to recognize the ways the structures that benefit us at the expense of others are not good for *anyone*? What if people with privilege asked ourselves "What have I bought into?" and learned to identify the hidden threads connecting our distress to our privileges?

20

"My Bad, My Bad"

BEING A RECOVERING PERFECTIONIST means that I'm also a recovering control freak. My visits with kids at the detention center expose my predilection for order over chaos. I noticed this penchant one day as I was attempting to corral my students and the residents into a circle so the mindfulness group could begin. Nobody was paying attention. My students were engaged in casual conversations with some of the youth. Three female residents stood in a corner of the gym, talking and giggling. A few male youth shot baskets with the *zafus*. The hoop was too small for the meditation cushions to pass through it. I watched as they hit the rim and fell on the dirty floor, scattering tiny clumps of dust and hair as they landed.

The mindfulness group proffers ample opportunities for me to practice letting go of my "law and order" inclinations. When it came time to break into small groups, the three girls who had been chatting in the corner wanted to stay together. I invited them to be in a group with me and one of my students. As we discussed the prompts, however, they kept having side conversations. Every time I interrupted their whispered chatter to remind them that paying attention during small group discussions was part of our mindfulness practice, they quickly apologized—"My bad, my bad"—and redirected their attention. Minutes later, they'd resume their distracting banter.

My frustration grew.

On the one hand, this is understandable because I wanted to preserve the integrity of the group by encouraging everyone to pay attention to what others were sharing. On the other hand, I could have just as easily invited these girls to form their own small group so they could continue their conversation in a way that was meaningful for them.

But, I wanted them to follow the rules. And if I'm honest—and this is hard to admit—I felt entitled to their respect. I took their distracting behavior *personally*, as if it was their job to make me feel like a competent facilitator. I made their side chatter about me and my preference for order over chaos, following rules, respecting authority.

I used to see my desire to contain chaos as a symptom of my neurotic personality. But now I also recognize it as a by-product of my White, middle-class, Catholic upbringing. In my family, church, and schools, moral judgments about "good" and "bad" mapped neatly onto "compliant" and "unruly" behavior.

Associations between virtue and obedience have deep roots in the biblical tradition. For centuries, Euro-Christian leaders invoked the Bible's "household codes" to convince slaves to obey their masters, wives to obey their husbands, and children to obey their parents. Obedience to authority, they preached, was God's will.

One of Western culture's founding myths—the story of Eve and Adam's fall from grace—associates sin with disobedience, and disobedience with punishment.[1] In this story, God warns the first couple not to eat the fruit from the tree of the knowledge of good and evil. They do it anyway. *They break the law.* God, who happens to be patrolling the garden, witnesses their sin and interrogates them. In addition to kicking them out of paradise, God punishes Eve for her transgression by making childbirth horrendously painful and making her pine for the very person who gets to rule over her: her husband. Meanwhile, Adam must pay for letting his wife lead him astray by having to work hard for the rest of his life trying to grow food from barren, weedy soil. These curses and punishments come swiftly. Neither Eve nor Adam has an opportunity to explain their actions or apologize—to say, "My bad." Nor are they offered a second chance. The couple is forever doomed by their worst mistake.

I'm not a biblical scholar, but it's hard not to notice how aspects of this creation myth echo in America's punitive justice system that mostly White Christians created. The story of the fall constructs a moral universe in which the most powerful and privileged authority (God) gets to make and enforce the rules. Since the highest judge doles out the rule breakers' sanctions, they must be necessary, effective, and just. In this narrative, expressions of remorse either aren't invited or can't be trusted. Meanwhile,

---

1. More specifically, in this creation myth, sin enters the world through a woman's disobedient appetite—a narrative whose broad cultural significance I explore in my other books.

the anticipation of retribution prompts the wrongdoers to blame others for their sinful actions (Adam blames Eve for seducing him into eating the forbidden fruit; Eve blames the sneaky serpent). Overall, there's not much compassion for the sinners, unless you consider the animal skins God gives them to be an act of mercy. But even this gesture underscores the disgrace of the first couple's wrongdoing, symbolized by their nakedness—a shame that will shadow their descendants.

My unorthodox interpretation of this ancient tale is not meant to suggest that the biblical authors intended this story to convey the dynamics of surveillance, sin, and punishment that are common in our criminal legal system today. Rather, my reading aims to illuminate how a religiously scripted, punitive response to wrongdoing echoes in the "law and order" approach to "justice" that resulted in mass incarceration. This reading also invites us to consider how the meaning of a biblical story is largely driven by the experiences and interests of the interpreters. How might we understand this classic story in a way that helps us break the spiritual habit of assuming that a person's wrongdoing is rooted in their moral depravity and that they need to be punished?

We might start by borrowing Denzel's question: "Why we do the things we do?" *Why* did Eve eat the forbidden fruit? Maybe she ate it not because of some inborn propensity for evil, but because she was intrinsically curious, willful, daring, or maybe just hungry? *Why* did Adam succumb to Eve's invitation to eat with her? What if he joined her because he was trying to meet his need for a sense of mutuality and belonging? What if the qualities that led Eve to commit the first sin (curiosity, willfulness, a sense of adventure) were seen as positive characteristics that, with the proper resources and support, would enable her to develop her talents and leadership potential in ways that would benefit others? What if the desire for mutual connection that motivated Adam to join in Eve's iniquity was validated as a sign of his willingness to be vulnerable? Alternatively, might Eve and Adam have made different choices if the needs that propelled their unruly behavior (for example, for nourishment, mutuality, belonging) had been sufficiently nurtured?

Maybe the story of the fall isn't the problem, but how we interpret it— and whose interpretation becomes the master narrative. Reading this story as evidence that humans are born sinful, that disobedience is immoral, and that our mistakes need to be punished says more about the "law and order" mindset of the religious leaders whose interpretations became prominent than it does about God's will.

If reimagining the story of the fall is too big of a stretch, you could turn your attention to the Bible's first creation myth, the one in which God creates the heavens and earth in seven days. In that story, there is no garden. No Eve or Adam. No forbidden fruit or fall from grace. No punitive consequences for disobedience. Indeed, the first creation narrative affirms the original, indelible goodness of every living thing. Moreover, this narrative starts with an acknowledgment of chaos—"the earth was formless and empty, darkness was over the surface of the deep, and the Spirit of God was hovering over the waters" (Gen 1:1)—and concludes by affirming the necessity for rest and unstructured time: the need for Sabbath. To me, this affirmation symbolizes our shared need and holy obligation to let go of the fantasy of being in control, to be willing to say, again and again: "My bad."

21

"Showing Your True Feelings Made You Look Weak"

As you read the last chapter, what color did you envision Eve and Adam to be? Another question: Did it strike you as odd that I placed Eve's name before Adam's?

The same systems of White supremacy and male dominance that encourage us to perceive Whites as the default humans and men as naturally coming before women intersect in ways that produce toxic narratives of manhood that poison the lives of American youth.

In *Patriarchy Blues*, feminist Frederick Joseph summarizes the lessons he absorbed from a racist, patriarchal culture about what it means to be a man: "I learned to travel through life without expressing certain emotions, which was supposed to make me a strong, dependable man."[1] By the time he was in college, anger was the only feeling he could access. Upon hearing that one of his friends had been murdered, he punched holes in the wall with his fists. At his friend's funeral, Joseph isolated himself in a corner, hands clenched, fantasizing about taking revenge on the killer. The dead boy's mother, who is also Black, saw Joseph standing by himself. She approached him and remarked, "You haven't cried once for my son." He responded by promising that her son's death would not go unpunished. The mother looked at Joseph, hugged him tightly, and said: "A bunch of boys who don't know how to cry is the reason my son is dead. More anger and violence won't bring him back."[2]

1. Joseph, *Patriarchy Blues*, 30.
2. Joseph, *Patriarchy Blues*, 31.

Much of the suffering the incarcerated boys I've met have survived and inflicted on others has roots in patriarchal myths about manhood and the toxic masculinity Joseph describes. "Toxic masculinity" refers to notions and performances of "manhood" that are harmful to men and to others. When being a "real man" requires boys and men to deny or suppress how they really feel; or to derive their sense of worth by dominating and/or belittling others; or to claim unearned authority, knowledge, resources, and/or status that position them as "natural" leaders—in short, when masculinity is predicated on denying all the vulnerabilities that are part of being human, the result is toxic. This toxicity draws on and intersects with habits of White supremacy, especially the habitual sense of entitlement to being the person "in charge," someone who's "in control," someone whom, like God, other people should simultaneously admire and fear. Toxic masculinity uses the same master/slave template as racism; hence the myths of White supremacy and male superiority intersect and reinforce each other.

A domineering vision of manhood manifests itself in varying degrees and ways among the boys in the mindfulness group. Sometimes it's evident in the aloof way a male resident carries his body—for example, in the don't-mess-with-me strut that communicates a vibe of not caring, of being "cool." In fact, "chillin'" is a common response when I ask boys how they're doing. It's as if they want others to know that they're not bogged down by the pain of being locked up or by the suffering that preceded their justice involvement. While "chillin'" may be an idiom for expressing resistance to carceral culture, my conversations with male residents indicate that this self-characterization often doesn't accurately represent how they're really doing.

I don't blame the boys for having absorbed the hidden curriculum of the popular culture—the movies, TV shows, sports coverage, music, video games, and social media messages that teach them the importance of hiding their feelings. I did the exact same thing at their age, albeit in relation to toxic femininity. Moreover, some self-protective aspects of the toxic masculinity they've embraced may well have originated as survival strategies.

Often, however, the strategies we develop as children to shield ourselves from emotional or physical harm stop working as we get older. Hiding our "softer" emotions may protect us from ridicule and rejection; but if this strategy for self-preservation becomes a habit, we become alienated from who we really are and aspire to be. Despite the aura of power, detachment, self-assurance, and status that toxic masculinity exudes, this gender performance is bad for men (and everyone) because being able to access the parts of ourselves that feel painful or tender is what enables us to cultivate the empathy we need to create authentic relationships with each other—and with ourselves.

I invited a racially diverse group of boys to discuss part of Paul Laurence Dunbar's famous poem "We Wear the Mask," the first two lines of which elicited the most discussion: "We wear the mask that grins and lies, / It hides our cheeks and shades our eyes."[3] The compulsion to conceal your true feelings struck a chord with the youth. Tyrell said that growing up, he understood loud and clear that "showing your true feelings made you look weak." The other boys nodded in agreement.

Oliver gave an example of the "mask-ulinity" (my term) that was modeled in his house. He said his dad never showed any emotions—except anger. "I guess that was because of what Tyrell just said—how showing certain feelings makes you look weak." When Oliver's dad got the news that his own father had passed away, he silently retreated to his bedroom, slamming the door behind him. "Then I heard him crying," Oliver said. "It was *loud*." When Oliver's dad came out of the bedroom, he announced that he never wanted to talk about it again. "We all knew not to bring it up. Not ever."

Where does the idea that being a man requires you to conceal your emotions (except for anger) come from? Why do we teach boys that their power and worth depend on transcending their vulnerable feelings and being superior to others?

I'm not proposing a blanket answer here. But as a feminist religion scholar, it's hard not to notice how toxic masculinity norms and narratives today recycle some prominent theological images that have shaped Western culture for millennia.

Some of the most popular images of "God" personify the creative power of the universe as a masculine warrior king who sits aloof in the sky, detached from the flux of human life that "He" judges and controls. Created by and in the image of powerful men, this patriarchal portrait of God sanctions a society in which privileged males are "in control" both of their emotions and of those ranked beneath them on society's hierarchy—people who supposedly embody the less than rational, unruly, uncivilized side of humanity. And let's not forget another important feature of this Father God who rules from on high and legitimates male dominance below: "He" is white—at least in our imaginations, shaped as they are by images ranging from Michelangelo paintings to Sunday school coloring books.

Repeated exposure to images of God as male reinforce male authority in society and in our brains. So, too, standard images of God as White bolster White supremacy in our minds and in the world. The threads connecting such images to the lives of the youth may be invisible, but that doesn't mean they don't exist. Consider, for example, how much conventional

---

3. Dunbar, "We Wear the Mask," lines 1–2.

views of God as the "almighty" White patriarch in the sky resembles those Whites who historically have assumed the right to control people of color, to monitor, judge, and restrict their movements, to dole out rewards and punishments for obedient or disobedient behavior. What about the common assumption that God is too powerful to have any feelings? If God were to show feelings of sadness, anxiety, or depression, would God look weak?

22

"I Hope My Daughter Grows up to Be a Lesbian"

ONE WAY THAT TOXIC masculinity pressures boys to "be the man" is by encouraging them to be sexually active at a young age. Research suggests that "justice-involved adolescent males [are] a group at heightened risk for sexual risk-taking."[1]

One day, Darius, who was seventeen, and Shaquille, who was sixteen, were telling a female student and me about how much they miss their daughters.

Shaquille was anticipating a furlough during which he'd be celebrating his daughter's first birthday. Darius pulled out a picture of his daughter—an adorable two-year-old with curly black hair. Both boys talked about their baby girls as a source of motivation to stay out of trouble once they were released. "I want to be the father to her I never had," Shaquille said, echoing a desire I've heard frequently among incarcerated boys with children.

At some point, our conversation morphed into a discussion of our favorite music. Darius told us about a rap artist he likes. He started reciting the lyrics to one of this artist's songs. "Sorry," I interrupted, "but my brain can't move that fast. Can you slow down a bit so I can understand what the words are saying." I didn't need to tell Darius that in addition to being White, I'm also more than four decades older than he, which means I grew up listening to Elton John and Joni Mitchell. He laughed and started over, this time more slowly.

---

1. Knowles et al., "Risky Sexual Behavior," 562.

I quickly realized that the song he was sharing had overtly misogynist themes and terms. I couldn't keep up with the details, but there were images of violence against women, with plenty of "b*****s," "c***s," and other sexist vocabulary. Before long, Shaquille had joined Darius's performance. The two of them grooved to the music together.

When they'd finished, my student and I thanked them for the song. I noticed that she was watching me to see whether and how I'd respond to the sexist lyrics. Back on campus, we'd talked about complicity, specifically about quietly supporting patriarchal oppression with our silence. But we'd also discussed various ways Whites claim dominance by speaking and acting as if our values are universal. Should I speak up and risk alienating the boys and enacting White supremacy by pontificating about the song's misogyny? Or should I bite my tongue and risk colluding with a culture in which violence against women is normalized with the help of popular music that Darius and Shaquille clearly enjoy?

I decided to take a different tactic.

"I know you both love your daughters so much," I said to Shaquille and Darius. "So, I'm curious: How will you protect them from the kind of violent sexism that song seems to glorify?"

The question seemed to take both boys by surprise. But they appeared curious. "Hmmm . . ." Shaquille said with a faraway look. "I honestly never thought about that."

"Me neither," Darius agreed, rubbing his chin with his fingers as he concentrated on the dilemma that the music that he loved might not be good for someone he loved.

Then Darius stopped stroking his chin and straightened up, as if he'd had an epiphany. "I ain't gonna lie," he said, looking at my student and me. "And no offense to y'all, but I hope my daughter grows up to be a lesbian."

Shaquille laughed in agreement. "Yeah, I feel the same way. I know what dudes are like, and I want my daughter to be safe from guys like me."

My student and I laughed too.

"No offense taken," I said. "There's nothing wrong with being queer. But," I added, "maybe when you guys get out of here, you can help create a world in which your daughters can love whomever they love and where women don't have to worry about needing protection from guys who might hurt them."

As I worried that my sermonizing encouragement expressed White supremacy, Shaquille replied, "Hey, if anyone can motivate me to do that, it's my daughter."

23

"I Come from Violence"

SOMETIMES I INVITE THE youth who attend the mindfulness group to create discussion questions for our small group conversations. One day, Moira offered the prompt: "What do you miss most from your childhood?" Her question generated a lot of interest. Ricky wasted no time answering: "I miss the innocent mindset." He said there was a time when he was very young, maybe four or five years old, that he felt carefree. "This was before I had to worry about things like money and guns and people getting killed." Everything changed the day police raided Ricky's house and found his mom's meth lab in the basement. He was six. "That's when I lost my innocence."

Later in that conversation, I asked Ricky whether he had hope for a different future. He didn't answer my question directly, replying instead: "I come from violence, and violence is all I've ever known. If I weren't in here, I'd be dead, like my two friends and two family members I lost just this year." Ricky said he didn't mind being in detention, despite missing his freedom. "At least here I'm safe." He said his most immediate goal was to make it into the facility's transitional program on the first floor. "If I can make it forty-five more days without a fight, I can be in that program. I've got so much anger inside me, though. I don't know if I can do it. But I'm gonna try."

A few months later, Jorge used the exact same phrase as Ricky—"I come from violence." Unlike Ricky, however, who had expressed determination and a goal of transitioning out of detention, Jorge said he anticipates a future with more violence and, eventually, prison time. "I just don't see how I'm going to get out of the hood. I don't see things changing much." He sounded hopeless.

I wanted to tell Jorge that his future was entirely up to him, that he could decide his own destiny. But I knew that was a lie.

24

"Hood Dreaming"

THE INCARCERATED TEENAGERS I'VE met have diverse and complicated relationships with hope about their futures. "Don't get your hopes up" is a common refrain among kids waiting for a court hearing that will determine the trajectory of the years ahead. "Hope for the best; expect the worst" is another common mantra. Despite their restrained optimism—or is it cautious pessimism?—many youth in the mindfulness group explicitly dream of a better future.

A group of residents and I were discussing what the "American dream" meant to us. Kaya, who worried that she might be tried as an adult and possibly face years in prison, said this: "The American dream looks very different where we come from." Her use of "we" seemed to convey both her sense of belonging with her Black community and the opportunity gaps that separate that community from my White students and me. "For us," Kaya continued, "it's about *hood dreaming*," which she described as the hope of escaping the cycles of drugs, gangs, poverty, and violence in "the hood."

Before visiting kids in detention, I barely knew that places like "the hood" existed. Back in 1991, I had watched John Singleton's film *Boyz n the Hood* so I had a Hollywoodized mental picture of that world as one of racialized poverty and violence. It might as well have been a foreign country, one that I had no desire to visit. The dangerous streets of the Inglewood area of Los Angeles that the movie depicted were so far removed from the corn field–lined gravel road that led to the house where I grew up that "the hood" existed only in my imagination, if at all.

In their creative writing projects, several Black male residents described their dreams of leaving "the hood." Drake envisioned a scene in which his family gathered in a big house (though "not a mansion"), with a pool, basketball court, and plenty of food:

> My mom, M[. . .], Aunty J[. . .], and my cousin A[. . .] are all cooking. Greens, corn bread, chicken (grilled or fried), sweet potatoes, mashed potatoes, steak for papa, ribs, baked beans, and pies are all being cooked. We're somewhere sunny, where there is no violence and I don't have to worry about my mistakes catching up to me.

The boys who talk about leaving "the hood" almost always mention wanting to take their family members and "homies" (friends) with them.

The invisible privileges that economically stable Whites take for granted insulate us from having to know, think, and care about the divine humanity of children who grow up dodging bullets, burying multiple family members and friends, and "living fast," as Bicky Boy Beno put it. America's economically/racially segregated system works so well that even naming these realities risks reinforcing stereotypes that perpetuate suffering for "them" and privileges for "us." For most Whites, the "American dream" is constructed through an unwitting "out-of-sight, out-of-mind" process of exclusion in which the things we'd rather not see, much less experience, are conveniently eliminated.

"Hood dreaming" is connected to what kids in the mindfulness group have told me about their tenuous relationship with "hope." Should they risk hoping for a more promising future? A related question: Should privileged people encourage that hope? When White people talk about hope, are we unwittingly showcasing both our privilege and our ignorance? To me, the answer feels complicated.

Some Black social justice advocates insist on the need for hope in the struggle for racial justice. "I think hope is our superpower," Bryan Stevenson says.[1] "Injustice prevails where hopelessness persists."[2] Hope is the energy that motivates us to speak up and stand up for justice, he says. Hope sustains our ability to imagine a more promising future. Hope strengthens our determination to heal a world in disrepair. Hope affirms the possibility that people and systems can change, that redemption is possible.

Rooted in his Christian faith, Stevenson's summons for those seeking a more just society to be hopeful is compelling. Yet so are the perspectives of nonreligious authors and activists whose skepticism echoes the youths' "don't-get-your-hopes-up" perspective. Ta-Nehisi Coates is suspicious of White people's tendency to want to talk about hope in conversations about

---

1. Stevenson, "Finding the Courage," 25:30.
2. Stevenson, "Finding the Courage," 24:50.

racial justice. In the opening scene of *Between the World and Me*, he describes an interview with a White CNN reporter who asked him to explain what he meant when he wrote that White Americans' disproportionate wealth was achieved through theft and violence. Coates responded by reminding viewers of America's history of forced labor, stolen land, and brutalized bodies. After his explanation, the camera zoomed in on a picture of a White police officer hugging a young Black boy who is crying. Pointing to this fantasy of racial reconciliation, the CNN host asked Coates to talk about *hope*. That's when Coates realized he'd failed to convey the depth of suffering that our nation's legacies of slavery and genocide have left in their wake.[3]

In the struggle for racial justice, the absence of hope raises the question: Why even bother? Yet White people need to ask another question: Why are we frequently in such a hurry to talk about hope? Maybe we gravitate towards hope because we don't understand what it's like to have store clerks follow us around when we're shopping, or cops pull us over for a broken taillight, or strangers tell us to "go home" to our own country. Perhaps we talk so easily about hope because we don't live in fear that our bodies or the bodies of our children may be shot because they are perceived as dangerous. Let's be honest, most middle- and upper-class Whites have never even been to "the hood," much less hoped and dreamed about "getting out." What right do we have to talk about hope?

The challenge for those of us who gravitate towards hope is its proximity to denial. This proximity led Karl Marx, a nineteenth-century German philosopher, to denounce religion as the "opiate of the masses."[4] Marx observed multitudes of hard-working Europeans acquiescing to their own exploitation with the help of Christian narratives that promised to reward their sacrificial work ethic with heavenly salvation. For Marx, the Christian hope of salvation in the afterlife functioned as pain-reducing sedative that pacified the revolutionary consciousness workers needed to unite and change the social conditions of their oppression. Without saying it directly, Marx's critique of otherworldly Christianity exposed the irony of a religion whose members fixated on the promise of the afterlife when the man they claim to follow was decidedly *this*-worldly in his revolutionary defiance of oppression.

Hope is complicated for incarcerated kids. It should be complicated for us as well.

---

3. Coates, *Between the World and Me*, 5–10.
4. Marx, "Critique," 54.

25

"I Want to Be Sure People Understand Me"

THE SAME DAY WE talked about toxic masculinity, Treyvon shared about the death of his brother. "He was shot in the streets two months ago," he said, looking at the floor. "What made it worse is that someone stole the money we raised for his funeral. All $5,000 of it." His voice was barely audible. "My brother never got a proper burial."

The other boys in the group empathized with Treyvon's situation.

"That sucks," Angelo offered.

"I'm sorry, man," Oliver added.

"Me too," I said. "Are your parents still alive?" (I've learned not to assume.)

Treyvon shook his head, "No, I'm basically a ward of the state." He seemed ready to change the subject and asked if we could talk about our zodiac signs. The other boys were enthusiastic about this suggestion. Not only did they all know their sign, but they each had specific ideas about what their sign said about them.

"I'm a Sagittarius," Treyvon confidently said, "which is why I always speak my mind."

Oliver shared that he's a Libra, which, he said, explained why it's always been "very important" for him to make sure he gets his point across when talking with others. "I want to be sure people understand me."

Angelo said he felt the same way about wanting others to understand him, even though he's not a Libra.

These boys' interest in interpreting their signs struck me as evidence of their desire for self-understanding—a longing to explore who they are behind the mask that White supremacist notions of masculinity require them to wear. This desire also points to the human yearning to feel understood by others, which Oliver keenly identified.

The Buddhist teacher Thich Nhat Hanh says that feeling understood is a "basic condition for happiness."[1] He also says that true understanding involves compassion. People with privilege cannot begin to understand the complex humanity of incarcerated youth unless we see the suffering caused by the systemic injustices and traumas they have survived. The more we bear witness to this suffering, the less punishment makes sense.

---

1. Hanh, *Love in Action*, 93.

PART II

Compassion

26

The Creative Power of Life

BY THE TIME I got to Harvard Divinity School, I no longer believed in the cliché portrait of the old White man in the sky who either just sat there while people "below" suffered, or who spent "His" time judging our every move. That God now struck me as a cross between Zeus and Santa Claus, neither of whom were compelling images of the sacred for me.

Fortunately, I took several classes with a theologian named Gordon Kaufman, who encouraged students to consider the difference between human concepts of the divine ("God") and the sacred power/mystery to which those concepts point. Dr. Kaufman cautioned us to think carefully and critically about how we imagine "God" because our God images function to reinforce power structures in society, psychic patterns in our minds, and humans' relationships with each other—for better or for worse. For example, images of a vengeful God reinforce relationships, mindsets, and institutions based on the threat of retaliation. Alternatively, conceptions of God as merciful encourage relationships, mindsets, and institutions that promote compassionate responses to harmful behavior.

One day in class, Dr. Kaufman rocked my world by inviting us to imagine "God" not as a noun—almighty king, ruler, Father, or abstract "Being"— but as an invisible, dynamic power. "What happens if we shift our concept of 'God' as 'Creator' to 'God' as 'creativity'?" This way of envisioning "God" as the creative spirit—the evolutionary power—of life itself made sense to me intuitively and intellectually. When I combined this understanding of the divine with the feminist and womanist theologies I'd been studying, I had another epiphany: the creative power of life was simultaneously *beyond* and *within* everyone and everything. With that insight, it didn't matter whether

I "believed" in God. What mattered was that I experienced and trusted this creative power in my life, perceived and nurtured it in others, and used this sacred energy to practice the kindness, bravery, and compassion I need to heal myself and the world.

When I refer to the "divine humanity" of incarcerated teens, I'm talking about the creative power of life embodied in each of them—the same power that dwells within and beyond everyone and everything, interconnecting us all in the sometimes brutal, sometimes beautiful mystery of life. When we recognize this creative power in "at-risk youth," they become *high-potential kids* who, with enough care and concrete support, can take accountability and heal.

To recognize the divine humanity of kids who have been judged guilty, it helps to hear the painful backstories that have limited their ability to flourish. By giving you a glimpse of some of the hardships that propel teenagers' harmful actions, I hope to awaken the creative power of life in all of us, particularly as this life force manifests in the energy of compassion.

27

What Is Compassion?

THE FIRST THING THAT needs to be said about compassion is that it's not the same as pity. Pity is about feeling sorry for someone, which may seem virtuous. But when you feel sorry for someone, consciously or not, you retain a sense of separation from—and superiority over—the "less fortunate" person. By contrast, compassion is the capacity to *be with suffering* (literally: com—*with* and passion—*suffering*)—to be sensitive and present to someone's distress, without judging or rushing to fix.

Whereas pity triggers the desire to solve, rescue, or cure someone's pain, compassion involves a wish to reduce suffering through presence and mutual connection. Whereas pity creates virtuous heroes and helpless victims, compassion is rooted in a sensibility—a felt understanding—that *everyone* suffers, including people with privilege. Cultivating a sense of our "shared humanity"[1] with incarcerated youth can help mitigate our desires to "save" them. Yet the mutuality that distinguishes compassion from pity isn't predicated on some cliché notion that "we're all the same." This mutuality stems from an awareness that in varying degrees, forms, and circumstances, heartbreak is an inescapable part of the human condition—*and* that some kinds of suffering are preventable and/or can be reduced.

Simultaneously a value, mindset, attitude, and practice, compassion enables us to see teenagers' destructive actions as *reactions* to the painful desperation they experienced in the wake of trauma. Compassion complicates the meaning of juvenile justice because it requires us to pay attention to the harm that happened to youth offenders *prior to* whatever harm they

---

1. Neff, *Self-Compassion*, 61–79.

imposed on others. Ultimately, bearing witness to the suffering that propels humans' hurtful actions—including our own—enables us to denounce those actions without diminishing anyone's divine humanity.

I considered myself to be fairly versant about compassion prior to visiting incarcerated youth. But if I'm honest, my understanding of compassion tilted in the direction of pity. I saw it as something a person *gives* someone else, as if it were a commodity to be gifted in a one-way exchange. I thought compassion was something you did *for* others, rather than something you experience *with* others. I didn't see that the foundation for sharing compassion with others is practicing compassion for yourself, which involves recognizing and holding your own tenderness and grief. Without awareness of our own need for healing, any "compassion" we extend to others is probably pity in disguise.

I didn't anticipate that spending time with young people who have survived multiple traumas, many of them related to systemic oppression, would require me to be more aware of and truthful about the difficulties in my own life. Yet every week during our check-ins, the youths' honesty about their struggles—difficulties with anger, anxiety, and/or depression; grief over loved ones they'd lost; worry about sick or addicted family members; anxieties about returning to "the hood"—invites me to be real. Their vulnerability prompts me to tell the truth about what's hard for me, to admit that sometimes I'm not really "fine." Without going into details, I talk about my struggles with anxiety, regret, self-doubt, and toxic stress.

Initially, I felt guilty sharing my challenges with incarcerated teenagers. My problems are ridiculously privileged compared to theirs. But over the years, the youth have taught me that withholding the truth about my internal distress is a barrier to authentic relationships with them. If I want them to trust my capacity to be present to their pain, I must be willing to trust them with mine. Moreover, if I want to encourage the youth to have compassion for themselves, I must do the same. Practicing self-compassion is a crucial element of compassionate justice because, to paraphrase restorative justice expert Fania Davis, the punishing systems we want to dismantle live simultaneously inside and outside of us.[2]

---

2. Davis, *Little Book of Race*, 68.

28

"Dead or in Jail"

When Jorge expressed a lack of hope for getting out of the cycles of violence, I didn't know what to say. Though uncomfortable, such moments of not knowing remind me that it's not my job to save the youth I visit. Assuming I can is insulting to them and depressing for me.

Consciously, I know this savior mindset is not only oppressive but nonsensical. For example, one of the residents whom I got to know well over the course of a summer was shot dead by his buddy as they were stealing a car just four months after his release from the detention center. This was a boy who, using the pen name "Polo," had written about wanting his family to forgive him:

> I did some fucked up shit in life, I want my mom to forgive me for all the trouble I been in. I want my Dad to forgive me because I didn't become a basketball star and I was running the streets and being hard head[ed] . . . But I can't keep saying forgive me. I gotta show it and be about it.

Polo was a boy who, five months before his death, told me: "Where I come from, you're either dead or in jail by the time you're my age. *You feel me*? I don't want to be dead or in jail, so I'm working on changing."

Another boy from that summer cohort killed an immigrant taxi driver in a botched robbery attempt eight months after his release. This youth, whose chosen alias was "Drake," had also written about his desire to get his "shit" together. He wanted to be a good example for five younger siblings, especially his seven-year-old brother, whom he affectionately described as "the second coming of me."

One boy murdered. Another a "murderer."

Compassion is not about saving. Getting close to the immense pain incarcerated kids carry doesn't lead to a happy ending. Proximity changes your mind about "justice" because it breaks your heart.

29

"Deep Streets"

THE IDEA THAT PURSUING justice is heartbreaking may sound counterintuitive, or even a bit fluffy. In the US, you frequently hear phrases like "Justice has been served" when someone who's committed a crime receives a harsh penalty, as if "justice" means "they got what they deserved." In this morally symmetrical scaling of justice, the more heinous the crime, the more painful the sanction needs to be.

Despite surveys indicating that most Americans support less punitive approaches to justice, a thirst for revenge is evident in widespread support for the death penalty. Sixty-four percent "somewhat" or "strongly" favor killing people who kill people (presumably to show that killing is wrong), even though 78 percent acknowledge the risk that innocent people might be put to death.[1] Prior to 2005, laws permitted capital punishment for children (under age eighteen).

Certain theologies within the Christian tradition appear to support an eye-for-an-eye approach to justice. Among the most familiar is the narrative warning that God punishes sinners for their wicked actions and that retribution is fair, appropriate, necessary, and effective. Variations of this storyline appear in the Hebrew Bible's familiar dramas. In the legend of Noah's ark, God punishes humans' immoral behavior by sending a flood that kills everyone except Noah's family and a bunch of lucky animals (Gen 6–9). In the Exodus story, this same God castigates Pharaoh for enslaving the Hebrew people by sending a series of plagues that culminate in the death of every firstborn Egyptian child and animal (Exod 12:29). These are just

---

1. Pew Research Center, "Most Americans Favor," para. 2.

two of the more well-known examples of the Bible's retaliatory depictions of divine justice.

The Christian Scriptures also contain narratives that characterize divine power as vindictive. Jesus himself reportedly warned "those who commit lawlessness" that they will be thrown "into the fiery furnace, where there will be weeping and gnashing of teeth" (Matt 13:41–42) and that those who don't follow his teachings "will go away into eternal punishment," while "the righteous" will inherit eternal life (Matt 25:45–46). The apostle Paul warned "ungodly" and "unrighteous" Christians of "the wrath of God" (Rom 1:18). Similarly, the author of Colossians stated that "the wrath of God will come upon the sons of disobedience" (3:6). This is a brief sampling of the New Testament's depictions of a punitive God. Like it or not, the entire biblical tradition includes narratives that equate God's justice with divine vengeance.

Listen closely, and you'll hear echoes of this storyline in the assumption that teenagers who break the law deserve to be punished. This belief is blatantly stated in the article "Not Kids Anymore: A Need for Punishment and Deterrence in the Juvenile Justice System." Citing the public's demand for harsher penalties for youth crime to promote public safety, the author advocates incorporating more punishing measures into the system to "balance" out its emphasis on rehabilitation.[2] This reasoning ignores the compassion-oriented questions Denzel wanted to explore: "Why are we the way we are?" and "Why do we do the things we do?"

Punitive responses to juvenile wrongdoing disregard biblical theologies that affirm a compassionate approach to justice. Both Testaments contain stories in which divine power is synonymous with compassion, liberation, and forgiveness. The same warrior-like God who's depicted as punishing the Egyptians by casting Pharaoh's army into the sea (Exod 15) has compassion for the Hebrew people's misery: "I have heard their cry . . . I know their suffering" (Exod 3:7). Later in the Exodus story, God's forgiving nature is revealed to Moses in a passage that describes divine power as "merciful and gracious, slow to anger, abounding in steadfast love and faithfulness" (Exod 34:6). Numerous Psalms depict God's justice and righteousness as compassionate and gracious (Pss 86:15; 103:8; 116:5; 145:8–9). In the writings of the Hebrew prophets, the connection between divine justice and compassion is explicit. For example, the author of First Isaiah describes God as "gracious" and "merciful" *because* "the Lord is a God of justice" (Isa 30:18).

---

2. Chamberlin, "Not Kids Anymore."

Jesus, who was Jewish, shared this ancient Hebrew view of divine compassion as an appropriate response to wrongdoing. In the Gospel of Luke, he instructs his followers to "Be compassionate as God is compassionate."[3] Compassion is a central teaching in parables like the story of the softhearted father who forgives his "prodigal son," embracing him with loving-kindness (Luke 15:11–32). Among the most famous Gospel stories depicting God's merciful response to sin is the one about the woman caught in adultery (John 7:53—8:11). A group of self-righteous men want to stone her—the "mandatory sentence" according to their law. But Jesus turns their judgment back on themselves: "Let anyone among you who is without sin be the first to throw a stone at her."

Ultimately, the Bible's diverging narratives of "justice" are reflected in Americans' equivocal attitudes about criminal justice. Despite broad support for the death penalty, most US adults say they believe that God "loves all people, regardless of their faults."[4] Eighty-six percent of self-identified Christians surveyed express strong or moderate support for a justice system that prioritizes "restoration for all parties, including the victim, the impacted community, as well as the person who committed the crime."[5] Yet half of Christians accept the idea of spiritual retribution for sin.[6]

Christians' broad (88 percent) support for restorative justice[7] also seems to conflict with data indicating that 53 percent of Christians surveyed "somewhat" or "strongly" agree that "It's important to make an example out of someone for certain crimes, even if it means giving them a more severe punishment than their crime deserves."[8] Yet other questions on the same survey reveal a more caring attitude: 91 percent of Christians "somewhat" or "strongly" agree that "it's important that prison conditions are safe and humane, specifically because [they] believe every person has intrinsic value and worth." Seventy percent "strongly" or "somewhat" affirm that "sending youth to prison will make them more likely to live a life of crime than to reform them."[9]

Ultimately, Christians' ambivalent attitudes about crime and punishment mirror the mixed messages about justice in their tradition. As

3. According to Marcus Borg, the English word "compassion" is a better translation than "mercy" given the context of this text (*Heart of Christianity*, 125).

4. Pew Research Center, "When Americans Say."

5. Barna Group, "Survey of Christian Perceptions," 6.

6. Pew Research Center, "When Americans Say."

7. Hadro, "We Must Speak," para. 20.

8. Banks, "Evangelical Leaders Push," para. 16.

9. Barna Group, "Survey of Christian Perceptions," 13. See also Spelman, "Limited Importance"; National Research Council, *Growth of Incarceration*.

Harvard professor of Christian morals Matthew Potts points out, the Bible is "divided against itself" about the meaning of justice. Some biblical texts justify retributive violence and punishment; others admonish forgiveness and freedom from reprisal.[10] To paraphrase Stevenson, whether we throw stones at youth offenders or try to catch the stones thrown at them depends on which narrative we embrace.[11]

What I noticed about Tyrell the first time he attended the mindfulness group was his keen ability to pay attention. The curtain of nose-length locks that partially covered his eyes didn't conceal that he was listening carefully as I welcomed newcomers and told them what to expect. It's unusual for the residents to give me their undivided attention, and I pointed to his example of deep listening as I explained what practicing mindfulness might look like.

Tyrell ended up in my small group that day. Instead of using the *zafus*, we stood for the entire forty-five-minute conversation because Roshaun said that was the only way he could stay engaged in the conversation because his ADHD and PTSD had been spiking. Nobody seemed to mind standing while we talked.

The prompt on the first discussion card asked: "What's been the most important year of your life?"

"That's easy," Tyrell responded: "Fourteen. That's when I started running the deep streets."

"Deep streets?" I asked.

"Those are the most violent places in the hood," Roshaun explained.

Tyrell said he'd started "running" those streets because it was easier to make enough money there than it would have been with legal employment. A "real job" wouldn't pay enough: "Running the deep streets gave me the money I needed to take care of the girls [his sisters] and I could also be there for them when they needed me—when my mom wasn't home, which was most of the time because she was with her boyfriend."

Tyrell also stopped going to school when he was fourteen. He "lost interest" when he realized that nothing he was supposed to learn seemed relevant to his life.

What if, when we asked what youth offenders "deserved," we were talking not about the level of punishment that "fit" their crime, but about their *basic needs*, like access to resources that support their mental, physical, and emotional health; safe neighborhoods; meaningful educational opportunities; parents who also had resources to support their well-being? And what

---

10. Harvard Divinity School, "Christianity, Race," para. 10.

11. This is a reference to Stevenson's encouragement to become "stonecatchers" (*Just Mercy*, 295–310).

if we understood their behavior not primarily as "delinquent," but as *desperate*—as a frantic attempt to meet their needs when no one else did?

In *Rethinking Incarceration*, Dominique DuBois Gilliard discusses the ambiguity inherent in the Hebrew word for justice—*mishpat*—which he loosely translates to mean "giving people what they are due."[12] This principle could imply that kids should be punished for their harmful behavior in proportion to what they did (a retributive approach). Alternatively, it could mean attending to the unmet needs that prompted their destructive actions in the first place (a distributive approach). Giving youth offenders "what they are due" could also mean restoring dignity, safety, and a sense of belonging to everyone impacted by that harm (a restorative approach).[13]

You don't have to be a religion scholar to recognize that the Bible's competing narratives of divine justice—punishment vs. compassion—have shaped Americans' beliefs about criminal justice. Nor do you need be a psychotherapist to appreciate the benefits of a kind of justice that gives kids who have committed crimes "what they are due" in the form of resources and services that help them meet their needs and develop their divine potential. Tyrell was fortunate to have access to therapeutic opportunities in the residential treatment program. He had the added advantage that he fully intended to use that program's tools to help him develop the self-knowledge and skills he'll need to stay out of trouble: "I'm actually glad I'm here," he told me, "because now I get the chance to learn from my mistakes and hopefully have a better future."

---

12. Gilliard, *Rethinking Incarceration*, 142.

13. Both Snyder (*Protestant Ethic*) and Gilliard (*Rethinking Incarceration*) see biblical notions of justice as resources for a restorative approach to justice.

30

"Bro"

Juan had a bright smile, twinkly eyes, and emphatic and candid way of expressing himself. He also had a strong habit of calling me "bro," as in, "You feel me, bro?" This street idiom wasn't specific to me. He said "bro" at the end of just about every third sentence. Still, there was something amusingly endearing when he used the term to address me.

One day, I pointed out this colloquial habit. "Juan, did you know you're the only one in the world who calls me 'bro'?" Before I had a chance to tell him that I enjoyed this moniker, he was apologizing profusely.

"I'm sorry, man. I didn't mean to disrespect."

"No worries," I assured. I clarified that, correctly or not, I took it as a compliment. I said that informal way of addressing me made me feel included, as if I weren't the White, almost sixty-year-old, geeky religion professor that I am. He laughed, but he didn't argue with my self-description.

Juan was in detention for many months, so I got to know him well. His playfulness was charming, his candor disarming. Whenever I asked him how he was doing, he never hesitated to tell me, whether he was feeling hopeful, depressed, anxious, or bored. He talked a lot about his past. His most painful memory was watching one of his brothers get shot and killed by a rival gang member. His other two brothers died in a similar manner. Mixed with his intense grief over these deaths was a desire for vengeance. "The guys who killed them never went to prison. They're still walking the streets!" he said in disbelief. "Someday they're gonna pay for what they did."

I asked Juan if knowing that his brothers' killers would suffer for what they did would relieve his grief.

He didn't answer directly. He just repeated, "They're gonna pay."

One day, Juan told me how he got into crime. "My dad was all alone trying to raise us five boys—there were five of us before my brothers were killed." Juan knew his dad was struggling just to get by, and he never wanted to ask him for money. "I decided I needed to get stuff for myself and help my dad provide for the family." He dropped out of school after eighth grade and started robbing people and stealing cars. "I'm not gonna lie," he said. "Stealing things and robbing people was pretty much my full-time job before coming here."

When he wasn't reflecting on his difficult past, Juan often gushed about his two-year-old niece. "She calls me 'uncle' and I call her 'uncle,'" he said, eyes gleaming with affection. His face relaxed as he talked about the frilly pink dress and princess crown with fake diamonds and rubies that his niece wore at her birthday party, which happened just before Juan was arrested. I told him that I see his love for his niece as proof that his heart still has a lot of tenderness, despite everything he's been through, and that I believe this tenderness is a crucial part of what makes us human and ultimately enables us to heal. I had a lot more to say about this, but I sensed myself sliding into saviorism and sounding more like a preacher than a "bro."

In *The Tactile Heart*, John Hull, a New Testament scholar who is blind, tells sighted people that he's not interested in their "suffocating surplus of compassion."[1] Rather, he wants able-bodied people to imagine what it's like to be blind, examine our assumptions about people with disabilities, recognize that the world we inhabit is designed by and for nondisabled humans, and build a more accessible, inclusive society.

Similarly, the youth who come to the mindfulness group aren't looking for excessive empathy. But they do want their suffering to be seen and understood. Juan told me, "The reason I talk so much about my past is because I want the world to know what I've been through."

This desire creates a conundrum that I haven't resolved. In the process of bearing witness to the pain kids like Juan have survived, privileged people run the risk of otherizing them. We may see incarcerated youth as so radically different than ourselves that we unknowingly dehumanize them. Hearing their backstories, it's easy to feel relieved that despite your own problems, "things could always be worse." You may find yourself counting your blessings and thanking God that you and your loved ones have been spared such calamities.

As you read about the painful backstories of incarcerated youth, pay attention to what arises in you. Be on the lookout not just for pity and self-reassurance, but shock, denial, problem-solving, judgments, and voyeuristic

---

1. Hull, *Tactile Heart*, 85.

intrigue—all are ways we unwittingly fail to recognize and honor these kids' divine humanity. If a story like Juan's is painful to read, see if you can stay present to that pain without turning it into a "suffocating surplus of compassion." Reflect on what that pain is asking you to do.

31

"When Kids Don't Have a Chance to Be Kids When They're Kids"

THE SENSE OF RESPONSIBILITY both Tyrell and Juan felt to help provide for their families, even if it meant resorting to crime, is common among the youth I've met. Imani, whose family immigrated from a war-torn country in Africa, stole food from the corner store because "all we had to eat was noodles" and there wasn't always enough for her five siblings, parents, grandparents, and her. "Sometimes," Imani said, "kids make bad choices because they don't have better choices."

What happens when kids are forced to grow up too fast? Jordan had a theory.

After reading the prompt on his discussion card—"What from your childhood is hard to talk about?"—Jordan paused. I reminded everyone that it's perfectly fine to pass on prompts they'd rather not answer. But Jordan decided to share.

"I was seven when my dad was shot . . . in front of me. From that point on, I was pretty much on my own." In addition to parenting himself, Jordan had to lend money to his mom so she could buy groceries and pay medical bills. He didn't say where that money came from or whether his mom ever paid him back. But he did share his self-described "theory" about what happens to kids who are forced to grow up too fast: "When kids don't have a chance to be kids when they're kids, they end up acting like kids when they're adults."

I asked him if, by "acting like kids," he meant "acting like a child" (having fun, acting goofy, being spontaneous)? Or "acting childish" (behaving in ways that are risky, immature, and likely to get you in trouble)?

He responded, "Probably both."

Jordan's hypothesis insightfully articulates the familiar truth that age and maturity level don't always correspond. His theory also alludes to the enduring impact of childhood adversity and trauma, including intensely unwanted, unexpected, threatening, and/or violating experiences that infuse children's bodies with feelings of helplessness, confusion, overwhelm, and danger.[1]

Decades of research demonstrate the long-lasting damage of "adverse childhood experiences" (ACEs) on physical, emotional, and community well-being. ACE scores are measured through a questionnaire that asks about childhood exposure to various kinds of trauma and toxic stress. Higher ACE scores are correlated with elevated risks for chronic diseases, mental health challenges, unemployment later in life, and incarceration.[2]

In *The Deepest Well*, Nadine Burke Harris describes the links between childhood toxic stress and compromised physical and mental well-being.[3] She discovered these links when working with children from an economically impoverished community of color, many of whom displayed symptoms like "poor impulse control," "inability to focus," and "difficulty sitting still." Frequently, these youngsters were diagnosed with ADHD. But Burke Harris noticed that their cognitive and emotional struggles had biological dimensions that stemmed from childhood trauma. For example, a seven-year-old boy she treated had stopped growing at age four when he started being sexually abused. As the connection between bodily illness and childhood trauma became increasingly clear, so did the link between poor health and poor communities: "We know that it's not just *how* you live that affects your health, it's also *where* you live."[4]

The vast majority of youth in confinement come from low-income communities and have survived multiple kinds of toxic stress. Of the 64,329 adjudicated youth surveyed in a Florida study, 50 percent reported scores of four or more ACEs (compared to 13 percent in the original research). According to this study, higher ACE scores increase not only the probability of a young person getting in trouble with the law but also the risk of

---

1. This definition of trauma draws on McBride, *Wisdom of Your Body*; Van der Kolk, *Body Keeps the Score*; and Menakem, *My Grandmother's Hands*.
2. National Center for Injury Prevention, "CDC-Kaiser ACE Study."
3. Burke Harris, *Deepest Well*, xv.
4. Burke Harris, *Deepest Well*, 3–9, 8.

re-offending.[5] Moreover, people who have experienced four or more ACEs are "thirty-three times as likely to have learning and behavior problems in school."[6] Other research indicates that youth incarceration—particularly among preteens—can itself become an adverse childhood experience that has long-term negative mental health consequences, including increased risk for depression and higher levels of suicidality later in life.[7] Thus the long-term damage of ACEs is not just physical, but existential.

Some of the residents who participated in the summer writing workshop wrote poems that alluded to experiences of childhood trauma, isolation, and invisibility. A girl who chose the alias "Mae" shared the following poem:

> Mama wasn't home
> so I had to grow up fast
> 3 siblings to take care of
> had to do it all alone
> 7 years old
> that ain't right
> heard mama screaming
> so I sat and prayed at night
> didn't have no food
> so we had to wait till school
> kids started staring
> but they didn't know the truth
> say the wrong thing
> get beat till you screamed
> mama acted like she was blind
> when she could clearly see
> thought getting taken away
> meant I was free
> cause you shouldn't have to fight for
> everything you need
> one thing that really mattered
> was taken from me
> but it's okay cause one day
> you'll acknowledge me.

What science reveals about the links between childhood adversity and physical, mental, and spiritual well-being challenges the bootstrap ideology/morality that pervades American culture. According to this popular creed,

---

5. Baglivio et al., "Adverse Childhood Experiences."
6. Menakem, *My Grandmother's Hands*, 44.
7. Barnert et al., "Child Incarceration."

with enough hard work, discipline, and willpower, you can do anything you put your mind to. But the ACEs studies create a much more complicated picture. Just as our "minds" are not separate from our "bodies," so we can't extrapolate ourselves from environmental influences. Put differently, science confirms that teenagers' antisocial behavior originates in the pernicious stress of situations over which they had no control—situations that forced them to grow up fast.

32

"The Reason Kids like Us Do Drugs..."

MOST OF THE YOUTH I've met are decidedly *not* happy to be locked up. Yet many know they need more than medication to help them deal with their childhood trauma and develop skills for navigating life post-detention. *They know they need help.* This was evident in what some residents told my students and me on one of our first visits to the detention center:

- "My dad's in jail and my mom doesn't want me. You tell me what I'm supposed to do!"
- "My anxiety's already off the charts! And I just found out they have to kick me out of this facility because where my family lives disqualifies me from being here."
- "I can't sleep at night because every fifteen minutes the staff have to shine a flashlight into our rooms to make sure we don't kill ourselves."

These residents lived on the facility's third floor, which means they didn't have access to the same level of therapeutic services as the youth in the residential treatment program, though many expressed a desire to get on that program's waiting list.

When I first started visiting the detention center, I didn't know that as many as 70–80 percent of youth in confinement are rearrested within three years of their release.[1] (Note: recidivism rates are notoriously difficult to

---

1. McCarthy et al., "Future of Youth Justice," 13.

measure.²) So I was surprised to see Brett, who had gotten out several weeks earlier, show up for the mindfulness group.

"It's nice to see you," I said, "but I'm sorry you're back."

"Probation violation," he responded, sounding more discouraged than angry.

Later that day, I asked the residents in my small group whether they think punishment works to help at-risk kids stay out of trouble. "We need rehabilitation," Brett emphatically stated, "*not punishment!*" He spoke with confidence as he elaborated: "The reason kids like us do drugs and get into trouble is that we're trying to escape our pain." Brett's pain included the death of his beloved grandfather, who had been his only reliable caretaker. "That's when I started getting into drugs and other trouble," he said. "When he died, I didn't know what to do. I basically had no idea what would happen to me and my little sister." In addition to the devastating loss of his grandpa, Brett's mom, who had not been in his life for over a decade, was dying of cancer.

Years later, in the summer writing workshop, Polo articulated a similar insight about the pain that drove his illegal behavior:

> When my auntie passed away, I was doing anything to take the pain away so I could stop thinking about everything she did for me. It made me mad more and more. So what I did to make me feel better [was] smoking weed and getting money.

According to Van der Kolk, "One of the prime reasons for habitual drug use in teens is that they cannot stand the physical sensations that signal fear, rage, and helplessness."³ I suspect it's this same intolerance for difficult emotions that prompts most of us to do or say things we later regret—whether or not we use illegal drugs and regardless of age.

Because of traumatic experiences kids like Brett and Polo have survived, it's easy to forget that *they are still children*. Interestingly, this is one of the cornerstone insights on which America's youth justice system was originally built.

---

2. Office of Juvenile Justice, "Research Central."
3. Van der Kolk, *Body Keeps the Score*, 356.

33

"Houses of Refuge"

It's an overstatement to say that compassion was the primary value that motivated nineteenth-century social reformers to create America's juvenile justice system. Yet historians generally agree that the religiously inspired humanitarians who first developed this system believed that children's problematic behaviors were rooted in the unstable environments from which they came, rather than in some inherent moral deficiency. Motivated by Christian convictions (every child is created in God's image) and Enlightenment principles (children's minds are a tabula rasa), reformers insisted that disorderly kids needed rehabilitation, not punishment.[1]

A brief history of this system starts in the early 1800s when philanthropists, civil leaders, and businesspeople recognized that lawless kids needed their own correctional institutions, separate from adults, and that such facilities should focus on meeting troubled kids' needs, rather than punishing their wayward behavior. These child advocates saw kids as less mature and thus less culpable while also more malleable and capable of reform.[2] This insight inspired members of the Society for the Reformation of Juvenile Delinquents to create the first "house of refuge" in New York in 1825. In the decades that followed, facilities were designed to take care of poor and destitute kids who were either already "delinquent" or thought to be headed for trouble.[3] By mid-century, the houses of refuge were replaced by a reformatory-style system whose "training schools" (also called

1. Drinan, *War on Kids*, 17; Pickett, *House of Refuge*, 187.

2. Pickett, *House of Refuge*, 187–88.

3. McCarthy et al., "Future of Youth Justice," 2; Bernstein, *Burning Down the House*, 38–51.

"industrial schools") were supposed to serve a rehabilitative purpose. By the late 1800s, every state had some kind of juvenile correction facility. However, growing problems with overcrowding and abuse suggest that the names for these institutions—"house of refuge," "training schools"—were at least partially euphemistic.[4]

Not unlike today, poverty, parental neglect, homelessness, and/or racial and ethnic "otherness" increased a child's chances of landing in one of these facilities. Irish Catholic parents were deemed particularly incompetent, and their children were grossly overrepresented in the system.[5] And even the most "progressive" reformers viewed Black youth as a "lost cause" who "lack[ed] the physical, moral, and intellectual capacity on which normalization would depend."[6]

Regardless of a child's "offense," at the end of the nineteenth century the state became authorized to decide what was in their best interest. A law based on the principle of *parens patriae* designated "the state as parent" for kids from abusive or negligent families.[7] This legal doctrine governed America's first youth courts. The system encouraged judges to prioritize rehabilitation and personalize interventions based on each child's unique situation, while states provided social services to assist youth.[8]

Despite the good intentions of those who created America's juvenile justice system, Bernstein points out that "the corrupting elements that plague the system to this day were right there in the blueprint from the very start."[9] Children from poor, immigrant families were more likely to be seen as threats to the dominant social, political, White Protestant moral order and thus more likely to be criminalized. Moreover, despite their stated aim of "rehabilitation," many reformatories relied on punishing and abusive responses to their residents' transgressive behavior, "ranging from loss of already scant 'play hours' to a bread-and-water diet and solitary confinement to . . . corporal punishment."[10] Listen closely, and you'll hear echoes of the colonial mission to convert everyone to the dominant White Christian norm in the youth system's "presumption of benevolence" and its pursuit of "rehabilitation"—often through coercive measures. Ultimately, Bernstein

---

4. Bernstein, *Burning Down the House*, 39; McCarthy et al., "Future of Youth Justice," 3.
5. Pickett, *House of Refuge*, 187.
6. Henning, *Rage of Innocence*, 244.
7. Bernstein, *Burning Down the House*, 39–45, 48.
8. Drinan, *War on Kids*, 4, 16–17.
9. Bernstein, *Burning Down the House*, 40.
10. Bernstein, *Burning Down the House*, 41.

concludes, a "tension between care and control—between rehabilitation and punishment was woven into the fabric of the juvenile [system] . . . from its very inception."[11]

This same tension continues to shape discussions, aims, and practices within the youth justice system today. Diverging views on effective responses to wrongdoing also show up in the perspectives of different youth within the system. While many, like Brett, explicitly hope and ask for a more compassionate response to the harms they've committed, some have internalized the belief that kids who do wrong deserve to be punished.

---

11. Bernstein, *Burning Down the House*, 46; McCarthy et al., "Future of Youth Justice," 2–3.

34

"Does Punishment Work?"

OVER THE YEARS, I'VE asked youth in the mindfulness group how they think and feel about the effectiveness of punishment as a response to youth crime. Here's a sampling of some written responses to the question: "Does punishment work?"

- "I'm not sure. Part of me thinks kids need to be punished for bad things we do, but part of me doesn't think it works. Because even though this is my first time in jail, I have friends who've been locked up a bunch of times, and it doesn't seem to help."
- "Punishment is absolutely necessary. Especially for younger kids. They need to learn early that they'll have to pay for their crimes."
- "Kids like us do need to be punished; but once we're locked up, we also need to be helped."
- "Punishment just makes things worse because it's like people are giving up on you. And when people give up on you, it's easy to give up on yourself."
- "When they punish me by taking away my freedoms, it makes me feel like less of a person. And when I feel like less of a person, I just get angry."
- "I know punishment doesn't work. Been locked up five times already and I'm only sixteen."

Though not exhaustive, these responses represent the diversity of views among residents in the mindfulness group. Interestingly, the skepticism some youth express about the efficacy of punishment is supported by research revealing a litany of problems with punitive approaches to youth justice.

One of these problems may seem relatively superficial, namely, the monetary expense of confining and caring for teenage offenders. Costs vary from state to state, but a 2020 Justice Policy Institute report found that holding a single youth in secure confinement costs states on average 588 dollars per day.[1] Perhaps spending exorbitant amounts to incarcerate adolescents would be worth it if outcomes were more promising. But with so many kids getting rearrested within a few years of their release, the monetary issue is not superficial.

Rather than serve as a deterrent, evidence suggests that locking up teens, particularly without therapeutic interventions, makes recidivism more likely.[2] Darius called himself "a perfect example" of why punishment doesn't work. Though this was his first time in a treatment program, he'd previously been arrested fourteen times and spent years in various facilities. "The problem is that we go back to where we came from. The gang doesn't care that we're trying to be different, trying to be good. The gang doesn't respect what we've learned. They expect us to pick up where we left off when we got arrested."

This cycle of release-and-return can be demoralizing. When invited to write about a favorite memory, one boy wrote about the delicious taste of freedom before getting arrested again:

> I'm feeling good. I'm happy. My family [is] happy that I'm finally home. I missed them and they missed me . . . It's been a long time since I have been out so I love the fresh air and the smell just has me shocked because I'm fresh up out of the bin. I don't have nobody telling me what to do . . . I was really feeling good and saying to myself that I would never go back to jail. Well I should've never said that because now I'm back in jail.

Besides the pain of recidivism, there's evidence that youth who have been institutionalized are more likely to commit *worse* offenses once they're out.[3] "I remember being locked up for small things, now it's changed to big things," this boy wrote.

On top of troublingly high rates of recidivism for *individual* youth, prison abolitionists point to *institutional* recidivism, arguing that efforts

---

1. Justice Policy Institute, *Sticker Shock 2020*.
2. McCarthy at al., "Future of Youth Justice," 12–13.
3. Heller de Leon, "Long-Term Juvenile Incarceration," para. 1.

to reform the carceral system have either failed altogether or had minimal impact.

The dire need for systemic reform became undeniable as horrific stories of abuse within locked facilities surfaced in the 1980s and nineties. Bernstein's chapter chronicling abuses inside youth prisons describes a range of domination tactics, including solitary confinement, unnecessary use of force by staff, sexual molestation, restraints that led to broken bones, and the lethal suffocation of a twelve-year-old boy.[4] Egregiously abusive practices were not isolated incidents. A 2011 Annie E. Casey Foundation report documented "systemic violence, abuse, and/or excessive use of isolation or restraints" in thirty-nine states going back to 1970.[5]

Many juvenile justice scholars, activists, and professionals see these abuses as an outgrowth of the punitive culture in youth prisons that intensified during the "law and order" decades. Some share Bernstein's suspicion that the system itself is broken beyond repair. She asks whether a system in which "large numbers of vulnerable young people are held captive far from the public eye . . . makes such abuses inevitable."[6] Abolitionists insist that the problem isn't individual leaders or facilities, but the notion that locking up traumatized kids will help them.

Critics of the system also point out that some teens are locked up for minor offenses. In 2019, 18 percent were confined for technical violations or status offenses.[7] In 2018, about three quarters of youth awaiting trial were in detention facilities for nonviolent offenses.[8]

Since the youth I visit are not supposed to discuss why they are being detained, I can't speak to the level of their offenses. While Brett said he was re-incarcerated for a probation violation, it's not uncommon for male residents to mention guns in conversations and in their writings. One told me he was being held for attempted murder. Another wrote, "What I did the first time wasn't too bad, but this time, what I did was very serious. If they try me as an adult, I'm looking at twenty years in prison."

---

4. Bernstein, *Burning Down the House*, 81–102; McCarthy et al., "Future of Youth Justice," 4.

5. Mendel, *No Place for Kids*, 4–7.

6. Bernstein, *Burning Down the House*, 85–86.

7. Sawyer, "Youth Confinement," paras. 20–21.

8. Campaign for Youth Justice, "Key Facts," 3.

35

"What Keeps Me up at Night"

FEAR OF ENDING UP in the criminal justice system, which is supposed to be for adults, is a top anxiety among many older residents I've met. Alberto shared, "What keeps me up at night is worrying that I'll be tried as an adult, even though I was seventeen when I committed the crime. If I'm convicted as an adult, that's twelve years in prison with a bunch of men."

Alberto's fears are justified when you consider that youth placed in the adult system are five times more likely to be sexually assaulted while incarcerated and, by some reports, thirty-six times more likely to commit suicide (compared to youth confined in juvenile facilities). Kids who are sentenced as adults are also 34 percent more likely to re-offend after their release—often more seriously.[1] Compared to their White counterparts, youth of color are more likely to be tried as adults.[2] Generally, teens in the adult system have fewer opportunities for therapeutic programming and are exposed to situations that they're not developmentally prepared to handle.[3] Secure juvenile facilities like the one I visit are better suited to care for youth who need out-of-home placement.[4]

The practice of placing kids in the adult system epitomizes a more punitive approach to youth justice. Beginning in the 1960s, "tough on crime"

---

1. Pilnik and Mistrett, *If Not Adult System*, 9–10, 19, 24; Howell et al., "Young Offenders," 1–3.

2. Pilnik and Mistrett, *If Not the Adult System*, 6, 9; Lahey, "Steep Costs"; Stevenson, *Just Mercy*, 152; Bernstein, *Burning Down the House*, 78.

3. Bolin et al., "Americans' Opinions"; Campaign for Youth Justice, "Blended Sentencing," 1.

4. Development Services Group, "Alternatives to Detention," 5.

politicians promoted policies that allowed minors arrested for committing serious crimes to be tried in the adult court system and subject to the stringent sentences given to older offenders.[5] By the late 1990s, every state had more punitive policies for kids, including trying and sentencing them as adults and sending them to adult prisons.[6]

Although most Americans say they support moving away from vindictive approaches to youth justice,[7] a 2019 study found that approximately one third to 80 percent favor or strongly favor "blended sentencing" for youth convicted of committing violent crimes, which allows kids to be incarcerated in the adult system.[8] Some legal scholars still call for "adult time for adult crimes."[9] And between 2019 and 2021, the number of arrested juveniles who were tried as adults grew—from 3.2 percent to 3.7 percent.[10] As of 2021, most states still automatically prosecuted older teens (eighteen- and nineteen-year-olds) as adults, and all have laws permitting (or mandating) adolescents arrested for serious crimes to be tried as adults.[11] For reasons described above—risk of abuse, suicide, lack of therapeutic resources, increased recidivism—many juvenile justice experts consider funneling youth into the adult system to be a worst-case scenario. Yet in states like Florida, prosecutors can charge children as young as fourteen as adults.[12]

In *A Question of Freedom*, poet R. Dwayne Betts recounts the nine years he spent incarcerated for a carjacking he committed when he was sixteen. This happened in the 1990s—the height of the "tough on crime" era. Though Betts never fired the pistol he used to threaten the man whose car he stole, the law "certified" him as an adult, which meant serving time in several adult prisons:

> My mom wrote letters asking me how I was doing, asking me if I was safe. I couldn't tell her how it was in there, couldn't tell her how many young boys were in there hurting from what they did and from what others did to them. Hurting from what the

---

5. Drinan, *War on Kids*, 16–24.
6. Howell et al., "Young Offenders," 1–3.
7. Abrams, "Juvenile Justice at a Crossroads," 726.
8. Bolin et al., "Americans' Opinions," 19; Campaign for Youth Justice, "Blended Sentencing," 1.
9. Grossman and Stimson, *Adult Time*.
10. Fatherree, "Criminal Injustice," para. 11.
11. Teigen, "Juvenile Age of Jurisdiction," paras. 2–3.
12. Fatherree, "Criminal Injustice," para. 6.

courts did every time they sent a young man to a place governed by fists and randomness.[13]

Betts's story illuminates the layers of hurt that are inflicted and buried when kids are not treated as kids and when they receive no therapeutic or educational resources. "I couldn't understand why the state would send me to prison for nine years where I'd get no rehabilitation, no skill training, no education training, but enough violent images to last a generation."[14]

---

13. Betts, *Question of Freedom*, 153.
14. Betts, *Question of Freedom*, 225.

36

"You Have to Believe In Jesus or You're Going to Hell"

WHILE SOME OF THE youth I've met doubt the efficacy of punishment to change behavior, others see it as just and necessary. Usually, the punitive theology supporting this view is implicit. But not always.

During our weekly check-ins, Donny said he'd been feeling guilty because he hadn't been reading the Bible enough. Curious, I asked him which teachings in the Bible were most helpful to him. He replied: "The ones that say you have to believe in Jesus or you're going to hell." Donny described his premonition that "something bad" was going to happen because of his self-described spiritual laziness. He referenced the book of Revelation, the biblical text that many Christians (misguidedly)[1] interpret as a prophecy that predicts the end of the world, when Jesus will return to judge the living and the dead and condemn sinners to enduring damnation—a fate Donny clearly wanted to avoid. He seemed to believe that the threat of God's wrath would motivate him to stay out of trouble and that his current punishment was warranted. "I deserve to be punished for what I did," he said. "That's what the Bible says."

Even if Donny's beliefs were helpful to him (emphasis on *if*), his exclusionary, punitive theology was bad news for the boy sitting next to him, who commented, "Well, I guess I'm going to hell. Because I'm a Muslim."

Throughout US history, images of a punishing God have been a cornerstone of Christian supremacy. In 1741, a charismatic White preacher named Jonathan Edwards fueled the surge of evangelical fervor that was

---

1. Rossing, *Rapture Exposed*.

sweeping New England in what would become one of America's most famous sermons: "Sinners in the Hands of an Angry God." With vivid images of spiders and worms, blood and fire, Edwards warned evildoers that God's wrath and excruciating punishment awaited them in the afterlife unless they repented of their wicked ways and accepted salvation through Jesus. Edwards's assumption that Christianity is the only path to redemption echoes in the theologies of many evangelical Christians today: 96 percent of evangelical leaders surveyed affirmed that "Christianity is the one, true faith leading to eternal life."[2]

During the mid-twentieth century, this exclusionary, rewards-punishments theology shaped the views of evangelical Christian leaders, who were at the forefront of national discussions about "juvenile delinquency." In *God's Law and Order*, historian Aaron Griffith recounts how these mostly White men saw teenage crime as a symptom of America's moral decline.[3] Despite occasional references to poverty, their approach generally presumed criminality to be rooted in *individual sin*, not unjust social conditions. They believed vulnerable kids were lured into immoral behavior by secularizing forces that were ruining US society more broadly. A prominent preacher named David Wilkerson argued that "delinquency and drug use were literally 'Satan's fiendish plan to drag today's youth into the pit of hell.'"[4]

If individual sinfulness was the root of adolescent misconduct, personal salvation—giving your heart to Jesus—was the cure. Organizations like Youth for Christ, which flourished in the mid-twentieth century, made converting wayward teens central to their larger mission to evangelize Americans. Among this crusade's leaders, saving the souls of convicted or would-be adolescent criminals trumped (without eliminating) concern about disciplining them. Some went out of their way to help arrested teens *avoid* criminal prosecution and imprisonment. Popular preachers like Billy Graham acknowledged lawless adolescents' need for nurturing, without critiquing the structural injustices that created less-than-nurturing environments for marginalized youth. For Graham and his evangelical colleagues, the universal remedy for kids' reckless behavior was not systemic social change, but conversion to Christ.[5]

This remedy recycled a colonial narrative by depicting the disproportionately Black and Brown youth whom evangelical leaders sought to save as uncivilized. Griffith describes a youth organization's brochure that featured

2. Pew Research Center, "Global Survey."
3. Griffith, *God's Law and Order*, 54–80, esp. 58.
4. Wilkerson, quoted in Griffith, *God's Law and Order*, 70.
5. Griffith, *God's Law and Order*, 56–60, 67.

a picture of a Black male teenager with a threatening look on his face against a background of street graffiti. The copy described the "squalor, deprivation, and perpetual hopelessness" of East Harlem, whose mostly "Puerto Rican and Negro" residents have "never lived outside the ghetto, never seen a normal middle class home or the grass and trees of an American suburb." Sympathetically, the brochure continues: "Most have never known traditional family life. They are untouched by the influence of Christianity."[6] The pamphlet's image and rhetoric paint a picture of "youngsters in the ghetto" that resembles colonial Christianity's images of uncivilized "heathens" and "barbarians" in the jungle.

According to Griffith, at least one evangelical leader condemned such parallel tropes. Tom Skinner was an African American, born-again, ex-gang member who recognized White Evangelicals' cries for law and order as a strategy for controlling Black people. Skinner criticized his White peers for preaching the gospel as a means for pacifying civil unrest among the Black community. He rejected Graham's notion that America's police force was charged with doing God's will and argued that crime and violence were rooted in social injustices.[7]

Donny's concern with not spending enough time reading the Bible echoes White evangelical Christian leaders' approach to teenage crime in mid-twentieth-century America. In a landmark sermon on "juvenile delinquency" in 1954, Billy Graham warned that adolescent lawlessness could be traced to a "deficiency" in the home—specifically, "an appalling lack of religious training" and a failure to read and follow "the teachings of scriptures."[8]

Listening to Graham's diagnosis of the problem, it's hard not to wonder *which* "teachings of scriptures" he was referring to. As we've seen, the Bible offers conflicting messages about God's character and what divine "justice" means in relation to unethical behavior. Not only that, but our *interpretations* of biblical texts are inevitably shaped by the particularities of our history, social privileges (or lack thereof), worldview, and myriad other variables. In the end, it's hard to see how reading the Bible more will save troubled youth, especially if its teachings are selected and interpreted in ways that foster personal fear and shame, while ignoring the societal roots of "juvenile delinquency" and the unhealed wounds that feed it.

---

6. Griffith, *God's Law and Order*, 88–89.
7. Griffith, *God's Law and Order*, 90, 145–47.
8. Graham, "Juvenile Delinquency," 3:58–4:28.

37

"I'm Afraid of God"

ONE SUMMER AFTERNOON, MOST of the residents were attending a CPR class. Of the six boys who were not doing the class, all except one—Sam—wanted to attend the mindfulness group. Normally, participating in the group is voluntary. But Sam ended up having to join us because there wasn't an extra staff person to stay with him one-on-one back in the pod.

As soon as he walked in the gym, Sam complained about being "forced" to attend.

"I don't blame you," I empathized. "I know you guys don't have many freedoms in here, and this is just one more choice you didn't get to make." Sam's face relaxed ever so slightly. I invited him to join the big circle we sit in for the first part of the mindfulness group, but he declined, opting instead to stand against the gym wall and watch from a distance as the rest of us did some short meditation practices. When we broke into small groups, I invited Sam to join mine—"Only if you want to." He refused, but moved closer to the corner where my group was sitting, close enough to eavesdrop on our conversation.

The other youth and I were discussing the question: "What are you afraid of?"

Bao was the first to respond. But he spoke so quickly and softly that I didn't understand him. I asked him a few times to repeat what he was saying, and I still couldn't decipher his response. It sounded like, "Dah!"—as in, "Dah! What a stupid question!" Finally, I asked him, "Are you saying 'dah'?"

Bao lifted his head and looked at me, brows knit together in a mix of puzzlement and frustration. "No," he said, speaking slowly and loudly now, "Not 'dah.' *God*. I'm afraid of God."

"Ooohhhhh—sorry. Do you mean you're afraid that God will punish you for your mistakes?"

Bao nodded, adding, "I'm afraid of what will happen, you know . . . when I die. I'm afraid I'll go to hell."

The belief that God chastises people who do "bad things" by sending them to hell is popular in many religious circles. This vindictive theology provides a conceptual framework for a justice system that punishes people convicted of crimes by sending them to prison, which may be a proxy for hell on earth. The scenes Betts describes in his account of coming of age in adult prisons are rife with violence, fear, insanity, indignity, and a chilling hopelessness:

> What happened in prison wasn't new, as people were getting beaten into comas around me, stabbed and worse. I couldn't let my mind get lost in their blood. I learned a language of violence and walked around like everyone else, as if the blood was the most natural thing in the world.[1]

Sounds like a contemporary analogue to scenes from Dante's *Inferno*.

A 2021 Pew Research Center study found that most Americans (62 percent) believe in hell. Among Christians, the numbers were notably higher. Over half think that people in hell "definitely" or "probably" experience suffering (psychological and physical) and that a person in hell becomes aware of the pain they caused others when they were alive, presumably adding to their sense of guilt and regret. Forty-nine percent believe people in hell are "definitely" or "probably" cut off from relationship with God, and 44 percent think that those in hell "definitely" or "probably" can meet Satan.[2] A 2015 survey on the same topic found that most (58 percent) Americans believe in a *literal* hell—a place "where people who have led bad lives and die without being sorry are eternally punished."[3]

These beliefs and percentages raise a litany of questions, starting with what "hell" really means. Is hell a place? If so, what kind of place is it? How do souls who are "sent" there get there?

Christians' widespread belief in hell is remarkable when you consider, as New Testament scholar Bart Ehrman demonstrates, that the notion of hell as a literal place of eternal torment and damnation "cannot be found either in the Old Testament or in the teachings of the historical Jesus," but

---

1. Betts, *Question of Freedom*, 201.
2. Nortey et al., "Few Americans Blame God," 28–29.
3. Murphy, "Most Americans Believe."

was developed centuries after the biblical period.[4] Moreover, biblical ideas like "hell" reflect the imaginations of ancient Hebrews and Christians, who didn't operate with a literal mindset. These historical people relied on metaphors, myths, and stories to express spiritual truths and encourage moral behavior.[5] This strategy is evident in the ministry of Jesus, who responded to his followers' questions with parables or figures of speech in which an object represented something else—"The kingdom of heaven is like a treasure hidden in the field" (Matt 13:44). Like other ancient people, Jesus understood the truth of fiction.

What if hell isn't a place "bad" people go when they die, but a way of describing certain kinds of suffering? Maybe the "unquenchable fire" of hell (Mark 9:43) is a metaphorical way of naming the feeling of being trapped in painful emotions, without exits or options. The Zen teacher Thich Nhat Hanh suggested that when you're stuck in anger, you're in hell.[6] The same could be said about grief, anxiety, depression, addictive craving, and other forms of inner turmoil that even those of us who are not just trying to survive may experience as overwhelming, tormenting, and imprisoning. Jesus reportedly said that the "kingdom of heaven is among you" (Luke 17:21). Maybe the kingdom of hell is too.

If "hell" is a fitting metaphor for agonizing *internal* states, it also aptly describes horrific *external* circumstances, like the prison conditions Betts chronicles, or the trauma-inducing situations incarcerated youth have endured. Using the fear of eternal damnation or the threat of punishment to deter young people from engaging in immoral behavior assumes that they were not already living in hell well *before* they created hell for others.

---

4. Ehrman, *Heaven and Hell*, 16.
5. Borg, *Heart of Christianity*, 49–57.
6. Hanh, *Living Buddha, Living Christ*, 75.

38

"I Would Talk about..."

A PUNISHING APPROACH TO youth justice obscures the *underlying reasons* for youth crime. On a structural level, these reasons include systemic injustices—especially poverty, racism, and sexism—that create hellish social conditions for high potential kids. On an individual level, "shame, isolation, exposure to violence, and an inability to meet one's economic needs" drive crime.[1] Essentially, teenage wrongdoing is rooted in suffering. Counterproductively, punitive solutions to hurtful behavior exacerbate that pain and leave its sources intact.

During the writing workshop, one of my student assistants invited the youth to imagine interviewing themselves: "What questions would you ask yourself, and how would you respond?" Rose Marie wrote:

> I would talk about being in JDC [juvenile detention centers] most of my teenage years and why I ran away. I would talk about my charges and why I did what I did... I would talk about my siblings and about my physical abuse. I would talk about my brothers dying and how it's affected me. I would talk about my DID [Dissociated Identity Disorder]... I would talk about my time in [a psychiatric treatment facility]. I would talk about how medications affected me. I would talk about how my mom left me... I would talk about the books I've read and... about being raised by drug addicts who abused children... about my Gram getting cancer and how that affected me when I was young... I would talk about my drug use... about "friends" who have betrayed me.

1. Sered, *Until We Reckon*, 3–4.

Does this sound like a girl who "deserves" to be punished?

So many of the painful backstories of the youth I've met involve traumatic and unjust circumstances over which they had no control. In response to a writing prompt consisting of a single word—"struggle"—Bicky Boy Beno wrote about growing up without a bed: "I was sleeping on the floor. My moms was out of the way. Granny did what she could, but bills needed to be paid. So I had to live fast to keep food in my stomach."

If we truly understood the suffering many justice-involved youth have survived, we'd feel more compassion than judgment.

Yet during the 2022 mid-term elections, many Americans supported "anti-crime" candidates who promised to restore "law and order" to our nation's streets.[2] Republican candidates stoked public fears of "soaring violent crime." Democrats promised more funding for police.[3] Members from both parties revived the "tough on crime" sentiments reminiscent of the era when punitive responses to "juvenile delinquency" intensified.

During that era, evangelical Christians started supporting harsher responses to teenage lawlessness. Whereas in the 1950s, leaders like Billy Graham stressed the need for personal conversion over punishment, by the late 1960s, Graham and others backed politicians whose policies were more retaliatory than redemptive. Graham galvanized White Christians' enthusiasm for Richard Nixon, the self-designated "law and order" candidate who promised to restore civility to the South on the heels of the civil rights movement. Leaders like Graham reconciled their faith in God's grace with their punishing approach to "justice" by insisting that church and state had different roles to play in maintaining America's moral order: while it was Jesus' job to forgive criminals, it was the government's divinely ordained duty to judge and sentence them severely.[4] Graham claimed to know not only what God wants, but also what "American people want," namely, "law, order, and security."[5]

But "American people" are not a monolith. How could Graham—or anyone—possibly know what each of us believes a more just, safe, and moral society entails? Has anyone asked Bicky Boy Beno or Rose Marie or their Black and Indigenous ancestors?

---

2. Price and Bedayn, "GOP Steps Up," paras. 5–6.
3. Linskey and Sotomayor, "Worries over crime," para. 3.
4. Griffith, *God's Law and Order*, 95, 120–22, 135–41.
5. Graham, quoted in Griffith, *God's Law and Order*, 141.

39

"I Already Died Once"

IF AMERICANS ARE NOT a monolith, neither are incarcerated youth. I've said this already, but the point can't be overstated. In the same conversation in which Bao said he's afraid of going to hell, Jordan shared that he wasn't worried about what will happen to him when he dies.

"I'm a Buddhist," he explained. "I don't believe in hell." Jordan said he wasn't exactly sure what he thinks happens after you die. "Maybe some kind of reincarnation; but I don't know if you get reincarnated into another person, or maybe an animal, or a bug or tree."

Sam—the boy who initially didn't want to participate but by that point was fully engaged—went next: "I'm not afraid of anything," he said. "I don't believe in God, and I already know what happens when you die: everything goes black. It's just black. There's nothing there."

"You sound pretty certain," I observed.

"I am," Sam confidently responded, "because I've already died once."

"Really?"

"Yeah. I was dead for seven minutes during a drug overdose. My heart stopped for seven minutes. They brought me back to life."

Bao instantly challenged this story. "That can't be true."

"No way," Jordan added.

Roshaun didn't say anything, but the astonished look on his face suggested that he was open to the possibility that Sam was telling the truth.

When the youth share hard-to-believe anecdotes, I'm more curious about how they think about whatever they're recounting than whether the incident really happened. I asked Sam: "Do you think you had a choice about coming back to life?"

He said he wasn't sure.

My best friend Theresa is a retired probation officer. She told me that when listening to the stories of the kids in her care, she found it helpful to distinguish what was likely to be *literally true* from what was more probably *emotionally true*. The challenge of identifying which is which points to the complexity in these kids' lives.

Regardless of whether Sam's story that he'd "already died once" was literally true, perhaps it was emotionally accurate as a metaphor—intended or not—not just for him, but for many incarcerated teens who have survived some version of a living death. So many of the youth I've met have endured the "trials of hell" and lived to tell about it.

But will we listen?

When asked how we feel when we hear about human suffering, 24 percent of Americans surveyed said they often need to "tune out" the bad news "because it's just too much to take." That nearly a quarter of us find it necessary to disregard the afflictions of others is bad news for kids who can't simply opt out of their grueling situations. Similarly troubling is the self-referential focus of the most popular response to the question above: 71 percent said that when they hear about others' suffering, they frequently feel "thankful for the good things" in their own lives.[1] Gratitude can be wonderful. But it's no substitute for compassion.

Perhaps the good news from this survey is that 40 percent expressed a "desire to help" those in need.[2] But even this desire is problematic if the attitudes and actions it fosters stop at charity. Giving to others *expresses* privilege, without challenging the structures that create privilege. Moreover, the desire to "help" people in need often downplays the need for healing among the "helpers."

In the original ACE study, which was based on the lives of well-to-do adults, over two thirds of the seventeen thousand plus surveyed reported at least one adverse childhood experience.[3] Recognizing the widespread presence of childhood trauma among nonincarcerated people with privilege doesn't imply that "we're all the same" or that we can fully understand painful experiences we've never had. Rather, this recognition creates an opportunity for us to behold our shared humanity, including our *mutual* need to reduce suffering in ourselves and the world.

---

1. Nortey et al., "Few Americans Blame God," 16.
2. Nortey et al., "Few Americans Blame God," 16.
3. National Center for Injury Prevention, "CDC-Kaiser ACE Study."

40

"All the Love in My Heart Went Out of Me That Day"

During the school year, eleven students from my Religion, Race, and Social Justice class help facilitate our small group discussions, which means that if there's a resident who needs one-on-one attention, I can spend time with them.

One December afternoon, as my students and the youth were transitioning into smaller groups, I noticed Roshaun standing off to the side of the gym, bouncing a tennis ball off the wall and catching it repeatedly. I approached him and asked if he'd prefer to have a conversation with just me. He nodded and explained that his PTSD and ADHD were "really bad" that day and asked if we could stand while we talked.

"Of course. Do you want to discuss the prompts I brought?"

He nodded again and read the first one: "How did the environment you grew up in shape you and your life?"

Roshaun talked about growing up in "the hood." His dad had been in jail since he was seven. He knew his mom loved him and worked hard to put food on the table for his sister and him, but sometimes there just wasn't enough. "Have you ever eaten out of dumpsters?" he asked in all seriousness.

"No, I haven't," I responded.

"There was always violence just around the corner." To illustrate his point, Roshaun pulled up the hem of his pants and showed me a scar from a bullet that had entered one side of his calf and exited the other. "I never wanted to leave the house after that," he said.

Later that month, when my students were on Christmas break, I arranged to bring cookies for the kids in the pods. When I got there, I discovered that most of the residents I'd gotten to know during the previous semester were on furloughs visiting their families for the holidays. Only a few kids from the mindfulness group were still there, including Roshaun. After having some cookies, he asked me to wait while he went to his room to get something. He returned with a photo album and opened it to a picture of himself standing with another Black boy. They were side by side facing the camera, long skinny arms draped around each other's shoulders, looking cool and happy. "This is my best friend," Roshaun said, pointing to the photo. "Or was." He turned the page to a picture of himself, dressed in stylishly torn jeans and a sharp red hoodie, standing over a closed coffin that was already in the earth. "That's my best friend in there," he explained, staring at the picture. "When I saw him being lowered into that grave . . ." He paused and swallowed hard. "All the love in my heart went out of me that day." As he said this, he put his hand to his chest and made a motion—as if he was pulling an invisible thread out of his heart.

The more I listen to the depth of the youths' painful backstories, the harder it is to judge their harmful choices. Whatever Roshaun did to get himself locked up, it was no doubt a reaction to his suffering. In this regard, Roshaun isn't so unlike people with privilege. In fact, to grow our compassion for incarcerated kids without otherizing them or sliding into pity, we must practice seeing how a cycle of harm operates in our own lives. Incarcerated or not, it's easier to spread hurt than to feel it. Social work professor Brené Brown observes, "When we're suffering, many of us are better at causing pain than feeling it."[1]

If we want to avoid passing our distress onto others, we have to be present to it. Without such presence, our suffering remains unvalidated, unresolved, and contagious. Resmaa Menakem refers to unhealed hurt as "dirty pain":

> Dirty pain is the pain of avoidance, blame, and denial. When people respond from their most wounded parts, become cruel or violent, or physically or emotionally run away, they experience dirty pain. They also create more of it for themselves and others.[2]

Despite the temporary relief dirty pain strategies provide, they invariably end up exacerbating the suffering they're meant to alleviate because this

---

1. B. Brown, *Braving the Wilderness*, 158.
2. Menakem, *My Grandmother's Hands*, 19–20.

anguish remains unaddressed. Compassion is directly related to healing because, as I discuss more fully in Part IV, being present with suffering—our own and others'—is the only way to transform the hurt. As Menakem says, "healing involves discomfort." But in the long run, "refusing to heal is always more painful."[3]

---

3. Menakem, *My Grandmother's Hands*, 19–20.

41

"Grievid"

NOT ALL THE YOUTH I've met have survived extreme encounters with violence. Yet each has endured the trauma of losing loved ones—siblings, grandparents, favorite aunties and uncles, cousins, friends, parents, and sometimes all of the above. On top of such excruciating losses, many justice-involved youth have experienced betrayals of trust from caregivers, including emotional, physical, and/or sexual abuse. In fact, most teens in the system have histories of *complex* trauma, meaning they've endured multiple, compounding, and often long-standing forms of childhood adversity that, left untreated, will compromise their physical, mental, and emotional health for years to come.[1] Even though a traumatic incident stops, the devastation it unleashes in a person's mind/body/spirit "keeps being replayed in continually recycling memories and in a reorganized nervous system."[2]

Without supportive interventions, trauma can short-circuit children's healthy development, creating challenges at school and relationship difficulties, and making them more prone to substance abuse and risky behaviors, such as truancy, running away, and sexual promiscuity. What may look on the surface like a teenager's hostile, apathetic, or disrespectful attitude, and what may appear to be their flagrant disregard for safety and/or laws, often masks an effort to deny trauma or to preempt additional abuse and distress. An Obama-era report from the attorney general's National Task Force on Children Exposed to Violence states:

---

1. National Center for Child Traumatic Stress Network, *Complex Trauma*, 1–3.
2. Van der Kolk, *Body Keeps the Score*, 159.

> Many youth in the justice system appear angry, defiant, or indifferent, but actually they are fearful, depressed, and lonely. They hurt emotionally and feel powerless, abandoned, and subject to double standards by adults in their lives and in "the system." These children are often viewed by the system as beyond hope and uncontrollable, labeled as "oppositional," "willfully irresponsible," or "unreachable." What appears to be intentional defiance and aggression, however, is often a defense against the despair and hopelessness that violence has caused in these children's lives.[3]

The report concludes that punitive responses to such attitudes and behaviors can drive children deeper into the youth and adult systems, possibly permanently severing their connections to their families and society.

I thought of this report when I met Denali, who initially struck me as either aloof or detached. As I got to know her better, it became clear that she wasn't so much disengaged as she was protecting herself from further hurt by pretending not to care. "Why should I care," she asked, "when every time I do someone dies or gets hurt?" I don't know all the details of Denali's backstory, but she told me that her little sister had been shot dead "by some guy." In a rage of vengeance, her dad had killed her sister's killer, which had landed him in prison. Denali told me that she wasn't looking forward to the one-year anniversary of her mother's death, which was coming up soon.

Denali is a poet. She said that writing helps her cope with her grief. Among various poems she shared with the mindfulness group, my favorite is one that contrasts how she sees herself and her life ("In my eyes...") with how the world ("reality") sees and treats her. It's called "In My Eyes, and in Reality":

> In my eyes everyone's equal, but in reality, slavery's not over
> In my eyes there's no such word as hopeless, but in reality, there's not enough sponges to
> soak up the tears of the helpless.
> In my eyes, color's the most beautiful thing ever, but in reality my skin is *disgusting*
> In my eyes I'm beautiful, but in reality, I'm *dangerous*
> In my eyes we all got problems, but in reality, color is killing different color.

Given her poetic sensibilities, it's not surprising that Denali was one of the few residents who took me up on the invitation to invent new words that enable us to express different feelings that sometimes arise simultaneously.

---

3. Listenbee Jr. et al., *Children Exposed to Violence*, 171–72.

Denali combined "grief" and "livid" to coin a new word that named the intense mix of loss and rage she felt over the circumstances of her life: *grievid*.

The tough and cool veneer some incarcerated youth project masks the pain of their unhealed "grievid." Unresolved "grievid" saturates Rose Marie's reflection on the meaning of love, which she composed in the writing workshop. Initially, she was reluctant to share what she wrote with the group—until Drake offered to read it out loud for her:

> Love gives people the advantage to hurt you. Love hurts. It tears you apart piece by piece and it never ends. It makes you go to the edge of the universe for someone who steps on and abuses you constantly. It's feeling weak and not able to function emotionally by yourself. It's having to lean on someone else who doesn't know how to care for you or anybody. It's fake and controlling... Love cheats and lies. It throws you on the ground and beats you until you're drained and then it moves on to someone and repeats in a never-ending cycle of misery and hurt. I hate love.

Sometimes when I listen to the experiences and perspectives of incarcerated youth, I hear the words of Fr. Gregory Boyle: "Kindness is the only non-delusional response to everything."[4]

---

4. Boyle, "Can You Really Conquer," 57:35.

42

"We Were Not Violent Girls. We Were Girls Who Were Hurting"

Many justice-involved teens have endured repeated threats to their own lives and/or to the lives of people close to them. Besides Roshaun, several other boys at the detention center have told me stories of being shot at—often in a tone that toggles between pride and normalcy.

The intense violence that most incarcerated girls have survived frequently includes sexual trauma, which is one of the most reliable predictors of their involvement with the youth justice system. The disproportionate number of girls in the system who have been sexually or physically violated is illustrated by a study of Oregon's youth justice system, which found 93 percent of females in its care to be survivors of such trauma. In cases involving sex trafficking, girls can end up in carceral placements *because* of their victimization.[1]

Rose Marie was a survivor of sex trafficking. By age sixteen, she'd spent most of her adolescent life in juvenile facilities. Although she had a record, most of her time in confinement was the result of authorities' efforts to protect her from further trauma. Given the addiction, violent deaths, and abuses in her family situation, sending her home was no doubt deemed unsafe. During the months she participated in the mindfulness group, I don't remember ever seeing her smile. In response to a prompt that asked her to describe her favorite time of day, she wrote: "When it's time to sleep," because "then my mind can finally go blank."

---

1. Saada Saar et al., *Sexual Abuse to Prison Pipeline*, 5–7.

Cyntoia Brown was even less fortunate. Brown was sixteen when she shot and killed a man who was paying her for sex, because she thought he was about to kill her. She spent the next fifteen years in prison. When interviewed about Cyntoia's situation, her maternal grandmother explained that she herself was the victim of ongoing rapes and beatings, as was Cyntoia's mother. "I pulled myself together, put on makeup. That's what abused families usually does to keep anybody from knowing it." The silence and shame that often shadow sexual abuse magnify the original wound. Cyntoia's grandmother said the anguish of her trauma followed her daily and that she likely transmitted this pain to her daughter and granddaughter. She speculated that the trauma was in their "genetics."[2] Her theory is supported by epigenetics research documenting that trauma can be passed down biologically from one generation to the next.[3]

Many of us don't think of sexual violence against girls and women as a form of historical trauma. But how can it not be? After all, some men have used this specific form of brutality to terrorize, punish, and control females not just for generations, but for millennia—often with the silent support of narratives from texts many believe to be sacred.

The Bible is among the most influential sources for Western cultures' gender norms and power dynamics, and there's no shortage of rape narratives in this holy text. These narratives tend to blame, dismiss, downplay, silence, or ignore the experiences of women who are violated. The story of Tamar, who is raped by her half-brother Amnon, illustrates this dynamic. Following the assault, "Tamar put ashes on her head, and tore the long robe that she was wearing; she put her hand on her head, and went away, crying aloud as she went" (2 Sam 13:19). When she goes to her brother Absalom for help, he tells her to be quiet. Tamar's father, David, knows about the rape but doesn't so much as reprimand Amnon. Tamar ends up leading a desolate life, shunned, shamed, and isolated.[4]

Biblical rape narratives have been recycled for centuries and continue to tacitly support the rape culture Americans inhabit today. Feminist theologian Gina Messina-Dysert defines "rape culture" as "a cyclical system where rape is viewed as inevitable and is accepted as a fact of life and impossible to change."[5] Rape cultures draw support from both popular and traditional gender/body norms, images, and narratives that encourage people to view female bodies primarily as sexual objects of male desire. These same

2. Joan Warren, quoted in Birman, dir., *Murder to Mercy*, 1:05:00.
3. Yehuda, "How Trauma and Resilience."
4. Messina-Dysert, *Rape Culture*, 5–25.
5. Messina-Dysert, *Rape Culture*, 61.

cultures shame women who are deemed insufficiently "feminine." With support from rape culture's norms and narratives, 25 percent of women in the US have survived physical and/or sexual violence at the hands of an intimate partner.[6] The same percentage of girls will be sexually violated by their eighteenth birthday. According to *The Sexual Abuse to Prison Pipeline*, a report connecting violence against girls and young female incarceration,

> Fifteen percent of sexual assault and rape victims are under the age of 12; nearly half of all female rape survivors were victimized before the age of 18. And girls between the ages of 16 and 19 are four times more likely than the general population to be victims of rape, attempted rape, or sexual assault.[7]

These numbers illuminate a cultural context in which girls are consistently vulnerable to being sexually violated. Girls who have been sexually traumatized are at elevated risk for physical, mental, and emotional health challenges. They are more prone to drop out of school and more likely to get into legal trouble.[8]

Although girls comprise about one quarter to one fifth of justice-involved youth, their numbers have been disproportionately increasing. Minoritized female youth are overrepresented in this increase, as are those who identify as LGBTQ (lesbian, gay, bisexual, transgender, and/or queer). The reality that nearly all of these girls are victims of physical and/or sexual abuse points to a "sexual abuse to prison pipeline." This phrase describes "the ways in which we criminalize girls—especially girls of color—who have been sexually and physically abused."[9] Some behaviors for which they are arrested, including truancy, drug abuse, and prostitution, are symptoms of unaddressed trauma. Moreover, despite efforts to protect youth from further victimization inside the system—such as the Prison Rape Elimination Act (PREA)[10]—some girls suffer further abuse by prison staff.

Tragically, girls' experiences of physical and sexual violence tend to be self-perpetuating: "Experiences of trauma, maltreatment, and victimization play a role in placing girls on the pathway toward delinquency, re-traumatization, and chronic exposure to complex trauma."[11] Compared to boys, girls experience higher rates of "complex trauma," meaning they have survived

---

6. National Coalition against Domestic Violence, "Statistics."
7. Saada Saar et al., *Sexual Abuse to Prison Pipeline*, 5.
8. Van der Kolk, *Body Keeps the Score*, 164.
9. Saada Saar et al., *Sexual Abuse to Prison Pipeline*, 5–8, 24.
10. Henning, *Rage of Innocence*, 104–5.
11. National Center for Child Traumatic Stress Network, *Complex Trauma*, 1–3.

five or more kinds of toxic stress experiences.[12] The use of punitive tactics on girls in custody is potentially very concerning in light of their trauma histories. Coercive tactics (such as shackling), even for protective purposes, can trigger memories of physical and/or sexual abuse, reinforce a sense of helplessness, and exacerbate feelings of shame and humiliation.[13] One of the girls quoted in the *Sexual Abuse to Prison Pipeline* report describes her experience:

> I was locked up ten different times within a two year period. Inside juvie I met other girls like myself who were there for prostitution, running away, and truancy. All of us were from the same neighborhoods, poor families, and seemed to have the same disposition of trauma, anger mixed with hopelessness. We were not violent girls. We were girls who were hurting . . . Being locked up all I could do was reflect on my life but it didn't seem to help. I became even more withdrawn and angry.[14]

A compassionate approach to youth justice requires privileged people to share the burden of this girl's anger—to rage at a culture that accepts catastrophic levels of gendered violence, as if it were inevitable. Ultimately, compassion and anger are not incompatible energies. As compassion researcher Kristen Neff reminds us, compassion is not only tender, but fierce. Sensitivity and presence with suffering entails both the nonjudgmental kindness of a wise grandmother and the protective potency of a mother bear.[15]

---

12. Saada Saar et al., *Sexual Abuse to Prison Pipeline*, 9.
13. Sherman and Balck, *Gender Injustice*, 4, 19–28.
14. Nadiyah Sheref, quoted in Saada Saar et al., *Sexual Abuse to Prison*, 22.
15. Neff, *Fierce Self-Compassion*.

43

"When Someone Is Beating up Your Mom"

SOME JUSTICE-INVOLVED BOYS HAVE been on the other side of violence against women—not only as perpetrators of physical and/or sexual abuse, but as protectors against domestic violence.

After shuffling the discussion cards, Jordan drew one that asked, "Is violence ever okay?"

"Yes," he responded, "but only in self-defense."

"Yeah," Lamar agreed. "But sometimes it's hard to know if you really need to defend yourself, or if you're just getting out your aggression."

I asked if anyone had an example of when self-defense might warrant the use of violence.

"How about when someone's beating up your mom?" Lamar offered. "Then you have to step in to protect her."

Tyrell had been quietly listening to the conversation. I asked him what he thought.

"Well," he said, "what Lamar just described is pretty much what happened to me." Then he told us about a night when his mom's boyfriend was "going crazy," and he "had to stop him."

"That sounds dangerous," I said, "and scary."

"It was. And there was a gun involved, which made it even scarier."

I deliberated what to say next. "I'm glad you lived to tell this story," I finally commented.

Tyrell gave me a funny look. "Nooooo," he said, "*he* didn't have a gun! *I* was the one with the gun. And I shot him. He was going crazy on my mom, so I shot him. Not to kill him. But to get him off my mom. And it worked." Tyrell explained that the boyfriend wasn't badly injured—the bullet grazed the side of his leg. "The next day he called me up and cussed me out for shooting him. I told him to stay away from my mom and then I'd leave him alone. So, yes," he concluded, "I do believe there's a time and place for violence, and that example proves it."

A punitive approach to justice assumes that youth offenders' destructive behavior stems from a lack of moral fortitude, while ignoring the moral injuries these kids have survived. The term *moral injury* names the harm that happens to someone when they experience, witness, or do something they know in their heart is wrong.[1] A young person can be morally injured, for example, by experiencing physical abuse, watching someone else experience abuse, or by abusing someone. Such experiences are morally injurious insofar as they damage a person's conscience, compromising their ability to make ethical decisions. When a child experiences, witnesses, or does something that violates their sense of what's right, their perception of themselves as a "good person" may be diminished. Essentially, they may lose a sense of connection with their own divine humanity.

The category of "moral injury" helps us see how experiences that jeopardize a child's safety, well-being, or even their life are not just traumatizing, but also potentially damaging to their conscience. Thus the concept of moral injury illuminates aspects of toxic stress that a PTSD diagnosis doesn't.[2] Whereas PTSD tends to generate painful feelings of anxiety, horror, and helplessness, the experience of moral injury tends to instill a sense of shame, guilt, and anger.[3] As a concept, moral injury helps explain why war veterans have higher rates of suicidality, substance abuse, and violent behavior—not unlike justice-involved youth. When your conscience has been violated by something you saw or did—or something someone did to you—it's easy to lose faith in your own integrity and worth. When that happens, your moral compass is more likely to malfunction. Someone whose conscience has been seriously compromised may struggle to find a reason to continue living and/or may resort to self-harm or violating others to avoid the excruciating pain of owning what they have done, seen, or experienced.

In fact, suicidality among youth in juvenile facilities is alarmingly common: "Incarcerated youth die by suicide at a rate two to three times higher

---

1. Brock and Lettini, *Soul Repair*.
2. Shay, "Moral Injury," 184–86.
3. Brock and Lettini, *Soul Repair*, xiii; Shay, "Moral Injury," 184–86.

than that of youth in the general population."[4] Educator Donna Dukes explains the logic surrounding many justice-involved kids' profound despair:

> Life is only precious to those who believe success is possible, and critically at-risk youth don't . . . because in order to believe success is possible, you have to have dreams. In order to have dreams, you have to have hope. In order to have hope, you have to feel safe. In order to feel safe, you have to feel loved, valued. And they don't.[5]

Duke's observation reminds me of Curtis's response when I asked a group of residents what they needed the most to help them learn from their mistakes and be successful after their release. Without mincing words, he answered: "We need somebody who cares about us. We need somebody who cares."

---

4. Abram et al., "Suicidal Thoughts," para. 1. See also Bernstein, *Burning Down the House*, 100.

5. Dukes, "Let's Address the Needs," 5:02.

44

"That's When I Knew That My Brother Was Dead Too"

When Polo told me that most kids who look like him—young, Black, and male—are "either dead or in jail" by the time they're his age, I assumed he was exaggerating. But four months later, he was dead. Clearly, he knew something I didn't. His words echo in my mind like a prophecy every time I think of him.

The phrase—"dead or in jail"—also echoes in the mouths of other Black youth I've met at the detention center. I've heard a few of them repeat this phrase like a rap music refrain. Whenever the topic of violence comes up in discussions, it's clear why this truism of the "deep streets" speaks to them.

A week after a teenage boy legally purchased an AR rifle to murder nineteen students and two teachers at an elementary school in Uvalde, Texas, I asked a small group of boys what they thought were the roots of gun violence. Their answers were immediate: anger, hatred, and a desire for revenge. They spoke with confidence, as if they were experts on the issue, which on some level they are. Each of them had been on both sides of the malice they identified as the cause of gun violence.

Later in the conversation, one of the boys said there was another source of the problem. Speaking directly to me, Jordan stated: "You wouldn't believe how easy it is to get a gun."

"Really?" I asked, probably sounding naïve.

The other boys confirmed Jordan's point. Antoine offered himself as an example: "I got my first gun when I was eleven, and I know kids who got guns younger than that. And," he added, "these guns weren't for hunting animals. There ain't no deer in the hood."

Several months later, a different group of boys were telling me about growing up in "the hood." They talked about losing people they love to guns, as if it were the most normal thing in the world. Jalen's dad was murdered when he was nine, though his mother didn't tell him about the death for several weeks. "I knew something was wrong," he said. "I could sense it even though I was just a kid." Looking back, Jalen believes his mom was trying to spare him some pain by waiting to tell him. He added that losing his father was not nearly as hard as the more recent death of his brother, who was also shot and killed. Jalen described looking out the window of his family's apartment and seeing his brother's best friend leaning on a car parked at the curb, holding his hands over his face, sobbing. "That's when I knew that my brother was dead too."

The other boys in the group listened attentively as Jalen spoke, slowly nodding their heads in empathy. They, too, had lost people they loved to gun violence, including Darius's three-year-old brother. "He was killed by a revenge bullet that was meant for me."

It's both easy and necessary to condemn the violent acts some incarcerated youth have committed. But we won't truly understand these actions—and thus won't know how to respond to the kids who did them—until we bear witness to their backstories of *normalized violence*. As Sered reminds us, "No one enters violence for the first time by committing it."[1]

---

1. Sered, quoted in Kaba, *We Do This*, 146.

45

"I Want to Give Him, Just like the Rest of My Family, the World"

BEING SENSITIVE AND PRESENT to the suffering surrounding the lives of incarcerated teens requires us to stretch our hearts and minds enough to behold their creative potential. Neither the hurt they've endured nor the harm they've inflicted needs to become their destiny. But it could if more Americans don't adopt attitudes and support policies, practices, and programs that nurture these kids' better angels, including their capacities for love, empathy, and caring for others.

One of the most common ways residents in the mindfulness group demonstrate their capacity for tenderness is through the appreciation and affection they express for their families. Many of them describe family members or relatives who they know love them unconditionally. Indeed, most of the youth I've met have a strong sense of "family values." Drake wrote about his five siblings in detail, each of whom was uniquely special to him. Here's his description of his younger brother:

> He's charming, and when he wants something, the way he asks, you'll want to give it to him . . . I just want to be around him and teach him because I grew up without my big brother in my life and I don't want my brothers to feel like they have to look to anybody but me when they are confused or struggle. But he's goofy, playful, fun, he just reminds me of what I was like as a kid. His laugh is something else and his smile melts hearts. I miss him so much. I talk to him and saw him on ft [Facetime] but I just want to hug him and squeeze him and never let go.

> He loves legos, cars, ninjas, dinosaurs, video games, outdoors, bikes, scooters, basketball, football, karate, just all of it. And I want to give him, just like the rest of my family, the world.

Many of the youth in the mindfulness group talk about not wanting to let their families down. Bicky Boy Beno wrote this letter of encouragement to his son:

> Be better than me. Take care of your moms 'cause I ain't takin care of her. Be there for your sister. I know I'm away right now and not really old enough to know what's going on. But when daddy comes home I'm giv[ing] you and your sister better lives than I ever had. I want you to know I'm always with you even when I'm not cause you're a part of me . . . I want you to forever be strong, baby boy.

Despite the unbelievable challenges their families have faced, most incarcerated kids I've met have at least one family member—usually their mom—who has nurtured their better angels. "My mom's my biggest fan and supporter," Antoine told me. "She writes, calls, and visits as often as she can, even though I know she's got her hands full with work and taking care of my younger siblings." Antoine's empathy for his overworked mother is not uncommon, especially among the boys in the mindfulness group. Drake credited his mother for his own compassionate response to his younger brother when he got into a fight at school:

> Instead of coming down on him I talked to him about what happened and why he felt like he needed to do that. My mother used to get in trouble when she was my age, so she speaks to me from a place of understanding and teaching.

Like all of us, kids learn to treat others based on the examples of how they've been treated. This truism is another reason why compassionate justice makes more sense than the foolishness of a system that, to quote Davis, "harms people who harm people, presumably to show that harming people is wrong."[1]

---

1. Davis, *Little Book of Race*, 25.

PART III

Accountability

46

"A Cold-Blooded Killer"

One November evening in 2022, I heard a National Public Radio report on the trial of Nikolas Cruz, the young man who shot and killed fourteen students and three staff members at a Parkland, Florida high school in 2018. The shooter injured another seventeen people during the same violent rampage. A former student at the school, Cruz was nineteen at the time of the massacre—literally a teenager but legally an adult. He pled guilty. His lawyer persuaded the jury not to recommend capital punishment, arguing that Cruz was mentally impaired due to his mother's alcohol and drug abuse while pregnant with him.

NPR's report included clips from some of the victims' impact statements. A father whose fourteen-year-old son was among the murdered was one of several family members who called the verdict unfair. He lambasted the defense attorney for suggesting that mental health struggles were the source of Cruz's sociopathic violence. A teacher who survived the rampage expressed anguish and anger that "a cold-blooded killer" like Cruz didn't receive the death penalty:

> The idea that you [Cruz] . . . can actually live each day, eat your meals and put your head down at night—it seems completely unjust. The only comfort I have is that your life in prison will be filled with horror and fear.[1]

Earlier that afternoon, I'd been working on the chapters in Part II—the ones encouraging us to bear witness to the suffering of teenagers who hurt people. This story made me wonder: Are there limits to compassion?

1. G. Allen, "Parkland Survivors," para. 3.

I don't know the answer to that question. But I do know that taking the suffering of crime *survivors* seriously is crucial to the process of youth justice. As Danielle Sered, founder and director of Common Justice, points out,

> We are misunderstanding Bryan Stevenson's teaching that "each of [us] is more than the worst thing we have ever done" if we take it to mean that the harm we have caused is not so big that it can be explained away, that it can be diminished.[2]

Similarly, Menakem writes: "'I had been traumatized' is never a valid excuse for committing a crime. Neither is 'My ancestors were traumatized.'"[3] To bear witness to the suffering and injustices that contribute to teenagers' destructive—sometimes horrific—actions is *not* to justify those actions. While compassion for hurting kids is a crucial component of youth justice, so is recognizing and seeking to repair the damage or devastation they caused. To honor the divine humanity of everyone impacted by teenagers' harmful actions, *accountability* needs to be an integral aspect of compassionate justice.

---

2. Sered, *Until We Reckon*, 96.
3. Menakem, *My Grandmother's Hands*, 212.

47

What Does It Mean to Be Accountable?

MERRIAM-WEBSTER'S ONLINE DICTIONARY DEFINES "accountability" as "an obligation or willingness to accept responsibility or to account for one's actions." Other dictionaries echo this description of accountability as taking responsibility and answering for one's behavior. Curiously, these definitions don't mention punishment or coercion as aspects of accountability.

Yet within America's justice system, accountability is frequently associated—if not synonymous—with punishment. The tendency is to approach accountability as an accountant, as if justice were a math equation in which the damage caused by a crime can be forgiven if the responsible party pays for their wrongdoing with the proper amount of shame and suffering.

This punitive approach poses a problem not only because kids who commit serious harm are already hurting, but also because punishment is counterproductive to the accountability that's needed to stop the vicious cycles of hurt and foster public safety. Punishment diminishes accountability in part because it's designed to humiliate the wrongdoer. "It can be hard to take accountability for things you feel shame [about]," Drake wrote in his journal. Like most of us, teenagers are more motivated to accept responsibility for their mistakes and stop blaming others when they're not worried about being harshly judged or punished. Fear of retribution doesn't exactly incentivize truth-telling. Nor does the threat of punishment instill the courage needed to fess up to and repair whatever harm we've committed.

Owning the hurt we've caused is the first of five elements of accountability that Sered identifies based on her work with survivors of violent crime. Here's her entire list:

1. Acknowledging responsibility for one's actions
2. Acknowledging the impact of one's actions on others
3. Expressing genuine remorse
4. Taking actions to repair the harm to the degree possible, and guided when feasible by the people harmed, or "doing sorry"
5. No longer committing similar harm[1]

I asked a small group of boys in the mindfulness group what they thought of this list. They concurred that these steps looked dauntingly difficult.

"The hard thing about showing remorse is that others are gonna think you're weak," Diondre said. "If I say 'sorry,' others could take advantage of that, because maybe they're not sorry for what they did to me."

"Number five looks the hardest to me," Terrence chimed in. "I'm trying to use my time in this program to change. I really am. But I also know that when I get out, I'm going right back to the same old, same old."

Drew added, "Not blaming someone else for my mistakes is really hard. Nobody role-modeled that for me."

For many of us, acknowledging and answering for the harm we cause others is an arduous and even agonizing journey. Yet the deep discomfort that meaningful accountability involves is therapeutic and transformative, rather than punitive and shaming. Mustering the inner strength to admit to having hurt others, feeling genuinely sorry, and seeking to repair the damage to the extent possible metabolizes the "dirty pain" Menakem describes and reduces the likelihood of repeating the same harmful behavior.[2] Indeed, by interrupting the pattern of passing unhealed pain onto others, genuine accountability enhances public safety.

By contrast, a so-called "tough" (punitive) approach to accountability makes society *less* safe by letting harming parties off the hook. Sered explains this irony:

> No one in prison is required to face the human impacts of what they have done, to come face to face with the people whose lives are changed as a result of their decisions, to own their responsibility for those decisions and the pain they have caused, and

---

1. Sered, *Until We Reckon*, 96.
2. Menakem, *My Grandmother's Hands*, 19–20.

to do the extraordinarily hard work of answering for that pain and becoming someone who will not commit that harm again.³

If we want to promote public safety and interrupt the vicious cycles of hurting kids, we need to bear witness to and address the pain justice-involved youth have survived without protecting them from the *moral obligations* that arise from the harm they've inflicted. Accountability requires us to take crime victims' experiences seriously.

A victim-centric approach to accountability distinguishes punishment from accountability. The following side-by-side comparison illuminates this distinction:

• Punishment perpetuates cycles of harm.	• Accountability addresses harm.
• Punishment is a strategy for enforcing rules.	• Accountability creates obligations.
• Punishment tends to be shaming and isolating.	• Accountability fosters honesty and connection.
• Punishment is designed to inflict suffering and is usually coercive.	• Accountability is voluntary and breaks the cycles of harm.
• Punishment encourages passivity—the punished person simply has to endure it.	• Accountability is proactive—requiring the harming party to take responsibility for wrongdoing.
• Punishment doesn't address needs for healing and repair.	• Accountability fosters healing and seeks repair.⁴

America's legal system and culture condition us to equate "justice" with punishment and conflate punishment with accountability. These associations resurrect certain religious narratives that glorify sacrificial suffering as the price of redemption.

---

3. Sered, *Until We Reckon*, 91–92.

4. This list, which draws on Sered's work, slightly paraphrases and summarizes ideas from the Virginia Sexual and Domestic Violence Action Alliance, "Punishment Is Not Accountability."

48

"The Wages of Sin Is Death"

It's common to think of America's justice system as a secular institution. Yet Christian notions of sin, punishment, and redemption echo in the way this system pursues accountability, namely, by making convicted people pay for the harm they've inflicted by suffering. A popular verse from Paul's letters—"the wages of sin is death" (Rom 6:23)—suggests that sin (and by proxy, crime) requires mortifying retribution. Whether Paul meant "death" to represent the eternal damnation that awaits unrepentant sinners at the end of their lives, or the soul-killing inner torment that harming others produces in the living, the idea seems to be that God requires pain and punishment as "wages" for wrongdoing. This idea lends conceptual support to a system that holds criminals ("sinners") morally accountable by chastising them. As theologian Nikia Robert observes, the story of Christ's sacrificial suffering echoes today in the torment of socially marginalized bodies caught up in America's carceral state.[1]

Paul's belief that God ordained the sacrificial death of Jesus to redeem human sin (see Rom 3:25; 1 Cor 15:3) informed the most prominent atonement theories later Christian leaders developed to explain how sinners are forgiven and reconciled with God. A medieval thinker named Anselm formulated one of the most influential of these theories: God required and thus orchestrated Jesus' agonizing death on the cross to pay the debt incurred by human sin.[2] Centuries later, Protestant Reformers like Martin Luther and John Calvin tweaked Anselm's theology to formulate the "penal substitution"

---

1. Robert, "Penitence, Plantation and the Penitentiary," 46.
2. Pogin, "Conceptualizing the Atonement."

theory, which held that God's forgiveness of human sins required some kind of punitive, sacrificial, virtuous payment, which Jesus offered on the bloody cross.[3] Within this narrative, "God's justice could not be satisfied unless somebody was punished," and in Christianity, that somebody was Jesus.[4] The ongoing popularity of sacrificial atonement theories among Christians today is evident in the familiar storyline that "God sent his only Son, Jesus, to suffer and die for our sins."

The beliefs that 1) torturous sacrifice is necessary payment for sin; 2) someone must be punished for wrongdoing to be forgiven; and 3) the pain of punishment is virtuous, redemptive, and reconciling reverberate in our justice system's tendency to reduce accountability to retribution as the "wages of sin." This system mirrors the beliefs of many Americans, including non-Christians. As Potts observes, for many of us, "It is a natural assumption that if you do something wrong, you have to pay for it." Yet, he clarifies, this assumption is *not* natural at all. Rather, it reflects "a particular account of sin from the Christian tradition" in which Jesus pays for our moral failures by being crucified.[5]

The idea that God needed Jesus to suffer and die as restitution for human sin has troubling implications for incarcerated youth. For decades, womanist theologians have critiqued the narrative of redemptive suffering, which has been used to justify or sugarcoat the bloodshed of Black bodies in America, from slavery to lynching to police killings. Other feminist theologians suggest that sacrificial atonement narratives glorify divine child abuse. Rita Nakashima Brock perceives "the ghost of a punitive father lurk[ing] in the corners" of traditional atonement theories.[6] God's supposed need for "his only Son" to be tortured and sacrificed to "pay for our sins" resembles other biblical accounts that implicate God in child abuse. Consider the story in which God orders Abraham to kill his only son, which Abraham nearly does—stopping in the nick of time when an angel informs him that God was just testing his faith (Gen 22:1–19). Rebecca Parker and Joanne Carlson Brown challenge Christians to reject theologies in which "divine child abuse is paraded as salvific and the child who suffers 'without raising a voice' is lauded as the hope of the world."[7] Implicitly, such theologies lend themselves to interpreting the traumas and injustices incarcerated youth have survived as potentially redemptive.

3. Gilliard, *Rethinking Incarceration*, 150–55.
4. Harvard Divinity School, "Christianity, Race," para. 7.
5. Harvard Divinity School, "Christianity, Race," para. 7.
6. Brock, *Journeys by Heart*, 56. See also Brock and Parker, *Proverbs of Ashes*.
7. Quoted in Pogin, "Conceptualizing the Atonement," 169.

Importantly, biblical scholars don't think sacrificial atonement theories can be traced to the teachings of Jesus. As Marcus Borg explains, Jesus was a wisdom teacher, healer, social prophet, and initiator of a movement to create a different kind of society based on love and inclusion. Though he understood the potentially fatal consequences of his countercultural ministry, he didn't see his life purpose to be dying to absolve the sins of the world. He was more interested in creating a just and peaceful society on earth.[8]

What happens if we shift the central narrative of Christian faith to one that doesn't gloss over the historical reality that Jesus was criminalized, unjustly arrested, brutalized, and murdered by the Roman Empire because of his outspoken opposition to Roman oppression? Like the brave civil rights leaders in 1950s and 1960s, early followers of Jesus risked imprisonment and even death not as a strategy to pay for anyone's sins, but as an expression of their commitment to a faith that challenged imperial oppression. As feminist Rosemary Radford Ruether argues, "Suffering is a factor in the liberation process, not as a means of redemption, but as the risk one takes when one struggles to overcome unjust systems whose beneficiaries resist change."[9] Similarly, womanist Delores Williams insists that it was Jesus' liberating practice—his willingness to challenge oppression—not his death by torture, that has redemptive meaning for his followers.[10] According to Borg, it is more historically accurate and less spiritually harmful for Christians to affirm that Jesus died *because of*—not *for*—humans' sins.[11]

Atonement theories that depoliticize Jesus' death deprive contemporary Christians of a valuable resource for critiquing the injustices that make some youth more vulnerable than others to being traumatized, criminalized, arrested, detained, and imprisoned. What if challenging systemic injustices was the embodiment—the ultimate expression—of Christian faith? Would this not be a faith that was truly accountable to both the life and death of Jesus *and* to kids who get in trouble with the law?

We can't unsubscribe from beliefs we don't know we have. To challenge the cultural/spiritual habit of associating punishment with accountability, we must practice noticing how the narrative that suffering is morally necessary and redemptive has shaped dominant understandings of "justice" in the West.

---

8. Borg, *Heart of Christianity*, 92–95.
9. Ruether, *Women and Redemption*, 279.
10. Dorrien, "Cannon, Williams, and Womanist Survival."
11. Borg, *Jesus*, 274.

49

"That's Two Years of My Life Down the Drain"

THE OPENING SCENE OF Michel Foucault's *Discipline and Punish* illustrates Christianity's historic power to legitimize state-sponsored coercive pain as the path for atonement. In this scene, an eighteenth-century French priest presides over the quartering of a man found guilty of trying to kill the king. Being pulled apart by his limbs was the final stage of a gruesome torture process that included ripping the convicted man's body apart with red-hot pincers and pouring boiling oil, burning sulphur, and scorching lead over his lacerated flesh. Besides functioning as a deterrent, this gratuitous ceremony of corporal chastisement produced the sinner's repentance. The disgraced, desperate, dying man cried out to Jesus for help, begged God for pardon, kissed a crucifix, and implored the parish priest to pray for him. This spectacle also gave the righteous a chance to shore up their virtue. According to the *Gazette d'Amsterdam*, "The spectators were all edified by the solicitude of the parish priest . . . who despite his great age did not spare himself in offering consolation to the patient."[1]

We've come a long way since the days when religiously sanctioned torture was a culturally acceptable method for extracting criminal "accountability" and protecting the power of kings. However, Foucault cautions us not to assume that the "more subtle, more subdued," less visible forms of suffering that the modern penal system generated eliminated its oppressive, dehumanizing tendencies.[2] The historically shifting methods of pun-

---

1. Foucault, *Discipline and Punish*, 3.
2. Foucault, *Discipline and Punish*, 8.

ishment—from physical torture to the less bloody disciplines of the prison system—masked the ruling classes' enduring power to round up and repress socially marginalized people, supposedly for their own good.[3] In Foucault's account, "justice" methods that brutalized criminals' bodies were replaced by penal institutions, policies, and moralizing practices designed to correct their souls. Incarceration functioned as a less gory but still oppressively grueling and shaming strategy for controlling society's underclass.

On one of our first visits to the detention center, Jason described his difficult childhood, including his parents' struggles with severe poverty and drug addictions. "My mom's drug habit was so bad that she got permanent brain damage and has to live in an institution for the rest of her life." Jason's father abandoned him when he was a toddler and showed up a decade later—about the time he started getting in trouble.

The previous day, Jason's hopes for a lenient punishment for his crime had been dashed when a judge had sentenced him to two years in a juvenile prison in another state. "That's two years of my life down the drain," he said in a tone of frustration laced with grief.

"That sucks," Alison offered empathetically.

"It does," Shevon concurred. "But," he said encouragingly, "I've heard that place [the youth prison] isn't as bad as some of them."

Bernie had also recently been to court and was much happier with the outcome. "I got lucky," he said. "My judge mandated me to participate in the residential treatment program downstairs, starting next week." He said if he successfully completed the program, he could be released in eight weeks.

Shevon agreed that Bernie was lucky—"Because being locked up has made me worse."

Prison abolitionists share Shevon's perception—and Foucault's suspicion—that incarceration is counterproductive as a strategy for holding responsible parties accountable. While imprisonment tentatively prevents offenders from inflicting further damage on the public (though not necessarily on each other), research indicates that the pain and punishment of incarceration fail to deter youth crime.[4] Deterrence presumes that people have hope, which many teens on society's margins do not.[5] If you have reason to believe that kids who look like you and/or live where you live end up "either dead or in jail," what's to stop you from engaging in desperate behavior? Quoting the youth she interviewed, Bernstein illustrates the dangerous despondency that drives teenagers to engage in harmful behavior:

3. Jouet, "Foucault, Prison, Human Rights," 208.
4. Holman and Ziedenberg, *Dangers of Detention*, 7, 15.
5. Sered, *Until We Reckon*, 63.

- "I don't give a fuck about me—no one else does, so why should I?"
- "I don't give a fuck about you—how can I, when I can't even care about myself?"
- "I don't give a fuck what happens to me—could it get any worse than it already is?"
- "Go ahead, lock me up. Bring it on."[6]

Without question, some incarcerated teenagers have committed serious violence. But without interventions that address the roots of their actions, locking them up is likely to exacerbate their antisocial tendencies. Indeed, the very factors known to foster violence on an individual level—shame, isolation, exposure to violence, and economic insecurity—are the daily bread of life in adult prisons. Ironically, Sered observes, America has created "a response to violence that is characterized by precisely what we know to be the main drivers of violence."[7]

Perhaps punishment itself is a form of violence, even if it doesn't involve bloodshed. Punishment is administered to make someone suffer the consequences of their wrongdoing. And isn't causing pain to another the very essence of violence?

The violence that's baked into punitive strategies for holding youth accountable isn't the product of anyone's malicious intent. It originates in retaliatory approaches to justice that desecrate the spirits of hurting kids, to the point where they "don't give a fuck."

---

6. Bernstein, *Burning Down the House*, 169.
7. Sered, *Until We Reckon*, 76.

50

"J'ai Dû M'Fuir de Chez Moi" (I Had to Run Away from My Family)

While Sered's analysis focuses primarily on the adult system, it's relevant for at least some incarcerated kids because at its worst, the system of juvenile confinement mirrors the adult system. One example is the use of disciplinary measures that resemble solitary confinement, which the United Nations deems a kind of "torture."[1]

The practice of isolating inmates from society and each other was central to the original design and purpose of America's first adult prisons in the late eighteenth century. The Christians who created the penitentiary system sought to spare convicted criminals from the gruesome bodily punishments Foucault described. According to historian Jennifer Graber, these reformers envisioned the prison to be a "furnace of affliction"—a place where "God-ordained sufferings paved the way for receiving grace and reforming behavior."[2] They believed that convicts who were forced to face their sins through prolonged solitude in their cells would, through prayer and penitence, experience the divine mercy needed to redeem their souls.[3] By the mid-nineteenth century, however, this strategy of redemptive suffering

---

1. Sered, *Until We Reckon*, 93.

2. Graber, *Furnace of Affliction*, 6. See also Dubler and Lloyd, *Break Every Yoke*, 39–40.

3. Davis, *Little Book of Race*, 59.

"J'ai Dû M'Fuir de Chez Moi" (I Had to Run Away from My Family)   159

through solitary confinement had failed to produce prisoners' mass conversion, and the system became more strictly punitive.[4]

In early 2016, President Obama's administration banned solitary confinement for youth offenders in federal juvenile prisons.[5] Prior to that, the use of "the hole" had been widespread in youth prisons.[6] Still today, room confinement remains a common method for isolating youth who are deemed dangerous to themselves or others. According to Betts, such isolating strategies make prisons prone to abuse: "One of the reasons we can do what we do to men, women, and children in prison is because nobody sees it, and nobody pays them attention."[7] Additionally, it's hard to imagine how a practice that resembles torture will motivate teenage offenders to take responsibility for whatever harm they caused.

Room confinement is an example of a disciplinary practice that makes abolitionists want to end incarceration altogether. Yet even strong critics of the current system acknowledge that secure facilities may be needed to serve some young offenders,[8] whether because they pose a threat to public safety or because their own security and well-being would be endangered by returning to the environment from which they came. For youth who have access to therapeutic services, confinement may also provide a rare opportunity for healing. A friend whose daughter was incarcerated for drug-related charges believes that the residential treatment program she participated in saved her life. Additionally, some kids are in detention not because they committed crimes, but because they have nowhere else to go.

One day, one of my students informed me that there was a girl in his small group who didn't speak English. He was pretty sure her mother tongue was French, which happens to be a language I know almost well enough to understand and speak (emphasis on *almost*).

I invited the girl, Leila, to join me for a one-on-one conversation. As we introduced ourselves, I apologized for my poor French.

"Pas de problème" (No problem), she smiled and responded.

In clumsy French, I asked her how she was doing. Speaking slowly, she said she was okay. The staff were kind and had been using Google Translate to communicate with her. She told me she was from out of state and that her parents had immigrated to the US to escape the violence in their

---

4. Graber, *Furnace of Affliction*.

5. White House, "Fact Sheet."

6. Published in 2014, Bernstein devotes a chapter to "the hole" in *Burning Down the House*.

7. Miller, "Talking Volumes."

8. McCarthy et al., "Future of Youth Justice," 17.

home country in Africa. "Mais, j'ai dû m'fuir de chez moi" (But, I had to run away from my family), she explained, because of violence at home. She had hitched a ride with friends who were traveling cross-country. They had dropped her off in a nearby town, where the police found her. Holding back tears, Leila said she didn't know anyone in the area.

Immigrant children are not the only ones who might find themselves in confinement after running away from abusive families. Greta fled home to escape her mother's abuse (her dad had long since abandoned the family). "I couldn't take it anymore. I ran barefoot to the high school about a mile away because I didn't know where else to go." Greta had been at the facility for six months. "The worst part of being here so long is that the friends I make—the other girls in the pod—come and go." Sometimes Greta shared her poetry and drawings with my students and me. She was one of the rare participants in the mindfulness group who wanted to do longer meditations. I wasn't surprised when she told me she'd been teaching girls in the pod who didn't attend the group how to meditate.

One day, as I was leaving the mindfulness group, I asked Greta what she missed most about life outside the detention center. Her answer: "Life."

I wish I'd had more time to ask Greta to elaborate on the meaning of her response. What is it that makes life worth living? This is a question for all of us: What about *life* would you miss if you were in confinement?

The dislocations both Leila and Greta experienced also remind me of the need for a sense of home that nonincarcerated people share with them. What does "home" mean? Is it a place? A group of people? An embodied experience? How might nonincarcerated people cultivate a sense of belonging that doesn't distance us from the needs of incarcerated kids?

While putting hurting kids in solitary confinement hardly seems like a good idea, neither does sending them back to unsafe environments. Girls in Leila's and Greta's situations are extremely vulnerable to sexual victimization (including sex trafficking) and other forms of physical violence, as well as substance abuse and mental health challenges.[9] As abolitionists work for a world without prisons, secure youth facilities must provide "developmentally appropriate"[10] strategies that make teenagers feel cared for while holding those who have harmed others accountable. All of us must prioritize protecting kids from situations—in confinement, in their families, in their communities—that exacerbate their sense of powerlessness, alienation, failure, and shame.

---

9. Davies and Allen, "Trauma and Homelessness."
10. McCarthy et al., "Future of Youth Justice," 17.

51

"I Wasn't Even Holding the Gun"

SHAME IS COUNTERPRODUCTIVE TO accountability because it tends to produce denial, defensiveness, hostility, and blame—all of which block our ability to own and answer for our wrongdoing. Shame—"the intensely painful feeling or experience of believing that we are flawed and therefore unworthy of love, belonging, and connection"—triggers fear of condemnation and exile, and this fear impedes the soul-searching moral transformation that accountability requires.[1] Shaming kids doesn't encourage accountability because it fails to engage their inherent goodness and capacity to evolve and learn.

Shame is also a known contributor to violent behavior. Feelings of humiliation, unworthiness, and alienation can be so painful that some of us will do anything to make them go away.[2] Our strategies for eradicating shame—whether we direct aggression toward ourselves or others—vary, depending on our social location and circumstances. My white, middle-class, Catholic upbringing taught me to associate shame with my body and its desires; as a solution, I punished my flesh. For most of the incarcerated boys I've met, shame tends to be associated with feeling vulnerable or weak. As a strategy for gaining power, some of them have resorted to dominating or violating those they perceive to be the cause of such feelings.[3]

Shame may play a role in some young offenders' reluctance to accept accountability for harms they've committed. Occasionally, one of the

---

1. B. Brown, *Atlas of the Heart*, 137. See also B. Brown, "Shame and Accountability."
2. Sered, *Until We Reckon*, 67–68.
3. Sered, *Until We Reckon*, 126.

residents will explicitly reject or minimize responsibility for the crimes with which they've been charged:

- "I was just in the wrong place at the wrong time."
- "I didn't do it."
- "I got busted for something someone else did."
- "I didn't mean to hurt anyone."
- "I wasn't even holding the gun."

I can't say whether such appeals to innocence are rooted in fact or wishful thinking. But I can relate to the need they indirectly express: to not feel bad about yourself. In fact, these deflections of responsibility remind me of my own habitual urge to escape, shift, or curtail the blame for something I wish I hadn't done, to emphasize the purity of my intentions, to avoid the discomfort of owning and repairing my mistakes. I suspect many of us can empathize with both the urge to evade culpability and the need for belonging and acceptance beneath this impulse.

Accountability requires courage, not shame. Courage to confess the hurt we've caused. Courage to see the impact of whatever harms we've committed and make appropriate amends. Courage to express regrets. Courage to become someone who will not repeat the same mistakes.

In *On Repentance and Repair*, Rabbi Danya Ruttenberg maps an approach to accountability that demands bravery and humility rather than the disempowering, shameful, vicarious suffering of others. The path she charts includes five aspects of accountability that resemble the five steps Sered identifies. Based on Ruttenberg's interpretation of a medieval Jewish philosopher named Maimonides, these steps for repentance and repair are:

1. Confession—naming and owning the hurt you've inflicted, preferably in a public manner
2. Working diligently to transform your harmful habits
3. Accepting the consequences for your behavior and making amends and restitution
4. Offering a sincere apology
5. Making different choices going forward

Like the accountability process Sered outlines, the one Ruttenberg proposes is victim-centric. It prioritizes repentance and restoration over forgiveness and reconciliation. The focus is on the harming person's willingness to do the difficult, self-transformative work of taking responsibility and repairing the damage, not on the harmed party's obligation to forgive.[4]

---

[4]. Ruttenberg, *On Repentance and Repair*, 4–5.

52

"Monster"

THE POCKETS OF MY black, polyester, knee-length skirt bulged with tips from working the late shift at an upscale restaurant in Harvard Square. Later I'd learn that the money might not have been what he was after.

It was close to midnight when I left the restaurant and headed north through Harvard Yard. A slight smell of salt from the ocean hung in the humid June air—a pleasant reminder that I now lived on the East Coast. I'd made this late-night trek back to my dorm dozens of times: passing the science center, crossing Oxford Street, walking to my room in Divinity Hall.

Looking back, I was naïve about my vulnerability to violence. I'd lived in Europe and traveled independently. I trusted my ability to handle unpredictable situations. Still, as I approached the part of my walk home that always made me slightly nervous—a thirty-yard stretch of unlit sidewalk with a six-foot fence on one side and the wall of a tall, redbrick building on the other—a gut feeling prompted me to turn around.

A boy was less than thirty yards behind me. His silhouette was darkened by the science center's lights behind him, but I could see that he was White with shoulder-length dark hair. Maybe late teens. Turning back to survey the dark sidewalk ahead of me, I quickly surmised that I wouldn't stand a chance at outrunning this guy who was giving me the creeps. So I reversed course and walked directly toward him.

Just before we passed each other, I sensed his nervous energy and veered to the edge of the path to give him space. That's when he grabbed both of my wrists and wrestled me to the ground. I fought like a wild animal, screaming so hard that my throat was sore for three days. Luckily, a graduate student who was walking down Oxford Street heard me. "What's going on there?" he yelled and started walking toward us. When my assailant saw him, he ran.

I was shaking so badly that when the grad student tried to comfort me by putting his hand on my shoulder, I frantically recoiled. Eventually, I let him walk me to the security guards stationed in the nearby chemistry building. The police showed up and asked me to ride with them as they drove around campus to see if I saw anyone who looked like my attacker. I thought this was a dumb idea, but maybe they just wanted to be sure I was okay. We didn't find him.

The next day, the cops came to my dorm and showed me a large book with hundreds of different kinds of facial features. Since I'd gotten a clear view of my assailant's face, they wanted me to pick out his eyes, nose, mouth, hair style, and facial shape so they could make a "composite" picture of him. I doubted the efficacy of this patchwork approach, but by the time we'd finished, the image looked just like the boy who attacked me.

About a month later, I received a voicemail from a man with a very thick Boston accent: "Hello, Micheelle. This is a caall from the Haarvaard Police. We'd like you to come down to the staation to make an ID."

The young man in the first picture they showed me clearly wasn't my attacker. The second absolutely was. "Not a doubt in my mind," I told the officers. "How did you find him?"

The officer hesitated briefly, then responded: "He was arrested last night for raping a young woman down by the Charles River."

I don't remember pressing charges. I don't even remember whether the police asked me if I wanted to press charges. Like so many survivors of violent crime, my memory of what happened in the aftermath of the assault is murky. I know I never testified against my assailant in court; but then, only a fraction of convictions end up going to trial. Thanks to mass incarceration, America's criminal justice system is so logjammed that 94 to 97 percent of guilty sentences are the result of plea bargains.[1]

What I do remember is a quiet desperation to put that traumatic event behind me. But my body couldn't easily forget. Neither could my mind. My image of the boy who had assaulted me and raped another woman was that of a monster. And, though I'm not proud of this, if someone back then had asked me what should happen to him, I would have recommended castration.

---

1. Sered, *Until We Reckon*, 30.

53

"My Brother Is Six Feet in the Ground"

DECADES LATER, MY REVENGE fantasies have faded. I no longer see my attacker as a monster; nor do I wish he'd been castrated. However, I do wish I'd known more about the juvenile justice system back then and about the reasons some young people resort to hurting others. I wish someone in authority had asked me what I needed in the wake of that traumatic experience and had presented me with resources and options.

Unfortunately, survivors of violent crime are seldom asked what they want and need. America's dominant narrative about these victims—most of whom are *not* white women but people of color (all genders)—is that they want the most painful penalty possible for those who hurt them.[1] This narrative makes for tantalizing news stories that feed our cultural predilection for revenge as a method for dealing with grief.

"Drake," the eighteen-year-old male who had participated in the mindfulness group eight months before he murdered an immigrant taxi driver, wept as he apologized to his victim's family at his trial. He said he hadn't intended to hurt anybody and wished he could change what happened. He asked the family for forgiveness.

I thought about what Drake had written about his desire to be a good example to his little brother as I watched a news clip that showed him tearfully trying to empathize with the family's grief: "I'm a brother just like him," he said, referring to the victim. "I'm a cousin just like him. I'm someone's role model just like him."

---

1. Sered, *Until We Reckon*, 20–22, 204–10.

The victim's family members who spoke appeared unmoved by Drake's appeal to his blameless intentions, his plea for forgiveness, his tears of remorse. They said their family had come to America in search of a better life, and that the victim had just been trying to make an honest living. The victim's brother said he couldn't fathom a person murdering someone for rent money, and that such a crime was beyond his forgiveness. His sister lamented that the killer "gets another chance at life while my brother is 6 feet in the ground."[2] In their view, twelve and a half years in prison for killing their loved one was not enough.

I can hardly judge this family for demanding a more severe punishment for Drake—not just because of the vengeful feelings I had harbored toward my assailant, but because wanting to punish those who hurt us seems thoroughly human to me. I don't know whether vengeful feelings are themselves immoral (I rather doubt it). The problem is, retribution rarely produces the relief victims seek.

America's justice system isn't designed to meet the needs of crime survivors. In this system, crime and delinquency are deemed violations of the law and the state—not offenses against the person(s) harmed. Correspondingly, the state determines the guilt and imposes the penalty that will hold the harming party "accountable." The goal of deciding and administering what perpetrators "deserve"—how much and what kind of pain is needed to pay for their crime—overshadows questions about what survivors want and need, what the responsible person might owe their victim(s), and what they might do to make amends.[3]

Curiously, parts of this system mirror the accountability process I learned as part of my religious education.

---

2. Baumgarten, "Slain," para. 11.
3. Zehr, *Little Book*, 12, 19.

54

"Bless Me, Father, for I Have Sinned"

IN THE CATHOLIC CHURCH, most children make their first confession (a.k.a. the sacrament of penance or the rite of reconciliation) during the second grade, just prior to making their first Holy Communion.

"The first thing you say to the priest is, 'Bless me, Father, for I have sinned,'" my Sunday school teacher instructed a sizable audience of seven-year-olds sitting in a stuffy church basement classroom. "Then you recite the 'Act of Contrition,' which you must learn *by heart*." Overwhelmed, yet ever the devout overachiever, I determined to not only memorize all six lines of the prayer, but to recite them with sincerity.

When the big day came, I thought I was ready. But as I entered the dark confessional booth and knelt on the kneeler, I became petrified. I didn't know the priest and couldn't see his face. Only the white square of his black collar, slightly covered by his freshly shaven double chin, was visible through the small screen in the middle of the wall dividing his side of the booth from mine. Luckily, his voice was kind as he cued me to begin.

I made it through the prayers, but when it came time to confess my sins, my mind went blank. I'd been so focused on learning my lines that I hadn't given any thought to what I needed to confess. Plus, I was only seven and hadn't exactly racked up a mountain of sins to choose from. Fortunately, I recalled a transgression that surely needed confessing.

"My sister and I share a bedroom and we have identical bedspreads," I explained to the stranger behind the screen. "Well, last month our cat pooped on my bed. I was afraid my mom would be mad because the cat's not supposed to be in our bedroom. So I used paper towels to clean it up. Then . . ." I hesitated before confessing the part I knew was most egregious, "I switched bedspreads with my sister."

The penance the priest prescribed was to recite ten "Hail Marys" and ten "Our Fathers." Which I dutifully did. But it was years before it occurred to me that I should have been confessing to my sister, not the priest.

Religious or not, confession is a crucial part of any accountability process. But for it to be effective in producing the spiritual or psychological repair, remorse, and transformation that accountability entails, it must be designed in a way that honors victims' needs. In this regard, the US justice system mirrors the structural flaws in the design of my first confession:

- The harm (crime or sin) is treated as a violation against the state/God, not the victim.
- The person (judge or priest) responsible for adjudicating the guilty party's wrongdoing and brokering the penalty is assumed to know exactly what justice/redemption requires.
- The penance (whether ten years in prison or ten "Our Fathers") is not designed to facilitate the difficult, soul-searching, reparative work that becoming someone different requires.
- The self-described needs of the victims are not part of the equation.

When crime survivors are asked about their needs, they say they want their pain to be validated, rather than being gaslit or judged or blamed for what happened. They need information that enables them to formulate "a coherent narrative" that empowers them to find or create meaning from what they survived.[1] Many victims want the opportunity to speak—and for their voices to have an impact. They want access to mental health care and other resources that facilitate their healing. They also want the harming party to attempt to repair what they did. And, of course, survivors need safety for themselves and others. In fact, amid the diversity of desires and needs they express, violent crime survivors' top priority is *"to know that the person who hurt them would not hurt anyone else."*[2]

The current system's tendency to pursue "justice" while ignoring victims' wants, needs, and experiences may explain why more than half of survivors (52 percent) have so little confidence that this system will address their pain, they don't even bother enlisting law enforcement's help.[3] Accord-

---

1. Sered, *Until We Reckon*, 24.
2. Sered, *Until We Reckon*, 30; emphasis original.
3. Sered, *Until We Reckon*, 34, 46.

ing to Sered, if those who do report a crime are given the option to pursue a restorative path to justice, as opposed to the conventional/punitive approach, 90 percent choose the alternative.[4]

Rooted in Indigenous traditions, restorative justice is a way of responding to wrongdoing that prioritizes the needs of victims and the responsibility of offenders for repairing the harm they've caused. Instead of producing punitive judgments and sanctions that "fit" the severity of the harm inflicted, restorative justice attends to the suffering of everyone impacted by a crime, starting with the victim.

While both restorative and retributive justice "share a concern for balance," a punitive paradigm reflects the sacrificial atonement narratives that "pain will vindicate," that the guilty party must suffer to compensate for their offense.[5] By contrast, a restorative approach holds the harming party accountable through a process of confessing and bearing witness to the harm they've inflicted, expressing remorse, seeking to repair the damage to the extent possible, and addressing the root causes of their hurtful behavior so they no longer commit similar harm.[6]

This process doesn't happen overnight. Those who have a stake in the situation (victims, offenders, community members) prepare for it well in advance, typically with the support of trained restorative justice facilitators. When all the stakeholders are ready, they meet face-to-face in a "circle" process—an inclusive, collaborative space and practice where everyone is invited to share their truth. Through this process of addressing the harms, needs, and obligations of all parties, the nature of reparations is determined. The responsible party may be required to get treatment for mental health issues, chemical dependency, and/or trauma. They may be subject to parole or probation supervision, community service, and/or other forms of repair.[7]

The differences between punitive and restorative justice are evident in the different questions they pursue. Whereas retaliatory justice asks: "What laws have been broken? Who did it? What do they deserve?," a restorative justice approach seeks to know: "Who has been harmed? What are their needs? Whose obligations are these?"[8] Whereas punitive justice caters to our all-too-human desire to see people who hurt us suffer, restorative justice engages our equally human wish to see people who hurt us change.[9]

---

4. Sered, *Until We Reckon*, 42.
5. Zehr, *Little Book*, 75.
6. Sered, *Until We Reckon*, 96.
7. Sered, *Until We Reckon*, 45.
8. Zehr, *Little Book*, 31.
9. Sered, *Until We Reckon*, 89–90.

The idea that we ought to try to repair the harm we've inflicted doesn't sound particularly radical. Yet this basic insight is missing from punitive approaches to youth justice, which fail to provide processes and tools to nurture teenagers' *internal motivation* to grow and make different choices. Without such motivation, it's easy for justice-involved youth to become not just hopeless, but passively fatalistic.

55

"Sleeping Bags of Self-Pity"

THREE RESIDENTS AND I were discussing Menakem's distinction between "clean" and "dirty" pain. Wesley was enthusiastic about this contrast because it clarified the difference between problems he's resolved by owning and dealing with them, and difficulties that continue to haunt him because he ignores them. Wesley was also intrigued by Menakem's perception that "dirty" (unmetabolized) pain contributes to racialized trauma. He'd witnessed this dynamic firsthand as a Black kid growing up in America.

The other two residents—Alex and Dan—seemed less engaged in the conversation. Their low energy, distracted glances, and slouching bodies communicated boredom. I was about to end the discussion early when Alex spoke up: "When it comes to pain from the past, I just shove it down. It's easier that way."

"I getcha," Wesley responded. "But ignoring it won't make it go away."

"Doesn't matter," Alex insisted. "As long as I can't feel it, it don't bother me."

I asked Alex on a scale of one to ten (one = least; ten = most) how much he really wants to change, take accountability, and learn from his mistakes.

"Probably about a three," he responded matter-of-factly. "I like my life in the free world," he explained. "I don't really want to change." The problem, he insisted, was not his life on the outside, but that he kept getting arrested. He was sixteen, and this was his fourth stint in different detention centers. He didn't seem to make the connection that the life he enjoyed "in the free world" was repeatedly leading to confinement.

Dan joined the conversation. "Some *small* part of me wants to change." He said he didn't want to end up like his mom, whom he described as "drug addicted" and who reportedly made no effort to get clean. Nor did he want to be like his sister, who did nothing to encourage his mom to stop using. "Both of them just lay around in their sleeping bags of self-pity," Dan explained. Despite this imaginative critique, however, he admitted to his own scarcity of motivation to change: "A lot of the time in here, I'm just going through the motions until I get my freedom."

The apathy and resignation both Alex and Dan expressed surprised me. Most kids in the residential treatment program say they appreciate the resources this program offers to help them deal with their trauma histories. To be sure, the residents I've met have varying levels of internal motivation to take responsibility for their wrongdoing, change unhealthy patterns, and grow from their adversities. I worry most about kids like Alex and Dan who seem to lack the inner resolve and sense of accountability they need to stay out of trouble once they're released.

That said, kids in the mindfulness group keep teaching me not to assume too much about their inner thoughts and feelings. One day Alberto, who walked with a strut, projected a don't-mess-with-me vibe, and assumed the role of "alpha male" in his pod, pulled me aside me. Looking me in the eye, he asked in a tone that verged on pleading: *How can I change?*

What motivates someone to change self-defeating thought patterns and behaviors? How do any of us develop the desire to become the kind of person who transforms our harmful habits?

Chastising youth for their wrongdoing may elicit fear and obedience; but punishment doesn't nurture the inner freedom, courage, and empathy that accountability requires. Whereas punishment relies on extrinsic motivations (external threats to our well-being), accountability depends on (and produces) intrinsic rewards, including a clean conscience and sense of agency, connection, and purpose. Developing a strong moral compass is a more reliable and effective motivator of prosocial behavior because, to paraphrase Sered, we might be able to escape the police, but we can't escape ourselves.[1]

In many ways, a punitive approach to accountability mirrors Alex's strategy of "just shov[ing] it down." Doling out painful consequences for a teenager's destructive behavior tends to suppress rather than liberate the truth not only about the harm they committed, but about *why* they did what they did.

---

1. Sered, *Until We Reckon*, 107.

56

"Nobody Asked Me *Why* I Did What I Did"

"I'M IN JAIL FOR a first-time offense," Marcus said in a can-you-believe-it tone. What upset him most about getting arrested was that, in his words, "nobody asked me *why* I did what I did. They just cuffed me and put me in the back of their car."

I asked Marcus what he thinks he needs most right now. Initially, he shrugged off the question. Then he explained that every time he's needed something, he's had to rely entirely on himself—"not just for everyday things," he said, "but to learn from my experiences." He said no one had ever mentored him or taken the time to find out why he sometimes acted out.

Jeff Wallace would likely empathize with Marcus's desire for the police—or someone—to ask him why he did what he did. Wallace is a juvenile justice advocate of trauma-informed care who's motivated "by a need to redeem [him]self, with an obligation to give back to society." At age seventeen, Wallace was arrested for beating a man, stealing his wallet, and attempting to run him over with a car. Tried as an adult, he was sentenced to eleven years in prison, where he was exposed to daily violence, fellow inmates' insanity, relentless banging and yelling, frequently flooded toilets, and other dehumanizing conditions. Whatever "rehabilitation" happened during his imprisonment was the result of his own efforts and growth mindset. To avert boredom, he learned to play chess, which taught him virtues like "respect everyone," "protect the weak," and "be humble." Wallace also read voraciously, which prepared him to pursue educational opportunities after being released, including graduate degrees in criminal justice. His current work on behalf of justice-involved youth is an ongoing expression of his repentance and repair for "mistakes [he] couldn't fix." This work taught Wallace the importance of understanding the backstories of justice-involved youth, which, he says, require us to ask, "What happened to you?" instead of "What's wrong with you?"[1]

Questions like "Why did you do what you did?" complicate the issue of accountability because teenagers' destructive actions are invariably rooted in unhealed pain—including suffering resulting from systemic injustices. Exploring such questions facilitates the *inner work* all of us must do to understand the roots of our harmful behavior and make different choices going forward.[2]

Later in our conversation, Marcus, Antoine, and I discussed a quote by Nadia Bolz-Weber, a Lutheran pastor and author who says that "ignoring [a painful truth] doesn't make it go away; it just makes it a refugee."[3] I asked the boys where they thought this "refugee" of unaddressed pain goes when no one pays it any attention.

Antoine responded: "It goes straight to your heart."

Marcus said: "It builds and builds until it explodes."

---

1. Wallace, "Insider's Plan," 12:11.
2. Ruttenberg, *On Repentance and Repair*, 43.
3. Bolz-Weber, *Shameless*, 156.

57

"When I Was in the Sixth Grade, I Got into a Fight at School"

THE QUESTION "WHAT HAPPENED to you?" played a pivotal role in trajectory of Monique Morris's life. Morris is a prominent scholar, educator, and activist. But her life could have turned out very differently.

"When I was in the sixth grade," Morris recounts, "I got into a fight at school." One day in gym class, a boy who had been taunting her for weeks stepped on her shoe and refused to apologize—the last straw. Though he was considerably bigger, she threw him to the ground, where they fought until a teacher intervened. Later, the principal called Morris to her office.

She didn't suspend Morris or call the police. She didn't prohibit her from going to school the next day. Instead, the principal asked: "*What happened?*"[1]

Turns out, in addition to being bullied, Morris had been suffering from a combination of sexual trauma, abandonment, and exposure to other forms of violence—the pain of which had become like a "refugee" that was building and building until it finally exploded. The empathy of the educators who worked with her in the aftermath of the fight made all the difference at that critical juncture in Morris's life:

> They knew me. They knew I loved to read. They knew I loved to draw. They knew I adored Prince. And they used that information to help me understand why my actions and those of my

---

1. Morris, "Why Black Girls," 0:00–1:16. See also Morris, *Pushout*.

classmate were disruptive to the learning community they were leading.[2]

If, instead of holding her accountable with compassion, these educators had suspended Morris or involved law enforcement, her bad day in school may have been the beginning of months, years, even decades of entanglement with the justice system.

Perceived as "too loud, too aggressive, too angry, too visible,"[3] Black girls are especially vulnerable to marginalization and punishment in schools. Compared to their White counterparts, they're seven times more likely to experience one or more out-of-school suspensions; compared to their White and Latinx peers, they're almost three times more likely to be sent to juvenile court.[4] While Black girls make up 16 percent of females in America's schools, they represent 43 percent of those arrested. These arrests are fueled by biases shaped by racist-sexist stereotypes depicting Black girls as more belligerent, promiscuous, and adultlike than their White peers, and as intellectually inferior and needing less nurturing, protection, comfort, and support.[5] Though there's no evidence that Black and Brown students of any gender break the law more often than their white peers, Black and Latinx youth comprise more than 70 percent of those who are arrested in school or turned over to police.[6] Like Black girls in particular, students of color are disproportionately impacted by the "school-to-prison pipeline."

The school-to-prison pipeline (STPP) is a metaphor for policies and practices schools use to severely discipline—in many cases, *criminalize*—students for behaviors that some teachers and administrators perceive to be harmful or disruptive. These policies and practices contribute to public schools' penal culture and increase the likelihood of kids becoming justice-involved.

Excessive punishment of K–12 students' disorderly or noncompliant behavior began during the "tough on crime" era. In the 1990s, schools nationwide implemented security measures that resembled those in prisons—metal detectors, security cameras, locked doors, and sometimes even drug-finding dogs. As school shootings became more common, security guards, law enforcement, and resource officers became regular features of locker-lined hallways. Meanwhile, schools adopted "zero tolerance" policies that automatically catalyzed harsh punishments for student behaviors that

2. Morris, "Why Black Girls," 1:21–36.
3. Morris, "Why Black Girls," 4:14.
4. Morris, "Why Black Girls," 2:58–3:07.
5. Morris, *Pushout*, 50, 11; Epstein et al., *Girlhood Interrupted*.
6. DiAngelo, *What Does It Mean*, 117–22.

many experts and parents alike believe are age appropriate, or at least not surprising.[7] Kids have been suspended, expelled, arrested, detained, and adjudicated for actions ranging from food fights in the cafeteria to fistfights on the playground. Playing music loudly, throwing Skittles at another kid, dress code violations, "inappropriate" hairstyles, possessing a nail clipper—or a knife—exemplify the wide range of behaviors that result in law enforcement involvement thanks to "zero tolerance" policies.[8] As recently as 2019, fourteen million students attended "schools with police but no counselor, nurse, psychologist, or social worker."[9]

Without any evidence that they make schools safer, STPP policies drastically increase the number of student suspensions, which compound the academic struggles many students already experience, particularly those struggling with learning disabilities, mental health challenges, childhood trauma, or racial and/or economic injustice.[10] In a vicious cycle, school suspensions increase the risk of dropping out of school altogether, which increases the prospect of incarceration. Residential facilities like the one I visit provide free public education for the youth in their care. Some of the residents have told me that school at the detention center has been the best education they have received. Generally, however, many kids in confinement don't complete high school, which diminishes their prospects for future employment and other educational opportunities.[11]

Schools' excessive disciplinary measures were designed to amp up student accountability for misbehavior. Yet these measures fail in the same ways punishment fails to motivate students to act responsibly because they don't facilitate self-examination or internal motivation to change antisocial behavior. Nor do they incentivize students whose conduct *is* harmful to make things right. STPP practices also ignore the underlying reasons for students' distracting or dangerous behavior, such as adverse childhood experiences. Moreover, harsh disciplinary consequences embody—rather than challenge—the structural injustices that often contribute to that behavior. Conveniently, such measures do nothing to hold nonincarcerated people with privilege collectively accountable for neglecting to prioritize quality education for every child.

---

7. Drinan, *War on Kids*, 46–48.

8. Baxter, *We Are All Criminals*, 152; Drinan, *War on Kids*, 48.

9. Whitaker et al., *Cops and No Counselors*, 4, 23–24.

10. Drinan, *War on Kids*, 50–51; DiAngelo, *What Does It Mean*, 117–22; Teske, "Zero Tolerance Policies."

11. Rapanut et al., "Patchwork Education System."

Our lack of accountability may take various forms—including *apathy*. We may accept (by ignoring) the gross resource disparities between schools in impoverished vs. affluent communities—inequities created by a system in which districts depend on property taxes as a major source of revenue.[12] Even in well-funded schools, classrooms are often overcrowded, teachers overworked, and mental health and disability services understaffed.

Do we care?

Do privileged people see it as our responsibility to help dismantle not just the STPP but the rote, teach-to-the-test kind of learning that squelches many young people's natural curiosity? Do we envision meaningful, holistic K–12 education as a national priority and guaranteed right for *all* children? Do we study candidates' views on education and vote for local, state, and federal leaders who care about students' intellectual development beyond standardized exam scores? Do we support the arts, music, and athletics as integral to the kind of learning all kids *deserve*? Do we ensure that every student has access to healthy meals? Do we support teachers, the majority of whom genuinely care about the welfare of kids in their classroom? All of us owe it to teachers and students to support educational policies, practices, and visions that foster not just academic achievement but well-being, equity, creativity, and appreciation for diversity.

Once we relinquish the assumption that punishment achieves accountability, we can design more respectful, effective ways to encourage youth to act responsibly—and learn. The Holistic Life Foundation is an example of a creative intervention that promotes adolescent accountability by providing therapeutic and other health resources for traumatized kids in low-income communities. Founders Ali Smith, Atman Smith, and Andres Gonzalez teach kids who are sent to detention (both after-school detention and juvenile detention facilities) how to meditate, do yoga, and take good care of their bodies, their communities, and the natural world. They aim to empower youth to cultivate a sense of inner stillness, empathy, and resilience that enables them to grow their intelligence, be responsible, heal themselves, and repair the world.[13]

According to Ashley Lipscomb, cofounder of the Institute for Anti-Racist Education, Christians must play a leading role in implementing holistic interventions in K–12 education. This work starts with owning and answering for the ways Christian narratives have tacitly supported the school-to-prison pipeline and confined students' imaginations. Lipscomb connects the dots between atonement theologies that depict humans as

---

12. DiAngelo, *What Does It Mean*, 117–22.
13. Smith et al., *Let Your Light Shine*.

"inherently deserving of punishment" and the penal culture of schooling in America. Since this culture originated in the mission to convert and assimilate all students to white Christianity, Lipscomb argues that Christians have a heightened moral responsibility to reject and abolish the toxic "carceral and punitive logics" embedded in school policies that criminalize children.[14] To that end, Lipscomb embraces an "abolitionist theology" that encourages us to "unlearn . . . the notion that punitive measures 'correct behavior.'"[15] She calls on all of us to demand that school officials replace vindictive policies and practices with pedagogies that foster critical thinking, relationships, healing, safety, and creativity in the classroom. This shift requires us to stop spending billions on police and other disciplinary tactics and instead invest in resources that nurture the genius of each student by supporting their mental, social, and emotional well-being.[16]

The incarcerated youth I've met would benefit greatly from the kind of liberating learning community Lipscomb describes. A lot of them haven't had good experiences in schools—*not* because they lack intelligence and curiosity. Although many struggle with learning disabilities, each possesses their own kind of genius. And while they are generally disenchanted with knowledge that feels utterly irrelevant to their lives, the majority express a desire to learn. Once I asked a group of six youth about their favorite subjects in school. Everyone had something to say:

- Art and English
- Art, social studies, and English
- Science
- Social studies
- History
- History and English

Even this short list gives us a glimpse of incarcerated kids' innate curiosity and ongoing desire for learning that empowers them to better understand the world and to express themselves so that the world better understands them.

---

14. Lipscomb, "Abolitionist Theology Can Help," 8.
15. Lipscomb, "Abolitionist Theology Can Help," 9.
16. Lipscomb, "Abolitionist Theology Can Help," 9–10.

58

"I'm Not Going to Apologize for Things I'm Not Sorry For"

Three residents and I were discussing the prompt: "What makes for a good apology?" Skirting the question, Musa shared his thoughts.

"I don't apologize to anyone." His tone was emphatic. "Especially not for things I'm not sorry for." Musa said sometimes people expect him to apologize for things he hasn't even done. But even when he's done "bad things" (his words), he won't apologize if he's not truly sorry.

"Maybe apologizing isn't for you," Bernie suggested. "Maybe it's for the person you hurt."

"Or maybe it *is* for you," Shevon offered. "So you can stop feeling bad about what you did."

"Doesn't matter who it's for," Musa was adamant. "I'm not going to apologize for things I'm not sorry for."

Listening to this conversation, I remembered when my own kids were young. After they did or said something harmful to each other and I was too preoccupied or exhausted to give the matter my full attention, I'd simply order them to apologize—regardless of whether they were truly sorry. "What do you saaay?" I'd ask with my stern mother tone that indicated there was only one right answer.

Many of us have felt the emptiness of a forced apology. Whether we're on the giving or receiving end of a hollow "I'm sorry," the lack of integrity doesn't feel good. In this light, I respect Musa's refusal to apologize for things for which he didn't feel remorse. The integrity in his unwillingness to say "sorry" when he didn't really *feel* or *mean* it challenges us to consider what an apology entails and its role in accountability.

In the steps for repentance and repair that Ruttenberg identifies, "Apology" comes relatively late in the sequence: step 4. The reason is simple yet profound: "Actions first. Words later."[1] *Saying* "sorry" means little if one hasn't been engaging in the actual *work* of repair that the first three steps embody: 1) naming and owning harm; 2) examining and starting to change harmful patterns; and 3) making restitution and accepting consequences for harm committed. In other words, expressions of regret and requests for forgiveness are most compelling when rooted in *prior* actionable efforts to own and answer for one's harmful behavior. More than a verbal expression of regret, an apology is the "natural outgrowth" of the repentance work already underway.[2]

The Jewish emphasis on repentance as something you *do*—rather than *say* or *feel*—syncs well with the effort-laden, action-oriented path to accountability that restorative justice follows. Both processes run counter to dominant cultural/religious tendencies to make remorse an internal or verbal affair. As Ruttenberg observes, this tendency reflects "a watered-down, secularized" version of the Protestant notion that "faith alone" is enough to "save" you.[3] In the sixteenth century, Martin Luther championed this belief in response to Catholicism's emphasis on performing virtuous acts as the path to righteousness. Luther saw how predicating salvation on "works"—performative, perfunctory actions to please God—led to corruptions like the sale of indulgences (a scam orchestrated by Catholic leaders who took money from the faithful in exchange for fast-tracking their dead loved ones out of purgatory into heaven). Luther didn't deny that good deeds are an integral part of Christian life, but he insisted there's nothing we can *do* (or *have* to do) to earn God's favor because only God's grace was powerful and pure enough to wash away sin. Over the centuries, and no doubt counter to his original intentions, Luther's repudiation of "works" as the path to redemption contributed to a culture in which grace became "cheap," as Dietrich Bonhoeffer pointed out.[4] Just say "sorry" and your sins are forgiven even without genuine repentance and repair.

I don't know why Musa wasn't sorry for whatever he refused to apologize about. Was he too proud? Did he feel justified in doing what he did?

---

1. Ruttenberg, *On Repentance and Repair*, 41.
2. Ruttenberg, *On Repentance and Repair*, 43.
3. Ruttenberg, *On Repentance and Repair*, 7.
4. Ruttenberg, *On Repentance and Repair*, 8.

Did he sense the hollowness of "cheap grace"—or perhaps recognize that kids in his situation are excluded from such easy forgiveness?

And/or, maybe Musa's defiance was rooted in some deeper sensibility that he's not just an offender, but a victim who, like nearly every other incarcerated kid, has survived various forms of trauma and systemic oppression.

And is anyone apologizing to him?

Are we aware that the teenagers many assume "deserve to be punished" are the same kids we've collectively neglected to protect and care for?[5]

Even if these weren't Musa's questions, they have become mine.

---

5. Sered, *Until We Reckon*, 89.

59

"Out There, It's 'Live by the Gun, Die by the Gun'"

IN AMERICA'S JUSTICE SYSTEM, the language of accountability typically revolves around "victims" and "perpetrators." But such binary and stigmatizing terms mask the complex reality that incarcerated teenagers are invariably both. Professor Cynthia Godsoe explains,

> The strong relationship between childhood victimization and later violent behavior deemed criminal has been so well-documented that it underlies the term "cycle of violence" as an empirical social science phenomenon.[1]

Ignoring the extent to which youth "offenders" are simultaneously victim/survivors perpetuates "a racialized narrative of individual blameworthiness"[2] and obscures the root causes of teenage crime: unmetabolized trauma and systemic injustices. Conveniently, such language fixates guilt on kids convicted of delinquency, while the rest of us are presumed innocent—a status that conceals our unwitting contributions to a society that fails to cherish and protect all children.

Juan was both ecstatic and anxious about his upcoming release. Ecstatic about regaining his freedom. Nervous about going back to "the hood." I asked him what strategies he planned to use to stay out of trouble. He responded frankly: "It'll be hard. Out there, it's 'live by the gun, die by the gun.'" He repeated this phrase several times in a cadence that reminded me

1. Godsoe, "Victim/Offender Overlap," 1320.
2. Godsoe, "Victim/Offender Overlap," 1322.

of the mantras football players in a huddle sometimes chant to psych themselves up before returning to a game they know they're losing. Juan seemed to be naming the daunting, violent conditions he knew he'd be up against once he finally gained his freedom.

Tyrell expressed similarly mixed feelings about his upcoming release. During the check-in part of a small group discussion, he said that what he was grateful for and what he was struggling with were the same thing: "I'm getting out soon." He smiled as he imagined out loud the day of his release: "I can't wait to see my mom and little sisters. Can't wait to be outside. Can't wait to eat something besides jail food." His face and tone turned serious. "But I'm not gonna lie; I'm nervous about getting out. I know it's gonna to be hard to steer clear of friends who got me into running the deep streets." I asked Tyrell if he had any friends who aren't running the deep streets. He mentioned a cousin who's in college. "That's where I want to end up—*college*," he said in a hopeful tone. "I know I need to finish my GED and get an education if I'm going to make something of my life."

With financial assistance, therapeutic resources, and family/community support, Tyrell has everything he needs to become a successful college student—intelligence, critical thinking skills, curiosity, a strong work ethic. But will his justice-involvement impede his dreams? Even after the question about criminal history was removed from the Common App (the standard college application form) in 2019, "70% of four-year colleges and universities require applicants to disclose a criminal record [as] a part of the college application process."[3] Research confirms that this question alone prevents nearly two thirds of applicants with a record from applying.[4] Though states vary in the extent to which they allow the public to access juvenile records, most make at least some information digitally available to the public, including college admissions offices.[5] There's not any empirical data indicating that students with criminal records pose a risk to their peers on university and college campuses, though there's ample evidence that education is among the most reliable and cost-effective ways to decrease recidivism, curb crime, and reduce financial instability.[6]

Impeding access to higher learning is just one of several ways that prior convictions can prolong the pain of punishment, communicating to a youth

---

3. National Conference of State Legislatures, "Admissions and Access," para. 2. See also Meade, "How 'Second Chance' Laws," 3:25.

4. Holmes, "Juvenile Records."

5. Rips, "Fresh Start," 217.

6. Scott-Clayton, "Thinking 'beyond the Box,'" para. 18; Baxter, *We Are All Criminals*, 22.

that their "debt to society" may never be paid.[7] Having a record can also make it harder for youth to find housing and/or jobs post-incarceration. Over 90 percent of landlords use background checks to screen potential renters, and over 94 percent of employers run background checks. For Tyrell, these potential obstacles are compounded by cultural perceptions of young Black males as "criminal by default"—in religious language, as "inherently sinful." One study found that White job applicants *with* a criminal record received more callbacks for interviews than Black applicants *without* a criminal record.[8]

As we encourage incarcerated youth to own and answer for the harm they've caused, nonincarcerated people with privilege have our own accounting to do. Are we examining whether our beliefs, values, mindsets, and actions ensure they support the well-being of *all* children, not just our own? Are we using our unearned advantages to dismantle the systemic injustices shaping the environments that propel some teenagers' desperate actions? Are we imagining and enacting ways to repair the harms caused by historical trauma? Are we open to hiring or renting to youth with a record? Will we welcome them into our classrooms, congregations, communities, and other public settings?

Do we understand our own need for repentance and repair?

---

7. Baxter, *We Are All Criminals*, 20.
8. Baxter, *We Are All Criminals*, 20–23; Meade, "How 'Second Chance' Laws."

60

"I Only Have Myself to Blame"

LAMAR HAD BEEN A regular at the mindfulness group. Usually, he was attentive and engaged. One day, however, his demeanor was down and withdrawn. When it was his turn to share, he spoke so softly that the rest of us had to lean in hard to hear him. "I've been feeling a lot of anxiety and depression this week." He added that his court hearing, which had happened earlier that day, hadn't gone well. "I thought I only had a few more weeks in here, but the judge gave me six more months." Sounding more defeated than angry, Lamar added that he planned to "make the most" of his time in the treatment program. "My therapist is teaching me how to talk about my feelings. But changing my thoughts in a more positive direction is hard."

Later in this conversation, Lamar drew a discussion card that asked: "What's preventing you from being a better version of you?" He shrugged, then said: "I have only myself to blame."

No doubt, accepting full responsibility for his actions bodes well for Lamar's accountability journey. But it doesn't address the obligations people with privilege have to own and answer for the hidden role we've played in Lamar's life's trajectory—how our everyday, cumulative actions (and inactions) helped shape a world that gave him few good options.

What prevents us from sharing the blame for whatever harm Lamar inflicted? Surely our cultural conditioning to "otherize" incarcerated youth—to see them as "bad kids"—plays a role. But so does our socialization to see ourselves first and foremost *individuals*. Many Whites are drawn to America's myth of individualism: the fantasy that each of us operates independently, making choices that are freely chosen. The upshot of this worldview is that wrongdoing is rooted in an individual's flawed character and failed willpower—not the historical and contemporary situations and systems that influence a person's decisions. Individualism says that people convicted of crimes are morally blameworthy and solely responsible for the harm they've caused.[1] This thinking lets the rest of us off the hook.

An individualistic worldview is neither universal nor timeless. Indigenous cultures around the globe, societies in the Southern hemisphere, and many minoritized people within the US understand a person's identity primarily in relation to their community. In the West, individualism gained traction during the modern era, thanks in part to the views of a seventeenth-century French mathematician named René Descartes. In his quest to "prove" the immortality of the soul, Descartes posited a categorical distinction between "body" and "mind." His famous formulation of this theory—"I think, therefore I am"—identified the essence of every person with their cognitive capacities (the thinking mind), which he said didn't require a body. Cut off from the body's history, desires, needs, circumstances, and cultural conditioning, the mind (the "soul" or "self") was presumed free to pursue its own destiny, operating as a purely rational, independent, sovereign will.[2] This view of a person as first and foremost a rational individual is a cornerstone of the "bootstraps" ideology I described earlier, which says that anyone who tries hard enough can achieve the American dream of happiness, wealth, health, and freedom. If you fail, *you have only yourself to blame.*

During the modern era, Descartes's conception of the "self" as an autonomous individual encouraged Christians to think of sin individualistically. In his historical account of Christianity's influence on America's justice system, Griffith explains how, during the latter half of the twentieth century, evangelical leaders embraced this individualized notion of sin to explain crime as rooted in a person's moral failure. Their assumption that lawless behavior was freely chosen implied that punishment was necessary and appropriate: "If criminals were morally accountable as individuals, then the response was clear: Punishment, and more of it."[3]

Descartes's understanding of humans as autonomous individuals continues to influence many Americans' beliefs about justice, morality, and accountability. Knowingly or not, many of us subscribe to what one scholar refers to as the "evildoer" theory of criminal activity. This theory assumes that youth who engage in illicit behavior are deliberately and freely choosing to do something wrong—that their choices are *fully intentional*

---

1. Kelly, *Limits of Blame*, 3; DiAngelo, *What Does It Mean*, 196, 201.
2. Descartes, *Discourse on Method*, 20–23.
3. Griffith, *God's Law and Order*, 28–29.

and *conscious*. But social psychology research reveals that people's seemingly personal choices are primarily guided not by "conscious deliberation or intentionality," but by our social environment, cultural conditioning, and personal/family histories.[4] This research calls into question the assumptions that 1) we act strictly as "individuals," and 2) that the decisions we make are "freely chosen."[5] Highlighting the powerful role teenagers' environments play in the decisions they make does not mean they should not be held accountable for their behavior; but it does complicate the notion of "personal responsibility."

A more nuanced and mutual approach to accountability for youth offenders requires us to examine our assumptions about "sin." Many White Christians still harbor the Descartes-influenced understanding of "sin" as a personal indiscretion—something you deliberately do that violates God's will. As a young girl, I learned that it was a sin to lie to your parents, take God's name "in vain," or have sex before you're married. Even this short list of behaviors I was supposed to avoid illustrates how common notions of sin emphasize individual wrongdoing, assume intentionality, and implicate immoral character. Missing here is any attention to the ways our "personal" intentions, decisions, and character are shaped by social systems. Also missing is concern about the ways our harmful actions/inactions foster or diminish the well-being of others. Including those on society's margins. Including incarcerated kids.

Individualized definitions of accountability also obscure the harm caused by our *indifference* and *inactions*. In his "Letter from a Birmingham Jail," Martin Luther King Jr. famously called out "white moderates" for their unwitting collusion with racial oppression. King lamented that so many White Christians sat silently and comfortably on the sidelines of the struggle for racial justice. They were, he said, "more devoted to 'order' than to justice."[6] American individualism assures us that if the status quo is working well enough for us, if we're sufficiently comfortable, we don't have to worry about the suffering of kids like Lamar. His pain is his problem, for which he alone is to blame. Yet, as King saw it, "injustice anywhere is a threat to justice everywhere. We are caught in an inescapable network of mutuality, tied in a single garment of destiny. Whatever affects one directly, affects all indirectly."[7] By calling out the immoral apathy and inaction of decent

---

4. Fondacaro, "Injustice of Retribution," 148–50.
5. Fondacaro, "Injustice of Retribution," 157–58.
6. King Jr., "Letter from Birmingham Jail."
7. King Jr., "Letter from Birmingham Jail."

people, King offers a way to think about sin that holds privileged people accountable for the suffering of those on society's underside.

King and other liberation theologians emphasize the *social* dimensions of "sin"—the abominations of racism, sexism, wealth inequality, colonialism, and other systemic injustices. Reflecting on "God" from the perspective of society's most vulnerable, theologies of liberation encourage people with privilege to recognize the *invisible* and *unintentional* ways we support structural oppression. The point of liberation theology is not to make privileged people feel guilty, but to spiritually motivate us to leverage our advantages to create a world in which everyone can flourish. Ultimately, liberation theologies imply that Lamar is not solely to blame for his choices. However remotely, each of us played a role in his decisions. Whether or not we find the language of "sin" to be useful, we must relinquish our view of ourselves as "innocent" just because we're not in prison.

Abraham Joshua Heschel, the Jewish philosopher and theologian who marched with King, famously said: "Few are guilty, but all are responsible." Elaborating this point, he wrote: "If we admit that the individual is in some measure conditioned or affected by the spirit of society, an individual's crime discloses society's corruption." Like King, Heschel warned that our indifference to this corruption is "more insidious than evil itself."[8]

And just how much should ordinary citizens burden themselves with the pain caused by immoral systems? How much should safe, comfortable, White people care about kids like Lamar? Heschel's response illuminates the connection between compassion and accountability: "Morally speaking," he says, "there is no limit to the concern one must feel for the suffering of human beings."[9]

---

8. Heschel, *Insecurity of Freedom*, 92–93.
9. Heschel, "Reasons for My Involvement," 7–8.

61

"We Are All Criminals"

SEVERAL YEARS AGO, A White lawyer named Emily Baxter was assisting a young man named Anthony to determine whether his criminal record was eligible for being expunged. Expungement doesn't destroy a record but "seals" it from public view, making it less likely to become a barrier to accessing employment, education, housing, and other rights and resources.

Looking at his file, Baxter was relieved to see that Anthony's charge was only a minor theft. Her client, however, didn't share her relief. Instead, he broke down under the weight of the colossal stress of everything he'd *already* lost due to his conviction—a job, house payments, and meals, not to mention the loss of respect from friends and family, as well as his own sense of dignity, self-worth, and hope. Anthony's grief reminded Baxter that even a minor charge could have massive consequences.

Which is precisely why Baxter had been diligently working to persuade employers, landlords, legislators, and licensing boards to give people with criminal records a second chance. But the typical response she got was some version of: *"You can't trust a con"* or *"Once a criminal, always a criminal."* Together with the anguish Anthony expressed, those refrains prompted Baxter to reflect on her own behavior: "How many times had I taken something that wasn't mine? *What would life be like if I didn't have the luxury to forget?"*[1]

These questions became the impetus for what would become a much larger project. Through further study and extensive interviews with non-incarcerated people, Baxter discovered that while 25 percent of Americans

---

1. Baxter, *We Are All Criminals*, 1; emphasis original.

have a criminal record, virtually all of us have a criminal history. But, depending largely on our level of social privilege, only some of us have been caught and convicted. Here's a sampling of the people Baxter interviewed and the illegal activities they had gotten away with earlier in their lives:

- A mechanical engineer who had committed fraud, assault, burglary, and substance abuse violations
- A bank teller who had stolen another woman's wallet when she was in college
- A teacher who had used illicit drugs
- A deacon/insurance agent who had engaged in reckless driving (including under the influence), disorderly conduct, disrupting the peace, and unruly assembly
- A program developer who, while in college, had used a fake ID to consume as a minor, stolen pizza, possessed marijuana, and engaged in sex in a public place
- A prosecutor who had shoplifted in high school and college
- A federal officer who had aided and abetted the sale of controlled substances in high school and college
- An attorney who had committed trespassing, felony burglary, disorderly conduct, and theft of services
- A pediatrician who, as a teenager, had committed arson and criminal damage to property[2]

What does "justice" mean if nearly all Americans have criminal histories, but only a quarter of us have criminal records? How is it possible that 75 percent of us face no legal consequences for our illegal behavior?

The stories Baxter collected, and the photos accompanying them, compel nonincarcerated people to reflect on our tendency to presume ourselves not just innocent, but morally superior to those who get caught. These stories also challenge us to behold the role of race and class in determining who gets convicted, and to reflect on the illusory binaries at the heart of punitive approaches to accountability, namely, that there are "bad" and "good" people, "sinners" and "saints." Ultimately, Baxter suggests, recognizing that "we are all criminals" disrupts "the 'us versus them' dichotomy

---

2. Baxter, *We Are All Criminals*, 6–71.

that plagues both our private thoughts and public discourse about crime and criminality."[3] As Alexander Solzhenitsyn writes,

> If only there were evil people out there insidiously committing evil deeds, and it was simply necessary to separate them from the rest of us and destroy them. But the line dividing good and evil cuts through the heart of every human being, and who among us is willing to destroy a piece of their own heart?[4]

---

3. Baxter, *We Are All Criminals*, 2.
4. Solzhenitsyn, *Gulag Archipelago*, 28.

62

"The Belief That I Won't Get Caught"

BAXTER'S PROJECT FURTHER COMPLICATES the issue of "accountability" for incarcerated kids. Many of the crimes to which her interviewees confessed—crimes for which they were never convicted—happened in youth and involved behaviors they eventually outgrew. Research suggests that most justice-involved teens would eventually "age out" of their unlawful conduct if provided the support needed for healthy adolescent development. The word for this trajectory—"desistance"—names the tendency for young people's reckless or illegal behavior to diminish as they get older.[1]

An abundance of evidence from neuroscience and developmental psychology confirms what many parents of teenagers already know: adolescent minds tend to be more rebellious and risk prone than prudent and judicious. To be sure, in circumstances where their needs are met, most kids can make sound decisions. But in distressing situations, their limbic system—the instinctual, fight-flight-or-freeze part of their brain—is easily triggered, inhibiting their ability to make wise choices.[2] Humans' prefrontal cortex doesn't mature until our mid-twenties. This means adolescent brains are fertile grounds for learning and creativity. But they're also more impulsive, impressionable, and susceptible to peer pressure, stress, and other mental health challenges.[3] Moreover, trauma can impede the brain's maturation,

---

1. Baxter, *We Are All Criminals*, 167. See also Holman and Ziedenberg, *Dangers of Detention*, 6–7.
2. Troutman, "More Just System," 205.
3. National Institute for Mental Health, "Teen Brain." See also Baxter, *We Are All*

especially if it remains untreated. Not surprisingly, given their trauma-filled backstories, teens who get in trouble with the law "have less capacity for self-regulation in emotionally charged situations; their sensitivity to environmental influences is heightened, and they have not yet learned to make decisions with a future orientation."[4]

In a small group, someone drew a discussion card that asked: "What beliefs do you have that keep getting you into trouble?" All of the youth had the same response: "The belief that I won't get caught." Their shared assumption that they could "do bad things," as one boy put it, without consequence, struck me as a textbook example of scientific research confirming that good judgment isn't most teenagers' strong suit.[5]

In a different conversation, I asked a group of three boys if there was a habit they'd like to break. Shaquille responded matter-of-factly: "That's easy. I'd like to break my habit of stealing cars." I thought he was trying to be funny and expected the other two boys to laugh. But instead of laughing, they agreed that this was the same habit they wanted to break.

During the past two decades, scientific research on adolescent brain development has influenced Supreme Court decisions related to youth justice. In 2005, the death penalty was outlawed for kids under the age of eighteen (Roper v. Simmons). In 2010, life-without-parole sentences were banned for juveniles convicted with non-homicide offenses (Graham v. Florida); and in 2012, mandatory life-without-parole sentences were deemed unconstitutional for youth found guilty of homicide (Miller v. Alabama).[6] Some criminal justice experts are now questioning whether it makes sense for a justice-involved teenager's eighteenth birthday to be the magical threshold into adulthood.[7] We know from both science and experience that the line separating adolescence from adulthood is far from solid. Moreover, neuroscience's discovery of "neuroplasticity"—the brain's capacity to evolve and learn throughout a person's entire life—exposes the arbitrariness of this demarcation.

At any age, exercise and healthy food are crucial for promoting brain health. Yet these basic needs are in short supply for too many youth in confinement. I've lost track of how many have told me they stole food because they (and/or family members) were hungry. Virtually none of these kids'

Criminals, 156.

    4. McCarthy et al., "Future of Youth Justice," 5. See also Troutman, "More Just System," 203–8.

    5. Stanford Medicine, "Understanding the Teen Brain," para. 1.

    6. Juvenile Law Center, "Juvenile Life without Parole," para. 2.

    7. Chu, "Dangerous Minds," paras. 6–7.

families can afford gym memberships; many live in neighborhoods where simply being outside is unsafe. Luckily, the detention center I visit has a gym and an adjacent room with weights. Male residents often tell me that working out helps them deal with stress, and youth of all genders say they enjoy playing basketball. None, however, are enthusiastic about what they commonly refer to as "jail food." During a writing exercise, I asked a cohort of residents to describe what "jail food" tastes like. Dario put down his pencil, looked at me, and exclaimed: "It's *jail* food. Don't taste like nothing. Like *nothing* is how it tastes!"

There's no question that our diet impacts our well-being—physically, emotionally, mentally, and even spiritually. For better or worse, what we eat influences our microbiome—the billions of microorganisms that inhabit, and to a surprising extent, constitute our bodies. Neuroscientific research shows that bacteria in our gut impact our moods[8] (our "spirits"). Thus, among other factors, the *quality of food* children and teens consume contributes to the *quality of their attitudes and behaviors* before, during, and after incarceration. The field of nutritional neuroscience is relatively new, but one study of young male offenders found that dietary supplements decreased reactivity, aggression, and impulsivity.[9]

Various other aspects of carceral institutions work against the healthy brain development on which accountability depends. For example, we know that every brain is wired differently, that stressed-out brains have a hard time learning, and that vision tends to be the strongest of human senses (for sighted people).[10] Yet in many institutional settings, everything from the uniform clothing, to the monotonous schedules, to the drab color of paint on the wall convey to a teenager how little their individuality matters. The trauma histories of most kids in the system make their brains acutely sensitive to precisely the kinds of environmental triggers that are common in institutional settings, including "long periods of isolation; harsh, sterile surroundings; bright lights; a constant din; and a near-constant threat of violence."[11]

It's easy to criticize the system of juvenile confinement as detrimental to an adolescent's healthy brain development. But judging this system is not the same as being accountable for its potentially negative impact. As Rabbi Ruttenberg reminds us, accountability entails *actions*. Drawing on the list of steps she recommends, we can:

8. Azab, "Gut Bacteria Can Influence," paras. 9–10.
9. Raine et al., "Omega-3 Supplementation," 389–90.
10. Medina, *Brain Rules*.
11. McCarthy et al., "Future of Youth Justice," 5.

- Own and confess our *collective* failure to nurture not just the brains but the divine humanity of kids who get in trouble with the law
- Strive to consciously interrupt our mental, emotional, and spiritual habits of binary thinking about "guilt" and "innocence"
- Do what we can in our own corner of the world to repair the damage (directly or indirectly) caused by our neglect of disadvantaged youth

Ultimately, accountability requires each of us to change—to become the kind of person who no longer contributes to the suffering of hurting kids. Put differently, accountability involves healing.

PART IV

Healing

63

"I Don't Know Why I Keep Ending Up in Jail"

"I DON'T KNOW WHY I keep ending up in jail." Michael sounded discouraged, frustrated, and exhausted. "Every time I get out, I think I've changed. But obviously I haven't. Because I keep ending up back in jail again."

Anyone who has ever tried and failed to change unwanted behavior can empathize with Michael's struggle. Why is making such changes so hard? More specifically, why do many previously incarcerated teenagers end up back in the system? What's missing from the "justice" they encounter there?

In the preceding chapters, I've addressed this question by critiquing a punitive approach to juvenile wrongdoing and advocating instead for a kind of youth justice that:

- Recognizes and challenges the structural oppressions (especially racism, poverty, and sexism) that deprive marginalized youth the opportunities they need to flourish
- Takes seriously the suffering that predates and propels teenage offenders' harmful behavior
- Holds *both* incarcerated kids *and* people with privilege accountable for the harms we've unknowingly perpetuated

In other words, the kind of justice young offenders need and deserve is social/systemic, compassionate, and accountable. In the chapters ahead, I explore a related dimension of that justice: the need for healing.

Within America's youth justice system, healing has often been framed as "rehabilitation." During the past two decades, in response to the harsher penalties adopted during the "law and order" era, there's been a growing emphasis on providing therapeutic resources and services. This trend is encouraging. Studies show that therapeutic interventions are far more likely than retaliatory strategies to promote the kind of transformation that keeps kids out of the system:

> Therapeutic techniques focused on behavior change, such as restorative programs, skill building, counseling, and service coordination, have larger impacts on recidivism than external control techniques and punitive models that use discipline, deterrence, and surveillance.[1]

Research suggests that trauma-informed programs like the ones offered to the youth in the mindfulness group are especially effective in helping kids in confinement heal from the toxic stresses that contributed to their destructive behavior. Meta-analyses of studies indicate that although long-term incarceration generally increases the likelihood of recidivism, youth who receive quality therapeutic treatment are less likely to re-offend.[2]

I prefer the word *healing* over *rehabilitation* to describe the transformation Michael is asking about. "Rehabilitation" has a normalizing ring to it that doesn't honor the irreducible diversity of the youth I've met. The term also implies that there's a healthy ("habilitated") state or environment to which incarcerated kids can return, which, in most cases, just isn't true.[3] The fact that upon release, many kids go back to the same *un*healthy circumstances that fueled their harmful behavior points to a crucial dimension of healing that rehabilitation doesn't address: the *social* transformation needed to support *individual* healing. The language of healing reminds us that there is no return to the garden—not for incarcerated youth, not for any of us. In a world as troubled as the one we inhabit, the well-being and wholeness we seek is likely to be imperfect, fragile, tentative, and difficult.

In his lament about "ending up back in jail," Michael recognized that staying out of confinement would require a kind of change he'd yet to embody.

What kind of change? What does healing mean?

---

1. Development Services Group, "Juvenile Residential Programs," 12–13.
2. Development Services Group, "Juvenile Residential Programs," 12–13.
3. Wallace, "Insider's Plan," 13:00–13:12.

64

What Does Healing Mean?

HEALING STRIKES ME AS one of those overused and underdefined words in America today. Talk about "healing" saturates wellness culture. The word shows up in books, podcasts, social media, and a dazzling array of commercial products, programs, and gurus that promise to alleviate our maladies and make us feel better about ourselves, each other, and the world. Whether enticements to restored health focus on weight loss, stress reduction, back pain, or something else, popular notions of "healing" are typically tethered to pictures of well-being characterized by mental, physical, and emotional freedom from suffering, achieved through individual willpower, and made possible by social privilege. In mainstream medical discourses and practices, healing is often equated with curing—the goal of which (to be "cured") reflects and reinforces commercial culture's fantasy of personal wellness. In this fantasy, healing is about eradicating psychological and/or somatic afflictions, usually by conquering disease, correcting abnormalities, or eliminating discomfort with the help of science, technology, and experts.[1]

Mainstream medical and commercial approaches to healing may reduce suffering and facilitate well-being among people with privilege. But they fail to address the needs of youth in confinement. Whether couched as "cure," "correction," or "perfection," both the fix-it trajectory of these versions of healing and the dream of wholeness they promise gloss over the tragic truths that permeate the backstories of young offenders: some losses can't be recovered, some pains may never be cured. For them, healing is a verb that may never become a noun.

[1]. I examine mainstream self-help, commercial, and medical discourses and practices of healing in Lelwica, *Shameful Bodies*.

Popular definitions of healing not only ignore the systemic injustices that damage the mental, physical, and spiritual health of vulnerable youth, but they often downplay an inconvenient truth about healing: it can be *hard*! Like accountability, healing entails some degree of discomfort. Not masochistic discomfort, but a courageous willingness to recognize, feel, and wrestle with the hurt from which we seek relief. In response to a writing prompt, Bicky Beno Boy described the healing process with images reminiscent of Jacob's wrestling match with the angel: "I'm at war with myself . . . But I finally get the meaning of fighting demons. Up all night thinking, just dreaming."

The chasm between popular visions of restored health as a transcendent state of comfort or cure and incarcerated teenagers' needs for wellbeing as a dimension of justice are evident in six boys' written responses to the question "What does healing mean to you?"

- "Healing means to me that you are taking time to let something process, or letting something go through the next stage of development."
- "Letting go of something or someone who caused a traumatizing memory or bad memory you will never forget and that affects you in a big way."
- "To grow up."
- "Healing to me is the ability to successfully move on from something that you've struggled with."
- "I consider healing a strong word because healing is a long and hard step to take in your life. Because some people want to heal but they don't know how and some people take the hard step of healing and in the middle of the healing step they quit because it is hard. I believe healing includes forgiveness and acceptance."
- "To forgive or forget the past or people who have put you down."

These responses suggest that healing is a transformative process that requires both effort and patience, both agency and acceptance.

Asked "What makes it hard to heal?," this same group of boys wrote:

- "Pain, grief, insecurities"
- "Sometimes you're not ready to heal or it's hard to heal from it."
- "Anger, anxiety, depression, and bullying"
- "The changes that come with it"
- "Not being able to let go of bad things and situations"

- "Accepting things for what they are and figuring out how to move on. What's next? What do I do now?"

These responses suggest that healing is hard because it requires us to be present to internal suffering, to embrace things we can't control, to bravely face the uncertainty surrounding the changes healing brings. Being present to loss, fear, anger, betrayal, and other painful emotions goes against the grain of our evolutionary programming to escape suffering.

As the boys discussed their responses to the prompts, Michael said they reminded him of a prayer he'd heard. Based on the words he remembered, I realized he was referring to the Serenity Prayer. Written by Reinhold Niebuhr, a twentieth-century Protestant theologian, it says: "God, grant me the serenity to accept the things I cannot change, courage to change the things I can, and wisdom to know the difference."[2]

Healing means different things to different people because our wounds vary, as do our social identities and locations. As the boys' responses suggest, healing is complicated. As we'll see in the chapters ahead, its multiple dimensions include both anger and gratitude, realism and dreaming, personal and social transformation, self-examination, self-love, nurturing, empathy, forgiveness, joy, resilience, and more. Ultimately, healing is the metamorphosis of pain, a process that, as the boys keenly perceived, requires both struggle and surrender. Incarcerated or not, this journey begins when we stop avoiding our hurt. As somatic psychologist Hillary McBride observes, "*We heal when we can be with what we feel.*"[3] Paradoxically, turning toward what hurts—in ourselves and in the world—is how we recover our divine humanity.

---

2. See https://proactive12steps.com/serenity-prayer/.
3. McBride, *Wisdom of Your Body*, 108; emphasis original.

65

"The Kinship of Heaven"

AMERICAN CULTURE DOESN'T ENCOURAGE us to turn toward the suffering within or around us. Alongside its endless programs and products that promise to restore well-being, our culture proffers a smorgasbord of strategies for numbing, denying, and distracting ourselves from dis-ease—from "retail therapy," to workaholism, to alcohol, drug, and/or social media addictions, to name a few. For many of us, the habit of looking away from suffering is strong.

Certain religious narratives quietly encourage our escapist orientation with promises of freedom from suffering in a transcendent utopia. In Christianity, the all-too-human fantasy of escaping pain is often mythologized in traditional visions of heaven—that celestial place in the sky to which "good" people (those who obey "God's laws") are admitted when they die. In this narrative, salvation is depicted as a future state of everlasting perfection in another world—a place where cravings and afflictions end, the lame shall walk and the blind shall see, and everyone is happy. Curiously, this otherworldly paradise resembles "secular" mythologies of healing. Whether couched in religious or secular vocabulary, *salvation*—a term that's etymologically related to the Latin, *salve*, meaning "good health," "wholeness," or "healing"[1]—is associated with living happily ever after, and well-being is a reward for righteous behavior.

Interestingly, biblical scholars say that otherworldly perfection wasn't the idea of salvation Jesus proclaimed and practiced. For him, restored health meant liberation from bondage (both internal and political), return

---

1. Borg, *Heart of Christianity*, 175.

from exile or alienation (both spiritually and socially), and the experience of forgiveness and acceptance. This experiential, embodied, *this*-worldly approach to salvation was evident in Jesus' healing ministry. He restored health to people's bodies, minds, and spirits, particularly those suffering on the edges of the social body. In fact, Jesus' political opposition to the Roman Empire, whose laws and institutions systematically disparaged the divine humanity of impoverished people, was integral to the salvation he practiced and preached.[2] For him, the "kingdom of God" and "kingdom of heaven" were metaphors for a liberating experience of wholeness, dignity, and belonging that was already available both among and within those who practiced his countercultural message of love and justice (Matt 4:17). In between the world that was and the world that could be—at the intersection of past, present, and future—healing was possible.

Boyle retranslates Jesus' references to the "kingdom" (*basileia*) of God as the "*kin*ship" of God.[3] This phrase more aptly captures the communal, egalitarian, and inclusive healing Jesus envisioned and embodied. In the Gospels, Jesus frequently eats and drinks with "sinners." In his parables, he likens the kinship of God to a festive banquet to which everyone is invited, especially people his society ignores or condemns (Luke 14:15–24; 22:1–14). In contrast to the Roman Empire's matrix of domination, Jesus compared the healing power of God's kinship to the hidden potential of a mustard seed, which despite its miniscule size, grows into tree large enough to provide refuge for a multitude of birds (Luke 13:18–19; Matt 13:31–32; Mark 4:30–32).

The mustard seed parable is one of my favorites. My maternal grandmother was a serious gardener, and so is my mom. I inherited their love of growing things—from tomatoes to zinnias. My mom and grandma also taught me the importance of composting—the process whereby decaying plants, food waste, and even animal manure become fertilizer that restores the soil with valuable nutrients and increases its ability to retain water in periods of drought. Just as seeds represent the creative potential of society's "little ones" (Matt 10:42), so composting provides an apt, earthy metaphor of the process whereby transformed pain becomes a resource that benefits others.[4]

---

2. Borg, *Heart of Christianity*, 90, 171–79; Brock and Parker, *Saving Paradise*, xiii.
3. Boyle, *Tattoos on the Heart*.
4. Bussie, *Love without Limits*, ch. 5.

66

"He Was Really Thirsty!"

My love for gardening prompted an idea. The college where I teach has some organic gardens on the edge of campus. Why not see if we could create a plot next to these established beds for residents at the detention center? Might the opportunity to plant, care for, and harvest their own vegetables support their healing?

Since youth in the mindfulness group are in secure confinement, I looked into involving youth in the facility's transitional program. This nonsecure program helps adjudicated older teens develop the life skills they'll need to transition from their out-of-home placements into their next living situation. Youth in this program have jobs in the area and do community service. Depending on their individual needs, they participate in educational programming, receive therapeutic support, and get help with practical tasks, such as getting a driver's permit. They also learn life skills like budgeting and cooking. Why not teach them how to plant, weed, water, and harvest their own veggies?

Fortunately, administrators at the college and the detention center agreed. In 2020, the college rototilled a twenty-by-twenty-foot plot for the youth to tend and hired a student garden mentor. Every week during the summer, a small van full of youth and their supervisor visit the garden, where the student mentor and I show them the ropes.

In *The Well-Gardened Mind*, psychiatrist Sue Stuart-Smith explores how growing plants, whether radishes or roses, offers an opportunity to grow ourselves. "Quintessentially, caring for a garden is a nurturing activity," one that can be existentially grounding and therefore healing for people who have experienced trauma and/or loss.[1] Paying attention to plants' needs for sunshine, water, and weeding cultivates our capacity to care. Watching seeds we've pushed into the soil sprout and evolve into something edible and/or beautiful enables us to behold the invisible life force that animates everything, ourselves included. (This year, the boys wanted to grow flowers). Gardening also connects us with the earth's resurrection-like rhythms of decay and renewal, which mirror the vicissitudes of our lives.

Not all the youth who participate in the garden visits are as excited as Stuart-Smith and me about growing things. While some don't hesitate to put hoe and shovel to work, others watch from the garden's sidelines and pet my yellow lab, Buck. And while there's excitement when the first tomato is ready for harvest, there's less enthusiasm for watering and weeding. Yet even the youth who aren't interested in getting their shoes or hands dirty seem to enjoy being outside. And the leisurely pace of growing things allows for interesting conversations—about challenges at work, difficult family histories, vocational aspirations. Cultivating organic vegetables is also conducive for discussions on planetary and personal health.

Various scenes from these garden visits illuminate the capacity to nurture as a dimension of healing: a trans girl bent over in concentration, diligently digging out dandelions that had invaded the watermelon patch; a boy who proudly displayed the bag of tomatoes, onions, peppers, and cilantro he'd harvested and was planning to use to make salsa that night; another boy who rescued the fragile violet plant he found growing in the middle of the garden, insisting that it was "not a weed."

So far, my favorite memory from these visits happened on a mercilessly hot day in July. Whether weeding or watching others work, all of us were moving slowly—except for Buck, who ran enthusiastically after the frisbee Jeremy threw to him. While almost all the youth enjoy my dog, Jeremy was especially attuned to him. So when Buck decided he needed a break from playing fetch, Jeremy looked for a container to give him water. Two other boys joined the search, but all the plastic pots in the shed had holes on the bottom. I went to my car to see if I could find something that might work. Nothing. But it didn't matter. By the time I returned, the boys had improvised a solution: Jeremy was slowly pouring water from his own thermos into another boy's cupped hands, from which Buck was sloppily and gratefully lapping. Looking up, Jeremy happily exclaimed, "He was really thirsty!"

---

1. Stuart-Smith, *Well-Gardened Mind*, 13–15.

These scenes of determination, pride, tenderness, empathy, and innovation remind us that justice-involved youth already have inside themselves the seeds they need to heal. Like Buck, they need to be watered.

67

"Being on the Run"

IN THE MINDFULNESS GROUP, we water the seeds of serenity inside us through meditation.

One day, Alberto told me that he'd used conscious breathing to stop himself from reacting when he got mad at his math teacher. "I was helping my buddy with a math problem, and the teacher accused me of cheating, when all I was doing was trying to help him."

"What was it like to not react from a place of anger?" I asked.

"What was hard was that I felt angry but didn't give in to it," Alberto responded. "That's not something I'm used to doing."

"Me neither," I replied. "I've been practicing mindfulness for decades, and I'm still just a beginner."

Lots of adults with comfortable lives and few if any ACEs struggle to tolerate disturbing emotions. Imagine how difficult it is for traumatized teens to stay present with fear, grief, anger, and other forms of distress without reverting to fight, flight, or freeze! By "stay present with," I mean *feel* the energy of those feelings in your body, without reacting to them. Incarcerated or not, composting pain takes tremendous inner strength because it requires us to stop running away from what hurts.

In that same conversation, Alberto broke the facility's rule by recounting what he did that landed him in detention. "I got in a fight with a kid at school. Beat him up pretty bad." Before I could ask him to refrain from sharing more details, he added, "But the night before, my dad was beating me up. And how come he's not in jail?"

I sensed the question was rhetorical, which was fortunate since I didn't have an answer.

"What other feelings besides anger are difficult to tolerate?" I asked the group.

"Regret," Donny offered.

"Say more," I invited.

"Mostly I regret being on the run." Turning to me, Donny clarified that "being on the run" meant running from the cops. "Running from them only made things worse," he continued. "I wish I'd never tried to get away."

"I've never had to run from the cops," I shared. "But I've spent plenty of energy trying to escape my problems. I think it's a natural thing to do. The bummer is, it never works. Every time I try outrunning my problems, they not only catch up with me, but they get bigger. Probably because when I'm running, I'm not dealing with them."

"Wait—can you say that again?" Alberto interjected.

I was about to repeat myself, when Donny helpfully offered a more succinct summary: "She said being on the run only makes things worse."

The Buddhist teacher Jack Kornfield says that there are two kinds of suffering: the kind we run away from, which continues to follow us, and the kind we turn toward, which we can heal.[1] The conscious breathing meditation we do in the mindfulness group is a method for learning to stop running. Paying attention to the sensation of our bellies inflating on the in breath and deflating on the out breath slows us down internally. Returning our attention to this sensation when our minds wander strengthens our ability to become present (note: breathing always happens in the present). The residents often describe this mind-body practice as "calming." It's no coincidence that "breath" and "spirit" are etymologically related: whether our inhales and exhales are shallow or deep, anxious or soothing, short or long, our breathing connects, reflects, and influences our mental-emotional-bodily states.

Our bodies are ground zero for healing because even when our wounds are invisible, they are rooted in our flesh. There are, after all, no solid lines dividing what goes on in our thoughts, feelings, bodies, and spirits. As McBride points out, "Our body hears everything we think."[2] Interestingly, neuroscientific research validates premodern Christians' view of human minds, bodies, and spirits as interconnected. Despite Christianity's anti-body reputation, a view of flesh and spirit as distinct but united prevailed until the seventeenth century when Descartes divorced the two, heralding the mind/body dualism that, to this day, causes us to overlook the embodied dimension of healing.

---

1. Kornfield, "Life of Greatness."
2. McBride, *Wisdom of Your Body*, 147.

The traumas incarcerated youth have survived necessitate a kind of healing that, in McBride's words, "happens from the ground up." Such healing unfolds "when we have a new experience of ourselves and hold our attention on it long enough for it to sink in."[3] Resmaa Menakem offers a series of steps that, practiced repeatedly, facilitate this transformative process. They include:

1. Soothing yourself by quieting your mind, calming your heart, and settling your body
2. Noticing the sensations, vibrations, and emotions in your body instead of reacting to them
3. Accepting the discomfort instead of trying to flee it, and observing when it changes
4. Staying present and in your body as you allow your experience to unfold, with its ambiguity and uncertainty, responding from the best parts of yourself
5. Safely discharging any energy that remains (via exercise, dancing, sports activities, physical labor)[4]

These practices counteract our tendencies to get stuck in "dirty pain" by avoiding our internal suffering, reacting defensively, and/or blaming, shaming, or pitying ourselves or others.[5]

McBride and Menakem are therapists, not theologians. Yet their healing strategies resemble the embodied wisdom found in diverse spiritual traditions. The thirteenth-century Sufi poet Rumi wrote that "the cure for pain is in the pain."[6] Contemporary Buddhist teacher Pema Chödrön describes "staying present" as the antidote to misery.[7] The most prominent icon of Western Christianity—the image of Jesus nailed to a cross—depicts a man who clearly did not run away from suffering.[8]

---

3. McBride, *Wisdom of Your Body*, 58–59, 13.
4. Menakem, *My Grandmother's Hands*, 168.
5. Menakem, *My Grandmother's Hands*, 166.
6. Rumi, *Essential Rumi*, 205.
7. This message pervades Pema Chödrön's books. See, e.g., *Welcoming the Unwelcome*.
8. Armstrong, *Twelve Steps*, 92.

68

"It's Been a Hard Week"

IN ADDITION TO BEING a nerdy religion professor, I'm also a "four" on the Enneagram (a typology of personality types). This means I belong to a category of people who like to talk about deep things. Sometimes this proclivity leads to amazing conversations. But it also means I'm often the most serious person in the room.

Spending time with the youth helps me appreciate the value of small talk. The chitchat that happens as we settle into small groups fosters a relaxed atmosphere. And I enjoy the icebreakers we do at the beginning of the mindfulness group—"What's your least favorite food?" "Who's your favorite superhero?" "What famous person would you choose to have dinner with?"

One afternoon, Keesha, two students, and I realized we were all wearing Vans, a brand of shoes that I didn't know was made for skateboarders. If you Google "What kind of person wears Vans?," you'll learn that surfers, skaters, rebels, artists, misfits, musicians, and athletes are among those sporting the "cool" these shoes represent. Though I relate to terms like "rebel" and "misfit," *cool* is not a quality most people would associate with me. So I was delighted to learn that Keesha not only loves Vans, but that she was impressed to see me wearing them. In the free world, clout by fashion seems superficial. In detention, it created a connection that supported a difficult conversation.

As we started the ritual check-ins, Keesha's tone and demeanor shifted. Her face looked tense and her normally upbeat voice was unsteady. "It's been a hard week," she said. "I started writing my trauma narrative, which I have to finish if I want to get out of here in two months." She paused, then continued, "The hard part is that I was sexually abused."

As I took a deep breath and considered how to respond, one of my students looked Keesha in the eye and gently said, "You're not alone . . . the same thing happened to me." The student thanked Keesha for having the courage to speak up and talked about her own struggle to name what had happened to her—how she didn't want to tell anyone, how her parents still don't know, how even though she knows in her head that it wasn't her fault, it's still hard not to blame herself. Keesha, who struggles mightily with attention deficit, was totally focused on what my student was sharing. Her face and shoulders had relaxed.

My student wasn't offering a cure or trying to save Keesha from her pain. Yet through the vulnerability they both risked, across the immense opportunity gaps separating their lives, there was a connection, a nonseparation that, in that moment, felt like healing.[1]

In traditional Christian theology, salvation is sometimes depicted as a rescue mission: Jesus delivers us from our sins like a superhero who saves ordinary citizens from the bad guys. But this *isn't* the model of healing Jesus practiced,[2] and it's not a realistic path for incarcerated kids. What I witnessed in the interaction between Keesha and my student wasn't an everlasting cure, but a micro-moment of relief made possible by Keesha's bravery and my student's empathy. Keesha doesn't need someone to save her. She needs safe spaces and relationships that support her innate ability, desire, and courage to heal.

Most of us don't associate "salvation" with *safety*. But research suggests that feeling safe is a basic condition for healing.[3] If you don't feel safe, you can't name what hurts. And to paraphrase trauma expert Bessel van der Kolk, what can't be spoken can't be healed.[4] According to neuroscientist Stephen Porges, our bodies/minds pick up cues from other people's vocal tones and facial expressions to assess a relationship's safety (or lack thereof).[5] Trustworthy relationships make it possible for us to disclose how we've been hurt. Naming our hurt is crucial for moving through it; and moving through pain is how we transform and learn from it. When we trust that our grief will be seen and validated, we can also be honest about how it impacted our decisions, including those we're not proud of.[6] Additionally, talking about what hurts dissipates the shame that frequently shadows

---

1. I describe this interaction in Lelwica, "Power of Proximity," 41.
2. Borg, *Heart of Christianity*, 80–100.
3. Van der Kolk, *Body Keeps the Score*, 315.
4. Van der Kolk, *Body Keeps the Score*, 332–49.
5. Porges, "Neuroscience & Power."
6. Sered, *Until We Reckon*, 122–23.

traumatizing experiences—the same shame that, left unresolved, can lead to violence. Paradoxically, then, feeling safe is both preventative medicine and a salve for hurting kids.

Safety is not only foundational for healing; it's a condition for learning, creativity, growth, and flourishing—all of which are antidotes to antisocial behavior. Instead of calling for "tough" (punishing) responses to teenage crime, privileged people ought to be asking what we can do to help kids feel safe in their schools, homes, neighborhoods, and communities.[7] If we understand the harm teenage offenders inflict as rooted in their undigested pain, it becomes clear why healing—not punishment—is the key to creating a safer society. Healing empowers youth to access the empathy that trauma threatens to destroy.

The trauma narrative Keesha mentioned is another method for composting pain. James Pennebaker was among the first psychologists to recognize writing's therapeutic potential. Writing enables trauma survivors to organize their experiences and empowers them to become the authors of their own stories. Determining the meaning of what happened—what you learned from it and how it shapes your self-understanding—restores the sense of agency that becomes eclipsed in traumatic situations.[8] As Holocaust survivor and psychologist Victor Frankl keenly observed, traumatized people experience relief and growth when they're able to find or discover meaning in what happened to them. Frankl is *not* saying that "suffering is redemptive" or that "everything happens a reason." He's simply encouraging us to be the ones who decide what our distressing experiences mean.[9]

---

7. Porges, "Neuroscience & Power."
8. Pennebaker, *Writing to Heal*.
9. Frankl, *Man's Search for Meaning*.

69

"You Go to the Margins So That the Folks There Make *You* Different"

Occasionally, someone asks me whether I have a chance "to share [my] faith" with the youth I visit. Honestly, I'm not even sure what that means. For me, "faith" is more about actions and questions than beliefs and answers, and I have zero desire to convert anyone to a particular religion. I'm far more interested in what the youth teach me about the need for *interfaith values* like compassion, accountability, liberation, and healing as dimensions of the justice they need.

White Christians' attempts to "rehabilitate" troubled youth by "saving" their souls are as old as the juvenile system itself.

In 1833, a ten-year-old Black boy named Austin Reed was found guilty of arson and placed in America's first house of refuge, where he lived until his release six years later. The following year, Reed was charged with larceny and sent to an adult prison in upstate New York. There he endured corporal punishment for his noncompliant behavior. One day he was anguishing alone in his cell after a harsh beating when a White chaplain visited him. Reed describes this visit in his memoir:

> As the chaplain stood in front of my iron grated door, he seemed to me like a new born angel, sent from the portals of the sky to come and unlock the prisoner's door, unbind his chains and let the prisoner free.[1]

---

1. Quoted in Dubler and Lloyd, *Break Every Yoke*, 36–37.

In *Break Every Yoke*, religion scholars Joshua Dubler and Vincent Lloyd highlight the ambiguity of the healing the chaplain facilitates. Reed himself says that the chaplain's comforting presence and message of forgiveness through Christ provided great spiritual relief. But the chaplain's visit did nothing to change the structural White supremacy and brutality Reed endured.[2] Even so, Reed resisted cliché narratives of redemptive suffering that permeate Christian prison ministry then and now. The more years he spent in confinement, the more Reed's scrutiny of his own moral failures morphed into a prophetic critique of the prison system's cruelty.[3]

Throughout the twentieth century and still today, many Christian prison ministries forego Reed's structural critique of America's punitive justice system in their hurry to save individual sinners. Not only did prominent evangelical leaders see personal conversion to Christ as the only cure for youth crime, but some viewed them as a "captive audience" for spreading the gospel.[4]

Evangelizing approaches to healing exclude the multitude of kids for whom Christian faith is irrelevant or unpersuasive—including those who see "God" as an "asshole." Moreover, such approaches assume that teenagers' unlawful behavior is rooted in their moral deficiency. Billy Graham's call for America to "pray her way out" of rampant teenage crime[5] epitomizes the "spiritual bypassing" that's common among White Christian leaders who talk about redemption without addressing the sources of suffering for socially marginalized people. These spiritualizing salvation narratives mimic White wellness culture's tendency to ignore the material inequalities that enable some but not others to heal.[6]

Admittedly, it's easy to criticize the exclusionary, individualizing, and spiritualizing approach to healing that characterizes most evangelical prison ministries. But it's harder to accuse people involved with these ministries of apathy regarding imprisoned people. Moreover, like Reed, many incarcerated people today appreciate Evangelicals' outreach to them.[7] Perhaps doing something, however flawed, is better than doing nothing?

Boyle's work with ex-gang members in Los Angeles represents an alternative way to accompany people on society's periphery: "You go to the margins," he says, "not to make a difference. You go to the margins so that

---

2. Dubler and Lloyd, *Break Every Yoke*, 36–37.
3. Yoder, "Prison Theology," 75.
4. Griffith, *God's Law and Order*, 213–16.
5. Graham, quoted in Griffith, *God's Law and Order*, 59.
6. Jackson and Rao, *White Women*, 114–15.
7. Griffith, *God's Law and Order*, 266.

the folks there make *you* different."[8] Boyle encourages "do-gooders" like me to abandon our ambition, conscious or not, to be the hero. Not only is a rescue-mission approach to healing condescending to those we would "save," but this orientation leads to burnout: "You burn out because you've allowed it to become about you. You've depleted yourself because it's about you saving the day." From Boyle's perspective, people who "go to the margins" are not called to be "successful." They're called to be loving. "I just want to delight in the person who's in my path and cherish [them] with every breath." With this kind of healing, "you stop caring about outcomes."[9]

In other words, you stop trying to be the savior. What a relief!

---

8. Boyle, "Can You Really Conquer," 1:45:56.
9. Boyle, "Can you Really Conquer," 1:46:17.

70

The Hula Dance

LETTING GO OF OUTCOMES doesn't come easily for an overachiever like me. But the detention center residents challenge me to revise my assumptions about what healing looks like.

I got the idea of playing charades with them after reading about community theater programs designed to promote emotional intelligence among inner-city kids who have been exposed to—and/or committed—violence. Obviously, an informal game of pantomimes is a far cry from the acting opportunities that well-designed drama programs like Shakespeare in the Courts provide justice-involved kids.[1] Still, I was curious to see what would happen if, every month or two, we changed the normal structure of the mindfulness group and practiced paying attention in a different way, one that involved improvisational acting—and having fun!

Acting can be a form of *play*, which psychiatrist and researcher Stuart Brown defines as "anything that spontaneously is done for its own sake."[2] Play is so central to healthy childhood development that the United Nations considers it a human right to which every child is entitled.[3] Scientific studies illuminate both how childhood play cultivates empathy and trust and how its dearth can lead to antisocial behavior. Brown's research found a clear deficiency, deviancy, or absence of play in the backstories of young men who committed homicide.[4] Other research links play acting to prosocial

---

1. Van der Kolk, *Body Keeps the Score*, 339–48.
2. S. Brown, "Play, Spirit, and Character," 7:50. See also S. Brown and Vaughan, *Play*.
3. Ginsburg et al., "Importance of Play"; Nijhof et al., "Healthy Play, Better Coping."
4. S. Brown, "Play, Spirit, and Character."

behaviors and feelings like sharing and empathy among youth.[5] Healthy play stimulates growth, learning, and healing among children who have experienced trauma.[6] Yet play requires a sense of safety—something kids in chronically unstable and/or violent environments can't count on.[7]

I returned the first charades game I ordered online. Though advertised as "fun for the entire family," most of its prompts assumed knowledge of TV shows, celebrities, or characters from movies, books, and cartoons representing mainstream White, middle-class, American culture. When I opened the second game, I worried that its prompts would be too easy. Turns out, the readily recognizable characters, actions, and objects on the cards, which are easy to act out and guess, contribute to feelings of success among actors and audience members of the mindfulness group. It's interesting to see how much the youth value this mutual success. To support it, they change the rules of the game. Instead of using the sand timer, actors have unlimited time to perform their prompt. Rather than create teams that would turn the fun of deciphering an actor's pantomime into a competition, anyone can guess the meaning of their nonverbal movements at any time—an approach that fills the room with chaotic excitement.

Some residents appear to be natural-born actors. Whenever it was Angelo's turn, he'd study the card he picked, hold it against his chest, and look at the ceiling while contemplating how best to pantomime the prompt. Then he'd throw himself into his performance, using wordless gestures to communicate that he was frosting a cake, impersonating a fashion model, or holding a baseball glove (all prompts he successfully acted out). The less theatrically inclined residents need more encouragement—at least initially. The first time Gary played, he reluctantly took the "stage" and half-heartedly acted out his prompt, which was "picking out clothing." The more we guessed the meaning of his mysterious movements, however, the more his confidence grew. Finally, a motion that looked like removing a hanger from a rack of clothes led someone to correctly identify what Gary was doing. Everyone cheered. Later in the same game, Gary volunteered for another turn.

The collective effort to interpret the meaning of what would normally be very strange movements fosters a feeling of belonging, and the silliness of those gestures provides a sense of comic relief—a temporary break from the stresses surrounding life in confinement. My favorite charade memory happened when the prompt I drew showed a cartoon image of "the hula dance." The kids and my students laughed hysterically as I waved my arms and bent

5. Development Services Group, "Arts-Based Programs."
6. Van der Weij, "Play Is the Natural Expression"; Felsman, "How Improv."
7. Henning, *Rage of Innocence*, 29–32.

my knees, rotating from side to side. But the funniest part was that although everyone seemed to recognize the dance, no one could remember its name. Tyrell skipped and jumped around the gym, as if this movement would dislodge the forgotten word from his memory, as the rest of us howled with laughter at the ridiculousness of the moment.

I left the detention center that afternoon with an expanded understanding of healing—one that wasn't defined by outcomes, saviorism, or eternal seriousness. Through the levity of a game of charades, the youth showed me the need for healing in the meantime between what is and what ought to be, the possibility, despite everything, of well-being in the here and now.

Between saving the world and doing nothing, behold, the hula dance!

71

"Because It Calms Our Amygdala"

It was the start of a new semester, and over half the residents who came to the mindfulness group were first-timers. After everyone introduced themselves, I told the new participants why my students and I were there (not to "help," but to learn) and what to expect regarding the structure of the group during the months ahead. I previewed the short mindfulness meditation practices we'd be doing, explaining how conscious breathing engages our parasympathetic nervous system and helps us feel safe.

When I'd finished, Clarisse enthusiastically raised her hand and confidently asserted: "I know what you're talking about. I forgot what it's called, but it's that small thing in the back of your brain that's shaped like an almond."

"You mean the amygdala?"

"Yes! That's it," she exclaimed. "It's where your fight, flight, and freeze comes from."

"It's wonderful that you know that!" I was genuinely delighted. "Where did you learn about the amygdala?"

Clarisse proudly responded: "In one of my trauma therapy sessions."

The following week, I asked the group if anyone remembered why we practice mindfulness meditation. Almost before I'd finished the question, Clarisse's hand shot up. With bright eyes, a beautiful smile, and shimmering self-assurance she said: "Because it calms our amygdala."

Rodney added: "Because it releases serotonin."

Then Jonas said he learned it takes twenty-one minutes for a craving to subside. "If you can distract yourself for twenty-one minutes, the urge will go away." Knowing this was important, he explained, because he struggles with addiction.

It's common to think of meditation as a spiritual practice and healing as an emotional process. But on some level, our spiritual and/or emotional experiences are rooted in the pinkish-grayish matter of our brains. For some residents in the treatment program, understanding the neuroscience of trauma is helpful. Of course, knowing the names of brain components and neurotransmitters doesn't automatically facilitate healing. But recognizing the neurophysiology of distressing emotions reduces the negative judgments associated with them.

These judgments reflect a long history of categorizing internal energies into "vices" and "virtues." In the late sixth century, Pope Gregory the Great identified feelings such as pride, greed, anger, laziness, and lust as "deadly sins," while patience, humility, temperance, charity, and kindness were designated "cardinal virtues."[1] As psychologist and pastor Melinda Contreras-Byrd observes, traditional Christianity's moral schema still informs our notions of "acceptable" and "unacceptable" feelings and their expression, depending on our race, class, and/or gender.[2] For example, women (especially women of color) are not *supposed to* feel or express anger; and men (particularly those in leadership positions) are not *supposed to* feel or show vulnerability. The moral overtones surrounding these expectations reveal their religious underpinnings.

Scientifically speaking, however, emotions are neither "good" nor "bad." From an evolutionary perspective, they are bodily messages that have helped humans adapt to and survive unpredictable circumstances. Anger enables us to assert or defend ourselves. Sadness prompts us to seek connection with others. Disgust cautions us to avoid something potentially harmful. Fear alerts us to possible dangers. Understanding the biological function of distressing feelings enables us to take them less personally and lessens the shame associated with them. Though they don't feel good, unpleasant emotions are not the problem. The problem is the moralizing stories we tell about them—that anger is bad, sadness is dangerous, and so on. These stories encourage us to deny or repress suffering, which prevents us from learning what difficult feelings might teach us.[3]

Understanding the neuroscience of trauma reduces the self-blame, shame, and stigma associated with trauma-induced feeling states and

---

1. *Britannica*, "Seven Deadly Sins" and "Seven Virtues."
2. Contreras-Byrd, "Introduction," 6.
3. McBride, *Wisdom of Your Body*, 109–11, 127.

behaviors (reactivity, hypervigilance, anger, depression, addiction).[4] Knowing the brain's territories and tendencies enables residents in the treatment program to see themselves not as "bad" or harmful delinquents, but as hurting yet resilient survivors. For Clarisse, Rodney, and Jonas, scientific knowledge is an empowering dimension of healing.

Whether we think of healing as a spiritual journey or a process of rewiring neural pathways—or both—justice demands that youth offenders have access to resources, knowledge, and an environment that destigmatizes their struggles so they can tell the truth about them.

---

4. McBride, *Wisdom of Your Body*, 70.

72

"What Have You Been Struggling with Lately?"

TRUTH-TELLING IS AN ESSENTIAL part of both accountability and healing. Whereas accountability requires us be honest about harm we've inflicted, healing demands that we confront the unresolved pain that propelled our harmful actions.

Being honest about how we're hurting goes against the grain of mainstream American culture. The nonstop busyness of our lives (work, school, relationships, housework) makes it difficult to even register inner distress, and commercial culture is constantly selling us stuff we don't need to alleviate discomfort. As Indigenous botanist Robin Wall Kimmerer observes, we've been conditioned to mistake our need for belonging as a desire for belongings.[1] If we turn to social media to meet our genuine desire for connection, we may find ourselves competing with others to see who's the happiest based on pictures of a friend's recent vacation or posts about their children's accomplishments. To keep pace with everyone else's "success," many of us work incessantly, which only further disconnects us from our inner truths, not to mention from each other. We may ask someone, "How's it going?" But rarely do we have the time or energy to listen to an extended answer.

In the mindfulness group, one way we interrupt our cultural habit of ignoring what's really going on within and among us is through the check-ins we do at the start of small group discussions. Everyone has a chance to share what they've been struggling with lately. While there's always the

---

1. Kimmerer, *Braiding Sweetgrass*, 308.

option to "pass," the youth rarely decline the chance to share. Their responses are often succinct, but seldom superficial. Some of the most common include:

- "Anxiety."
- "Depression."
- "Controlling my anger."
- "I just found out that my mom [or other family member] has cancer [or another illness]."
- "One of my friends [or family members] was shot last week."
- "I really miss my siblings."
- "My biggest struggle is being here [i.e., in detention]."
- "I can't sleep."
- "Other kids in the pod are annoying."
- "I keep getting in trouble with the staff."
- "The anniversary of [a family member]'s death is coming up."

The ease with which the residents share what's hard for them bespeaks the benefits of an approach to justice that prioritizes healing. The therapies these kids participate in enable many of them to talk about their problems with a freedom that those of us in the free world seldom feel.

Indeed, the youths' honesty pulls back the curtain on our collective habit of pretending everything's "fine." Without question, "positive thinking" can foster health and healing.[2] But when such thinking is predicated on pretense, it becomes "toxic positivity." My college students taught me that term to describe the pressure they feel to "be happy," "stay positive," "look on the bright side." Compulsory happiness feels oppressive to young people who are grappling with mental health issues. Incarcerated or not, the well-being we seek is not achieved by concealing our distress, but by increasing our capacity to name, embrace, and compost it.

Students in the Religion, Race, and Social Justice course often say they admire—and even envy—the residents' candor. Relatively speaking, my students are among the most privileged young people in America. Yet many of them feel less free than the incarcerated youth we visit when it comes to telling the truth about their lives.

I often leave my conversations with incarcerated youth wishing our culture provided more spaces for truth-telling. Perhaps if privileged people

---

2. Corliss, "Staying Positive," para. 6.

were honest about what we struggle with, we'd be less inclined to avoid the suffering of others. And maybe if we made more of an effort to see and validate the wounds of others, we'd feel less afraid about confronting the painful parts of our own history.

73

"If I Can't Learn to Control My Temper..."

NIKAN TOLD OUR SMALL group that his anger kept getting him in trouble with the staff and other kids in the pod. "If I can't learn to control my temper, I'm gonna be locked up forever."

What is the role of anger in the process of healing?

Remember, "wrath" is one of the "deadly sins." The medieval church fathers' moral concerns about anger are understandable given the violence to which unmanaged ire can lead. Yet demonizing our fury and forcing it underground can contribute to depression and/or explosive aggression.[1] Disparaging our anger also deprives us of the chance to learn from its energy and use it to facilitate healing.

I don't know the details of Nikan's backstory, but I imagine he had good reasons to be mad. Socially disadvantaged, high-potential children don't ask to grow up in poverty. They don't get to choose whether their ancestors were enslaved, raped, and/or forcibly removed. They can't count on access to the resources and opportunities they need to develop their creative potential. Nor can they control whether their bodies will become targets of another unhealed person's aggression. There are good reasons why anger is among the most prevalent emotions with which incarcerated youth struggle.

Even if we grant that wrath itself *isn't* sinful, the question remains what to do with it. Nikan's probably right that he needs to learn to control his temper if he wants to stay out of the system. But, to paraphrase Contreras-Byrd, we can't expect him to bravely turn toward the pain he's survived while

---

1. Busch, "Anger and Depression"; Sahu et al., "Depression Is More."

insisting that he remain calm, composed, and conflict free in the process.[2] He deserves a chance to express and discharge his anger. Helping him develop skills and providing venues to vent his wrath nonviolently would go a long way in delivering the healing justice he needs and deserves.

I thought about the role of anger in the process of healing when Angelica told me about the time she put tampons in the gas tank of the man who had raped her for eight years, starting when she was five.

I confess that I had to stifle an urge to cheer when Angie told me about sabotaging her rapist's gas tank. Still, I don't know whether her retaliatory act facilitated her healing. As Sered suggests, vengeful behavior is an expression of unhealed pain. The desire for revenge is a clarion call for one's suffering to be *seen*.[3] As Martin Luther King Jr. observed, "Violence is the language of the unheard."[4] Healing anger depends on one's wrath being witnessed, validated, and ventilated.

Contreras-Byrd believes that expressing anger can mobilize healing action, especially among people most harmed by systemic injustices. Rage is "an appropriate and psychologically empowering reaction" to the dehumanizing conditions in which Blacks have been forced to live, she says. Not only are Blacks entitled to their fury, but they have a holy mandate to rage against injustices, even if that means taking their rebellion to the streets. Like James Cone, a pioneering Black theologian, Contreras-Byrd understands Black people's furious responses to racial oppression as a manifestation of divine power. Simply put, their rage is *holy*.[5]

Perhaps this holy rage is what Jesus felt when he lost his cool and flipped the tables of money changers and merchants in the temple (Matt 21:12–13). For Christians who spiritualize Jesus' teachings, this disorderly conduct may seem out of character. But the historical Jesus was a fierce critic of both the temple religious leaders, who profited from the sacrifices of the poor, and the Roman Empire, whose economic structure and policies concentrated wealth in the hands of a few, leaving countless people to survive on crumbs. He must have been furious to see the empire's profit-driven ethos infiltrating the sacred space of the temple. Indeed, Jesus' example suggests that, channeled as rebellion against injustice, wrath may be a destructive virtue, or perhaps a redeeming sin.

Either way, Jesus' rage legitimizes anger's power to mobilize social critique, activism, and personal healing. People claiming to follow Jesus must

---

2. Contreras-Byrd, "Black Christians," 18–19.
3. Sered, *Until We Reckon*, 105.
4. Quoted in Wright, "Time for Pious Words," 57.
5. Contreras-Byrd, "Introduction," 7–8; Cone, *Black Theology*, 38.

share the burden of Nikan and Angelica's anger by protesting the brutalizing poverty, sexism, and racism that fueled it. What if we stopped fearing or demonizing the anger of incarcerated youth and read this energy as a prophetic sign that something isn't right? Without sanctioning violence, can we join them in revolting against a society that's failed them?

Kids need opportunities to feel and metabolize their fury in ways that prevent further harm and initiate healing. After Nikan shared, I asked the group, what are some good strategies for dealing with anger? Bao answered, "Working out." Nikan elaborated: "Lifting weights is a good way to get your aggression out, especially when you can't play football." Exercise can be a healthy method for metabolizing anger because it allows the energy of frustration to be released without fanning the flames of hostility. As Ruth King suggests, anger without animosity can catalyze positive change.[6]

I asked a group of residents what anger without hatred looks like. Daryan responded: "When my mom found out about my crime, she was angry with me, and she said so. But she also told me that she still loves me." Daryan's example suggests that love plays a role in healing anger. When someone we love does something that triggers our wrath, our love is bigger than the anger, leaving little room for hatred.

Almost a year after Angelica told me about her vengeful act, I was attempting to use a self-scanning machine at the grocery store, hoping to save time by doing my own check-out. I should have known better. The machine wasn't cooperating, or, more probably, I'd unwittingly entered an invalid code. "See a store attendant," the screen flashed. Looking around, I spotted a young woman wearing a store uniform. She was on the other side of the self-scanning area, so I waved my arms, smiled apologetically, and mouthed the words "Can you help me?" As she walked toward me, my brain became the scanning machine. She looked familiar, but I couldn't remember how I knew her—until she was standing in front of me, grinning widely. It was Angelica.

"Hi, Michelle," she said, still smiling.

"Oh my gosh!" I blurted out, "It's so good to see you!" No longer bound by the detention center's "no touch" policy, I asked if I could give her a hug. She laughed and held out her arms.

I asked her how she's been. "I'm doing very well," she replied reassuringly. She told me she liked her job, which paid well, and that she felt hopeful about her future. "I still think about the mindfulness group," she said. "It helped me learn how to calm myself. Sometimes I still meditate on

---

6. R. King, *Mindful of Race*, 222–24.

my own." Even if she was just being polite, I was thrilled to hear and see that she was doing well.

Angelica easily resolved my problem with the scanner. I wanted to stay all afternoon to hear more about how she was doing, but other shoppers were waiting in line to use the machine. Another hug, and we said goodbye.

What does healing anger look like?

The conflict-avoidant part of me still gravitates to a vision of salvation characterized by eternal peace—a time and place beyond anger and other painful mental, emotional, and spiritual states. But teenagers like Angelica and Nikan are teaching me that there's more to healing than a fantasy of never-ending harmony and reconciliation. There's not just room for rage on the path of healing; there's a need for this redeeming sin.

74

"I Was Thinking That I Probably Need Forgiveness from You"

OVER THE YEARS, THERE have been a handful of residents whose behavior in the mindfulness group was so repeatedly disruptive that, for the sake of the group, I made the difficult decision to ask the director of programming not to let them participate.

Evan was one of those kids. So I was surprised to see him show up one afternoon (the staff hadn't gotten the memo). I worried about what his presence would mean for everyone else. Before we got started, I pulled Evan aside and told him that if his behavior was as distracting as it had been the previous weeks, I'd ask him to leave.

"I'll be good," he said with a grin.

I made sure Evan was in my small group that day. As promised, he was "good" during check-ins. He shared his gratitude and struggles for the week and listened to others do the same. I was second-guessing my original intention to exclude him when Evan picked a discussion card that asked, "Is there anyone from whom you need forgiveness?" Pausing briefly, he looked at me and said: "Actually, I was thinking that I probably need forgiveness from you."

"From *me*?"

"Yeah," he smiled sheepishly, "because I know I've been some trouble in this group."

I appreciated Evan owning and apologizing for his conduct. But his sense that he needed *my* forgiveness felt wrong. After all, the roots of his disruptive behavior—whatever trauma, poverty, and racism he has survived—are my responsibility. Minimally, the need for forgiveness flows both ways.

My conversations with the residents have complicated my views on forgiveness. I used to think it was the alpha and omega of healing *for everyone*. I was raised on the teachings of Jesus, who preached that if you forgive others, God will forgive you (Matt 6:14). Jesus instructed his followers to forgive "seventy-seven times," implying that mercy should be unlimited (Matt 18:21–22). And he walked the talk—famously forgiving those who crucified him, saying they didn't know what they were doing (Luke 23:34). As a graduate student, I was drawn to Martin Luther King Jr.'s take on forgiveness. For him, forgiveness doesn't mean denying or disguising someone's harmful action; it means that that action is no longer a barrier in the relationship. King suggested that to withhold forgiveness is to withhold love, which corrupts a person's own soul, distorts their personality, and inhibits the wholeness they seek.[1]

I still believe that pardoning someone and letting go of anger, resentment, and hurt can be important dimensions of healing. But the youths' diverging views and experiences illuminate the complexity of forgiveness on the path to wholeness. Some explicitly recognize their need for absolution not just from their victims but from their own families. "What I did was stupid, and the victim didn't deserve it," Bernie said. "But I also hurt my mom. I need her forgiveness too." Others affirm the need for *self*-forgiveness: "I forgive myself," Tauri said, "because I've survived so much." And some struggle with the vulnerability surrounding forgiveness. Trey wrote:

> I don't want nobody to forgive me for the mistakes I made. Did too much to even want forgiveness. I wouldn't want the offer. I can't forgive because that's not me . . . I don't want nobody to forgive me so I'm not forgiving.

Ironically, Trey's refusal to accept, offer, or even desire forgiveness involves a recognition of the severity of the harm he's caused, which bodes well for accountability. That said, Trey describes this refusal as rooted in his character ("that's not me"), rather than the accumulation of pain that's gone unseen, unvalidated, and thus unhealed.

Maybe Trey declined forgiveness because he intuited what poet David Whyte observes: whether accepting or offering pardon, forgiveness is not just hard but heartbreaking because it requires us to return to "the original wound." To forgive "is to close in on the nature of the hurt itself." Indeed, the healing relief of forgiveness comes from accepting our pain, reimagining

---

1. King Jr., *Strength to Love*, 50–53.

our relationship to it, and "assum[ing] a larger identity than the person who was first hurt."[2] Whyte acknowledges that sometimes, forgiveness may not be possible—or even desirable. He likens the part of us that refuses to forgive to our body's immune system: the part that's tasked with remembering threats to our well-being, and even our life; the part nature designed to protect us from future attacks; the part that's "not actually meant to forget."[3] Even as I yearn to expand my own capacity to forgive, I suspect that Trey had good reasons for not sharing this desire.

Forgiveness can be tricky in a culture where it often feels compulsory—more like an expectation than a gift. As we've seen, prioritizing forgiveness over repentance can lead to a "cheap grace" that demands little from the responsible party. Moreover, while forgiveness can free us from the pain of the past, its absence doesn't mean we can't move on. Incarcerated youth are teaching me that there are *multiple* pathways for healing. Forgiveness is one of them. But so is the holy rage Angelica expressed by putting tampons in her rapist's gas tank. So is the nurturing Jeremy showed my dog. And so is the empathy Trey expressed in another part of his writing project. Asked to describe a time when he noticed someone else's suffering, he wrote, "When my brother broke his foot, I damn near felt it in my foot." Some youth may refuse to walk the path of forgiveness, but this refusal doesn't mean they're incapable of healing.

Instead of jumping to conclusions about juvenile offenders who find it impossible to offer or accept forgiveness, we would do well to focus on our own need for forgiveness. King keenly observed that forgiveness is not just an act but a "permanent attitude,"[4] and I think the same can be said about *the need for forgiveness* among people with privilege. Whites in particular must adopt a "permanent attitude" of *needing* forgiveness both for the historical atrocities our ancestors have inflicted on people of color and for the subtle and not-so-subtle ways we continue to recycle that shameful legacy.

To recognize that we/privileged people need forgiveness is *not* to suggest that we're entitled to it. That would be like expecting a gift from someone you or your ancestors stole from. To cultivate an attitude of needing forgiveness we must soften our hearts enough to empathize with the anger, hurt, and resentment many minoritized people carry, to see these feelings as *valid*, rather than something they should "get over" so we can feel more comfortable. Adopting a "permanent attitude" of needing without expecting

---

2. Whyte, *Consolations*, 77–78.
3. Whyte, *Consolations*, 77.
4. King Jr., *Strength to Love*, 40.

forgiveness would reduce our defensiveness when someone expresses the pain that racial oppression has created in their life.

Recognizing our ongoing need for forgiveness is not about groveling in guilt; it's about examining how our mental, emotional, and spiritual habits have unwittingly contributed to the suffering of those on society's margins. In the work of racial justice, self-examination doubles as an opportunity for personal growth and collective healing. "When we cause harm," Sered reminds us, "we are . . . damaged by it in ways we rarely talk about."[5] Perhaps one reason why many White Christians, including church leaders, are reluctant to talk or teach about the sin of White supremacy is because this legacy feels shameful. But, as Ruth King suggests, feeling ashamed is not nearly as helpful as interrupting and dismantling unjust systems.[6] Transforming racial oppression requires us to think and act in ways that respect the lives of people of color, redistribute the wealth and privileges we've accumulated at their expense (through reparations), and teach our children the less flattering facts of American history. Whites must pursue this reckoning, King suggests, not just for the sake of those suffering under the weight of White supremacy, but for our own freedom.[7]

---

5. Sered, *Until We Reckon*, 125.
6. R. King, *Mindful of Race*, 198.
7. R. King, *Mindful of Race*, 197–201.

75

"I'm Thankful to Be Here and Not under the Ground in the Cemetery"

During the check-in part of the mindfulness group, everyone's invited to share something they're grateful for. The youth almost always have something to say, which is mind-boggling when you consider what they've been through. Their responses tend to be brief, but sincere. Among their most common reasons for gratitude:

- A parent or caretaker who hasn't given up on them
- Knowing that they'll be getting out soon
- A chance to Zoom with a family member
- A recent or anticipated furlough
- A visit from someone they love
- Being in the treatment program

What role does gratitude play in the process of healing for incarcerated youth?

For millennia, religious traditions have encouraged their members to be thankful, even—and perhaps especially—in the worst of times. When life feels relentlessly hard, consciously appreciating something or someone can bring relief, reminding us that suffering isn't the only story. Brother David Steindl-Rast, a Zen-influenced Benedictine monk, emphasizes the connection between gratitude and happiness. By "happiness," he doesn't mean the pleasures and satisfactions that come and go, depending on external factors. The kind of happiness that gratitude cultivates is a deep sense of aliveness and well-being that incorporates—rather than transcends, eradicates, or conquers—sadness and struggle.[1]

Contemporary science validates the life-giving role of gratitude in humans' search for wholeness. A report that summarized over 270 studies on thankfulness confirms that people experience greater mental and physical health, social connection, vocational success, and relationship satisfaction when they "live gratefully." Thankful kids do better in school and are less likely to get into fights.[2] One study found that teenagers who did short gratitude exercises over the course of one month experienced increased satisfaction and motivation in their lives.[3]

Both traditional spiritual wisdom and contemporary science resonate with my own experience of gratitude's power to facilitate happiness and healing. But when I compare my gratitude inventory with the list of things for which the youth are thankful, it's clear that my grateful feelings mirror my privileges. Spiritually inclined people who are financially comfortable often describe our privileges as *blessings*. But doesn't that description suggest God plays favorites? Often the "blessings" for which I'm thankful are not just spiritual gifts, but social advantages. Moreover, my conscious feelings of appreciation don't actively challenge systemic injustices. What prevents my gratitude from deepening the sense of entitlement I've been conditioned to feel? How can I be grateful without ignoring the plight of people who don't appear to be so "blessed"?

These questions surfaced when Roshaun—the youth who showed me the picture of himself standing over his best friend's grave—shared that he was "thankful to be here and not under the ground in the cemetery."

I used to think of gratitude as an unassailable virtue, feeling, and practice. But now it seems just as complicated as forgiveness because of the inequity it exposes. Moreover, like forgiveness, thankfulness becomes especially problematic when it's obligatory. Though I tell the youth they can opt out of the gratitude sharing, what if they feel pressured to participate? What if the invitation to express thanks sends a message that they *should* feel thankful for *something*—and that there's something wrong with them if they don't?

Ever since Roshaun's comment, I've wrestled with the ethics of inviting participants in the mindfulness group to identify something for which they feel grateful. For now, this invitation is still part of our weekly check-ins

---

1. Steindl-Rast, *Essential Writings*, 40–41.
2. Greater Good Science Center, "Gratitude"; S. Allen, "Science of Gratitude," 1–2.
3. Armenta et al., "Satisfied Yet Striving."

because most of the youth seem to welcome the chance to consciously appreciate some aspect of their life—both in spite of and because of the adversities they face. Nonetheless, I now approach gratitude with a deeper appreciation for its complexity as a dimension of healing and with a clearer sense that my "blessings" are also responsibilities.

76

"Those Who Cannot Be Redeemed Have No Place in a Civilized Society"

NOT EVERYONE SHARES MY assumption that youth offenders need and deserve the chance to heal. I was reminded of this when I read the responses to an opinion piece about a case involving two Minnesota teenagers accused of murdering the twenty-three-year-old mother of a one-year-old. This horrific act was premeditated. The case received considerable publicity, partly because the state's left-leaning governor made the unusual move to take it out of the hands of an elected county attorney, who had planned to prosecute the fifteen- and seventeen-year-old defendants as juveniles, and give it to the state's attorney general, who promised a more punitive response: trying the boys as adults.

The author of the opinion piece, a law professor and senior district judge, acknowledged that "there is no good solution for such a miserable situation."[1] Then he explained why harsher punishments don't promote the accountability that victims and their families deserve. He called for justice that supports *both* public safety *and* humans' "capacity for healing and growth."[2] A considerable majority of the 126 responses to the article rejected the restorative approach to justice the judge advocated and doubled down on need for punishment. Here's a small sampling of those reactions:

- "Murderers should receive life sentences and no rehab is needed."

1. Peterson, "Judge," para. 4.
2. Peterson, "Judge," para. 21.

- "Rehabilitation is not possible . . . protecting the public with long prison sentences is all we have."
- "Lock [murderers] up for life. They forfeited any hope for redemption when they killed someone. And that includes teenager killers."
- "The Murderer should be locked up until they're carried out of prison and buried."
- "Those who cannot be redeemed have no place in a civilized society."[3]

Some of the pro-punishment comments argue that perpetrators are *criminals*, not *victims*. Many insist on prioritizing public safety above all else, suggesting that the best way to prevent recidivism is to keep offenders locked up for life. As the comments above make plain, several authoritatively declare that some wrongdoers are simply beyond redemption.

Reading these responses, I understood why even a left-leaning governor of a state known for its "liberal" sensibilities used his power to ensure a more stringent response to the boys' heinous act. Appearing "soft on crime" could jeopardize his own (and his party's) chances to remain in power. This pressure underscores the pivotal role ordinary people can play in turning the tide of our culture—and its justice system—in a less punitive direction by supporting policies that promote public safety through healing and restorative practices, rather than vengeance, shame, and banishment from "civilized society."

But do we believe that no one is beyond redemption?

This is a moral question—the kind no amount of data can answer absolutely, which may be why social science researchers and policy makers tend to avoid focusing on it. But whether we agree that a person's divine humanity cannot be erased—even if it becomes temporarily eclipsed—will impact the kind of justice youth offenders receive. Because politicians who shape that justice are listening, whether or not we speak our values.

---

3. Comments responding to Peterson, "Judge."

77

"All of Them Have Some Type of Involvement with the Juvenile Justice System"

THE IDEA THAT SOME teenagers are beyond redemption runs counter to the youth justice system's mission of rehabilitation. In the wake of the "law and order" decades, many scholars, professionals, and activists have sought to revive that mission with strategies that lighten the juvenile system's footprint on the lives of the youth it serves. These strategies include: 1) *diversion* for kids who don't pose a threat to public safety, and 2) *community-based programs* for nonviolent youth offenders. Both represent promising possibilities for healing justice.

"Diversion" keeps kids out of formal processing and confinement by using less punitive consequences to hold them accountable. Methods range from "warn and release" (e.g., parents, guardians, school staff, and others address the problematic behavior), to restorative justice mediation, to interventions involving intensive treatment services and check-ins with the court system.[1] Compared to formal processing through juvenile courts, research suggests that diversion *increases* public safety and supports educational/vocational achievements, while *reducing* recidivism, racial disparities, aggression, and future justice involvement.[2]

---

1. Development Services Group, "Diversion," 1; Annie E. Casey Foundation, "What Is Diversion," para. 1.

2. Mendel, "Protect and Redirect," para. 1; Development Services Group, "Alternatives to Detention," para. 1.

Community-based programs are another alternative to the carceral system for court-involved kids. These programs replace locked correctional facilities with a network of residential and nonresidential services that provide therapeutic resources. For kids who are allowed to stay with their families, community-based programs offer wraparound services to support their healthy development and prevent further justice involvement.[3]

The case for community-based alternatives is compelling. The alternatives are typically more cost effective and less disruptive to a young person's education and their family and community relationships. There is evidence that community-based programs lower youths' aggressive and delinquent behavior, improve their well-being, and increase their chances for finding jobs, which in turn decreases the likelihood of recidivism.[4]

Many experts point to Missouri as a model of success for community-based youth justice. Several decades ago, the state replaced its juvenile prison system with a well-staffed network of smaller "treatment centers." These residential facilities provide a homelike atmosphere for justice-involved youth (e.g., family-style meals, personal clothing options, sleeping quarters that are more like bedrooms than cells). While they vary in their level of security, the centers provide trauma-informed treatment that aims to develop residents' prosocial skills and support their educational progress and vocational training. Facilities encourage parent-family engagement (kids are placed near their communities) and close, caring relationships between residents, their peers, and well-trained staff. The supportive quality of these relationships motivates cooperative behavior, reducing the need to rely on punitive methods. As the director of a New York facility that adopted the Missouri model stated, "If I can't talk to [the youth], I'm in the wrong business."[5] Recidivism rates in Missouri are impressive: only 6.6 percent of youth reenter the youth system or go to adult prison within three years.[6]

Several states are currently adopting policies that favor healing over punishment for justice-involved kids. Lawmakers in Minnesota propose to create a new office of restorative justice for youth that aims to enhance public safety while reducing court involvement and confinement.[7] California plans to permanently close its youth prisons and implement a system

3. Kraut, "Community Based Alternatives," para. 2; National Juvenile Justice Network, "Keep Youth at Home."

4. McCarthy et al., "Future of Youth Justice," 22; Mendel, *No Place for Kids*; Orendain et al., "Juvenile Confinement Exacerbates," 5–6.

5. Bernstein, *Burning Down the House*, 147–150.

6. McCarthy et al., "Future of Youth Justice," 18, 24–27; Mendel, *Why Youth Incarceration Fails*.

7. Serres and Sawyer, "Minnesota Lawmakers," para. 2.

of community-based services. Admittedly, transitioning to less punitive approaches will not be easy.[8] But reducing the justice system's footprint on young offenders' lives and providing them resources for healing lessens the chances of adult incarceration.

Recalling his work as a county attorney, Judge Johnnie McDaniels noticed a pipeline from youth to adult incarceration: "As I stood in the courtroom prosecuting young people between the ages of 18 and 21, one of the first dynamics that I absolutely encountered was, all of them have some type of [prior] involvement with the juvenile justice system."[9] McDaniels concludes that if we want to promote public safety and address mass incarceration, we must help youth offenders heal.

---

8. Reséndez and Washburn, "Crisis before Closure," paras. 1–3.
9. McDaniels, "Why Changing Juvenile Corrections," 1:38.

78

"You Can't Be Happy If You Have PTSD"

Keesha read the prompt on her discussion card: "What does happiness mean to you?" She frowned, as if disagreeing with the question, and responded, "You can't be happy when you have PTSD. Because there's no cure for that."

One of my students in the group, who is in the army, offered another view. "Actually," he said, "I've seen some of my peers in the military—war veterans—be cured of PTSD."

"Well," Keesha replied, "I don't think it's possible for me."

"I'm no expert on PTSD," I said, "but maybe it's helpful to distinguish between 'curing' and 'healing.'"

"What do you mean?" Keesha sounded curious.

I told her that I'd learned about the difference between curing and healing when I was doing research in the field of disability studies.

"From what I understand, some people with physical or cognitive disabilities resist able-bodied people's obsession with trying to *cure* them—both because a lot of them have conditions that can't be cured and because the pressure to be cured assumes there's something wrong or shameful about them or their bodies. Whereas curing is about eliminating disease and/or making you 'normal,' healing is about learning to manage and metabolize suffering that may never entirely go away. With healing, you're not fixated on getting rid of something you can't control—for example, PTSD. Instead, you put your creative energy into projects and relationships that are meaningful and life giving. With healing, your so-called abnormality—whatever mental or physical challenge you struggle with—is one of the things you bring to the world. It's part—but not all—of what you makes you *you*."¹

I thought about Keesha later that evening when I heard one of my favorite Indigo Girls songs: "Happy in the Sorrow Key," by Amy Ray.² The lyrics call attention to the fortitude and fragility of life within and around us, bearing witness to the tension between our humanity and divinity and how sorrow changes us. Ray's song gives us language for naming the complexity of healing for those of us who struggle to integrate grief that may never go away into the wholeness and holiness of who we are.

---

1. See Lelwica, *Shameful Bodies*, ch. 5.
2. See https://genius.com/Indigo-girls-happy-in-the-sorrow-key-lyrics.

79

"Which Wolf Will You Feed?"

COMPLEXITY PERVADES THE MIGRATION incarcerated youth struggle to make from the person they were and are to the person they want to be. One afternoon, Darius asked me: "Is it possible for me to have both violence and calm inside myself?"

What a beautiful question!

"I think it's not only possible," I responded, "but your ability to notice these different energies inside you suggests that you're developing the capacity for introspection and self-knowledge. Now, the challenge is: Which wolf will you feed?"

Darius nodded and smiled.

The wolf-feeding question was a reference to a story I'd shared with the mindfulness group the previous week. In it, a Native American boy asks his grandfather about the two wolves hanging from the necklace he's wearing. "One wolf represents the capacity for love, harmony, kindness, and peace," the grandfather tells the boy. "The other symbolizes greed, arrogance, self-pity, and vengeance." He goes on to elaborate that the two wolves are constantly fighting each other inside each of us.

"Grandfather," the boy asks, "which wolf will win?"

The wise grandfather replies: "The one you feed."

This story circulates widely in popular books and on the internet. Perhaps the reason it resonates with so many people is that it affirms both the complexity and the agency in each of us. Like Darius, each of us harbors multiple propensities. Some create pain for ourselves and others. Some foster serenity and well-being. Healing requires us to become intimate with our interior landscape, to get to know the various wolves that roam the territories of our heart so we can be intentional about the one we feed.

Yet choosing which wolf to feed can be more complicated than the story suggests. Victor Frankl is often credited with an illuminating observation regarding human agency: "Between stimulus and response there is a space. In that space is our power to choose our response. In our response lies our growth and our freedom." Agency is a crucial aspect of healing. But the decisions we make are inevitably shaped by the question our bodies are constantly asking: "Is it dangerous or safe?"[1] The trauma the youth I've met have survived makes this question urgent because toxic stress shortens the space between "stimulus and response." Not surprisingly, many of them struggle to feel inwardly spacious and safe enough to deliberately choose which wolf they'll feed. We can't just tell Darius to make better choices. Healing justice requires people with the power to do so to create the social conditions in which he can feel safe.

This last point may seem obvious, redundant, and impossible. After all, if we knew how to construct a society in which no child was endangered, wouldn't we have done so by now?

It's easy to get discouraged in the work of healing the social body. For many of us, "accepting the things we cannot change" often means resigning ourselves to an unjust status quo. But like Darius, privileged people have to decide which wolf we'll feed: The one telling us that nothing we do will make a difference? Or the one that emboldens us to do whatever we can to create a culture in which Darius can feel safe enough to heal?

Considering the wolves of apathy and agency raises questions about faith. Many Christians operate as though "faith" were simply a matter of what you *believe*. In this paradigm, being a "person of faith" means subscribing to a series of propositions—for example, agreeing that the Bible is the "word of God," that Jesus is "God's only Son," that his death "washed away your sins." This belief-centered, doctrinally oriented approach to faith corresponds to otherworldly visions of redemption and healing. Having the "correct" convictions in this imperfect life becomes an entrance ticket to the heavenly hereafter. That many Christians equate faith with doctrinal belief explains the tragic gap between the love they generally profess and some Christians' lack of loving actions toward people who are suffering and/or different than them.

Jesus admonished his disciples to feed the wolf of loving action—to embody their faith by clothing the naked, feeding the hungry, welcoming the stranger, caring for the sick, sheltering the unhoused, visiting the

---

1. Menakem, *My Grandmother's Hands*, 6.

imprisoned (Matt 25:35–45). The kind of faith Jesus advocated and practiced had more the quality of a verb than a noun. This faith reflected his spiritual roots, particularly the Jewish idea of redemption as the work of *tikkun olam*: repairing the world.

In *Against Purity*, philosopher Alexis Shotwell cautions us against getting stuck in perfectionistic visions of world repair. Fantasies of a flawless future are illusory, and even our best efforts to heal the social body are not free from complicity with the injustices we seek to transform.[2] Still, both despite and because of suffering that seems insurmountable, those of us with privilege have a responsibility to give youth offenders the justice they deserve—the kind that, in the words of Davis, is about "getting well," not "getting even."[3]

Which wolf will we feed?

---

2. Shotwell, *Against Purity*, 4–5.
3. Davis, *Little Book of Race*, 14.

80

"No One Ever Taught Me How to Love Myself"

THREE RESIDENTS AND I waited as one of my students reflected on the prompt: "When do you show up as your best self?"

"It's funny," she said, "but I think I'm my best self when I'm rooted in self-love. That's something I've been working on lately. Because I don't think I can be any good to anyone else if I can't love myself."

Jordan went next: "It's pretty much the same for me. But no one ever taught me about self-love, so I feel like I'm having to learn it now, and I'm already eighteen. I think learning to love myself is going to require me to forgive myself." The rest of us waited to see if he wanted to say more, but he passed the card to me.

"At this stage in my life," I said, "what self-love looks like is authenticity. I've wasted too much energy seeking other people's approval. It's exhausting. And you lose touch with who you really are."

Lamar said he shows up with his best self when he's helping others. "That's something I like to do. It makes me happy to make others happy."

Tyrell was last to share. "I'm my best self when I'm keeping it real. That's when I like—or love—myself most. But it's hard to do that here in detention. Actually, it's hard on the outside too. People expect you to act a certain way."

On my drive home that afternoon, I thought about the needs for self-love, helping others, and "keeping it real" that the youth, my student, and I identified. In different ways, these needs underscore the importance of self-care as a dimension of healing. Caring for yourself is an expression of self-love that provides the energy you need to care about others and the courage you need to "keep it real."

Understandably, some social justice advocates are suspicious of calls for self-care as a dimension of healing. Co-opted by commercial wellness culture, "self-care" has been reduced to juice cleanses, going to a spa, getting a manicure, or some other luxury activity or product that caters to privileged people's personal well-being and sense of entitlement. But psychiatrist Pooja Lakshmin says that's not what self-care really means. Based on clinical research and her work with clients, she understands self-care as an internal, introspective journey in which we strive to align our lives with our core values through our daily decisions and the relationships we cultivate with ourselves and others. The self-care guidelines she advocates—setting healthy boundaries, practicing self-compassion, identifying our deepest values, and using our power wisely—aim to empower us to heal ourselves and the unjust systems we inhabit.[1]

The problem isn't self-care, but that people with privilege tend to hoard healing and self-care for ourselves. Our lives are too deeply interconnected for this hoarding habit to foster anyone's well-being. Lamar recognized what research suggests: happiness is *relational*.[2] Our own contentment is inextricably tied to the well-being of others. So is our healing. Disregarding other people's pain trains us to avoid what's unresolved in ourselves. Indeed, the psychological distress affluent people commonly experience is often rooted in the emptiness and isolation that come from pursuing our private goals, comforts, and interests without concern for others.

Liberating ourselves and supporting the freedom of others are not separate journeys. When we're imprisoned in our own little silos of striving and stress, pain and self-pity, we're less inclined to care about what others are going through. But when we feel sufficiently nurtured, we're more likely to have the bandwidth to be present to the hurt in ourselves and others. Practiced with attention to life's fundamental interdependence, self-care provides a foundation for healing ourselves and repairing the world. As dimensions of healing justice, self-care and community care are two sides of the same coin. They are how we love and honor the divine humanity we share. And, as the womanist poet-writer-activist Alice Walker reminds us, "Anything we love can be saved."[3]

---

1. Lakshmin, *Real Self-Care*.

2. Titova and Sheldon, "Happiness Comes"; for a summary of findings from the Harvard Happiness Study, see Mineo, "Good Genes."

3. A. Walker, *Anything We Love*.

81

"When We Were Dancing"

BEFORE SPENDING TIME WITH incarcerated youth, I didn't notice the various dimensions of healing (self-care, nurturing, anger, etc.), each offering a kind of entry point on the path of wholeness. Nor did I fully appreciate the nonlinear and sometimes transitory quality of this transformative journey.

In a small group of female residents, Callie shared that her highlight of the week was "when we were dancing." The other girls erupted with laughter. They clearly remembered the scene Callie was recalling.

Speaking through giggles, Ella explained: "The other night, we had a dance contest in the pod."

"No one won," Maggie clarified, still laughing.

"I think we all won," Callie suggested as their giggling continued.

If the dance contest they were describing was even a fraction as fun as their collective memory of it, it must have been a very good time!

Later in that same conversation, Callie picked a discussion card that asked: "What are your best qualities?" She said she couldn't think of any. By then, the mood had shifted. Callie looked like she might cry. I asked the other girls what they saw as Callie's best qualities.

"I like how you're spontaneous," Ella said. "I mean, without you, we'd never have had the dance contest."

Callie looked up and briefly smiled.

Maggie said she admired Callie's ability to sleep through anything.

"Yeah," Ella concurred. "You slept until two in the afternoon last Sunday. That's impressive!"

Callie responded that the reason she sleeps so long is that she's up all night with nightmares. "Just last week, I dreamt I was shot in the head four times."

I can only imagine the trauma behind Callie's nightmares. If her ability to dance and laugh isn't a testament to the resilience of the human spirit, I don't know what is. Even in confinement, in the makeshift community of girls in the pod, Callie and others improvised a way for their spirits to be free, a way to momentarily transcend their suffering. The delight their impromptu dance contest generated didn't cure whatever trauma was preventing Callie from sleeping. But that doesn't make the deep happiness the girls experienced less valuable or real. Joy is a dimension of healing, even when it's fleeting.

Growing up immersed in church culture, I sang hymns and recited prayers that repeatedly described salvation as "eternal" or "everlasting." Without realizing it, this forever-and-ever language fostered my expectation that happiness and healing are—or ought to be—permanent states. But the expectation for never-ending bliss sets you up for perpetual disappointment—at least if you're if interested in serenity and wholeness in this ever-changing, far from perfect life.

In her memoir, *Bipolar Faith*, womanist Monica Coleman explores a different kind of "salvation," one that highlights the embodied, impermanent, complex, and imperfect nature of healing. She recounts moments of profound joy punctuating her enduring experience of depression—an abiding sense of grief she describes as a "lifelong companion."[1] This "river of sadness" is at least as old as her great grandfather, who died by suicide, and as young as her twenty-one-year-old body, raped by an ex-boyfriend.[2] Sometimes she's able to answer the "What's wrong with me?" feeling that shadows her depression[3] with an intuitive wisdom that says, "There's nothing wrong with me."[4] Sometimes she exercises to generate endorphins. Sometimes she dances. Coleman further composts her heartbreak by creating for others what she needed for herself: a guidebook to support survivors of sexual violence (*The Dinah Project*). She recognizes the complicated mix of joy and sorrow that pervades her life in the image of Jesus entering Jerusalem, weeping as enthusiastic crowds surround and celebrate him.[5] Eventually,

---

1. Coleman, *Bipolar Faith*, 287.
2. Coleman, *Bipolar Faith*, 260.
3. Coleman, *Bipolar Faith*, 67.
4. Coleman, *Bipolar Faith*, 340.
5. Coleman, *Bipolar Faith*, 106–7.

Coleman realizes that sometimes it's "okay not to be okay."[6] Refusing to separate brokenness from wholeness, happiness from unhappiness, physical well-being from political activism from spiritual growth doesn't resolve her suffering, but it brings some relief.

Coleman's journey illustrates the provisional, nonlinear, incomplete quality of healing. Her story reminds us that the process of "getting better" is not a before-and-after photograph—the "after" being a perfect version of you. Healing is an ongoing commitment to turn towards what feels painful and/or unredeemable in ourselves and to transform our hurt so we don't dump it on others. Precisely because this path can be uneven and messy, we may need to dance every now and then.

---

6. Coleman, *Bipolar Faith*, 167.

82

"It's a Huge Slap in the Face to Enjoy the Little Things"

For kids in the mindfulness group, the dynamics between suffering, joy, and resilience overlap with another dimension of healing: creativity. In response to a prompt that asked, "When do you feel most brave?," Adrian, a self-described artist, replied: "When I'm standing in front of a big blank canvas that I'm about to draw or paint something on."

The connections between artistry and healing are evident in the youths' creative writing projects. During the writing workshop, several of the Black boys wrote rap music, which they proudly performed for us—together! Here's a section of a rap Drake composed about his favorite auntie, who tragically passed away:

> I love you and miss you, I hope you doin better,
> If you thinking about me I'm trying to get my life together.
> It hurts me every day known that we separate,
> But distance don't matter cuz love is forever.
> Since you've been gone I've met a lot of new faces,
> But I'd give all of it up just to trade places.
> To get one more day w/you I'd do one hundred years,
> And do a hundred more for everyday you were still here.
> If you're thinking about my mom she's doing good
> With everyone but you I still feel misunderstood.
> I got unresolved feelings that won't never change,
> I know you disappointed with the ways I tried to cope with pain.
> They on the outside lookin in my tinted windowpane,
> I lost the one I loved the most now I can't feel the same.

Not all the creativity expressed in residents' writing project materialized as songs. Asked to describe their favorite time of day, a girl who adopted the pen name "Scarlet" created this lucid scene:

> The stars are getting ready to shine and twinkle in the eyes of stargazers later that night. There's the procrastinator who waited till last minute to mow the grass, and a family. Brought together by the sizzling sirloins on the grill. Kids are laughing and running to get home before the street lights glow . . . I look at and just pay attention to the here and now, pay attention to every single detail, the color painted in the sky, the blades of green grass floating in the wind . . . all of the little things that are so easy to ignore in a world that's always moving so fast, it's a huge slap in the face to enjoy the little things.

Whatever form they take, opportunities for creative self-expression generate the transformative energy of healing, including the transcendent joy that's available, if only fleetingly, when we "pay attention to the here and now" and "enjoy the little things."

83

"I'd Create a Program for Kids like Me"

IT WOULD BE so easy for incarcerated youth to stop dreaming of a life in which they could develop their creative potential and put it to good use in the world. Luckily, most of the kids I've met haven't abandoned this aspiration. Neither should we if we want them to heal.

Understandably, some residents at the detention center define their dreams in relation to their current situation. Responding to a prompt that asked, "If you could change one thing in the world, what would it be?," Shaquille answered, "Better food for kids in jail," and Darius added, "Get kids like us decent lawyers." In his creative writing project, Trey wrote about his "dream of being free . . . I would love getting out [of detention]."

Often, however, the youth aspire to something beyond their immediate needs. In the same piece of writing, Trey wrote, "I would love leaving the hood with all my boys." One of the first things Moira told me when I met her was "I want to be a lawyer, because I like to argue." Listening to her describe the educational inequities she witnessed having gone to schools both on and off the reservation, how alcohol is poisoning her community, and how she's tired of seeing Indigenous women mysteriously disappear, I had no doubt that Moira has both the intelligence and the compassion needed to be an effective attorney. She did note, however, that if she decides not to go to law school, she wants to study botany.

The future dreams the youth have shared during the mindfulness group are diverse. Some of their vocational aspirations include:

- Tattoo artist

- Poet
- Plumber
- Trauma therapist
- Astrologer
- Truck driver
- Rap musician
- Barber
- Nurse
- Welder
- History teacher
- Motivational speaker

Such dreams may motivate the youth to do the hard work of healing. Yet meaningfully pursuing these ambitions depends on their ability to do that work—and that ability requires more than willpower and grit. Justice-involved teenagers need moral support, mentors, and therapeutic resources that enable them to develop the emotional stability and skills they'll need to weather the challenges surrounding any goal that's worth pursuing.

One of the most common aspirations I hear from the residents is the desire to use what they've learned from their adversities to benefit kids like themselves. Listen to how a group of three boys responded to the prompt "What kind of job would you enjoy doing so much that you'd do it even if you didn't get paid?"

"That's easy," Tyrell replied. "I'd create a program for kids like me."

"Heeeey," Lamar intervened, "that's what I was gonna say."

"Me too," Jalen added. "If I could do any job, it would be to work with kids like me, to help them stay out of trouble so they wouldn't have to go through what I'm going through, so they wouldn't end up in jail like me."

When I asked the boys to elaborate on how they would help kids like themselves "stay out of trouble," Tyrell said he would "organize activities for them, so they have things to do besides running the deep streets."

"I wouldn't just *tell* them to stop getting in trouble," Jalen added. "Because when someone tells me what I should do, it just makes me want to rebel even more."

"So, what would you say to kids in your program?" I asked.

"I wouldn't give advice," he reiterated. "I guess I'd just share my story."

The contemplative-activist Catholic priest Richard Rohr observes, "*If we do not transform our pain, we will most assuredly transmit it.*"[1] Tyrell, Jalen, and Lamar's shared dream of mentoring "kids like me" expresses both confidence in their capacity to heal and a vision for how to stop the cycle of hurting kids. Their aspiration also reveals their sense of what was missing in their own backstories and an understanding that they weren't destined to end up in jail. Ultimately, their shared longing to create a program for kids like themselves points to their desire to compost their suffering into empathetic action that helps heal their communities. Both despite and because of everything they've survived, these boys understand Sered's insight that "healed people heal people."[2]

---

1. Rohr, *Spring within Us*, 120–21; emphasis original.
2. Sered, *Until We Reckon*, 227.

84

"You Can't Trust Anyone until You Trust Yourself"

As a college professor, I value intellectual knowledge. But when it comes to transforming suffering, academic learning will only take you so far. Because healing is an embodied journey, *holistic* knowledge—wisdom borne from lived experience—tends to be more useful in the process of transforming pain.

I don't recall why Tyrell and I ended up in a one-on-one discussion, but I remember the conversation well. It started with a prompt: "Who is the biggest 'devil's advocate' in your life?"

Looking perplexed, Tyrell asked, "What's that mean?" He'd never heard the expression "devil's advocate." I explained that the term describes someone who challenges your beliefs in a way that requires you to clarify or defend them.

Tyrell said his biggest devil's advocates are his own self-doubts and fears. "What I mean is, part of me knows I can make it out of the deep streets and become the kind of person who helps kids like me. Then there's another part that doesn't believe I can do this. This is the part of me that thinks I'll end up like my dad."

We both laughed at the magnitude of the next prompt, given that we had only a few minutes left to discuss it: "What does love mean to you?"

Tyrell didn't waste any time answering. "I'll break bread with anyone. Know what I mean?"

"I love that image," I replied. "Say more."

"I mean, I love humanity. I love everyone, so I'll break bread with anyone. *But*," he continued, "that doesn't mean I trust everyone. The deeper kind of love is for people I really trust. But you can't trust anyone until you trust yourself. Just like you have to love yourself before you can love others, the same is true with trust."

While not every youth who attends the mindfulness group articulates such wisdom, many express the kind of knowledge born from experience that can facilitate healing. Several residents shared their hard-won life lessons in their writing projects. Mae wrote about self-respect:

> Self-respect isn't something someone else can give to you . . . It's something that takes time and courage. Some people think self-respect is based on how you act, and that's right, but that's only half of it. Self-respect is when you . . . don't base your self-esteem on what another person says to you. You base it on what you truly think.

On the topic of empathy, Moira wrote: "Be kind, you never know what other people are going through." She believes that kindness is contagious: "Being kind to someone can make that person be kind to someone else."

The youths' writing projects were full of various seeds of wisdom. Asked what advice they would give to a ten-year-old version of themselves, they responded:

- "If you need to calm down, you can count your inhales and exhales."
- "Strength comes from weakness . . . from using all of your experiences, hardships, and losses and letting them empower you, and encourage you to live better, and stronger . . . nobody can take away your strength."
- "You should never say 'I love you' without meaning it."
- "Don't let people get under your skin."
- "If you happen to get abused, you get as far as you can away from them."
- "Be strong for any circumstances."
- "Be yourself."
- "Push yourself to a higher standard in life."
- "Don't let your pain consume you."
- "Whatever you're going through will pass and you'll be stronger from it."

- "Keep yo head up stay strong and don't give up on anything, you gone be successful don't let anyone tell you different bro."
- "Don't follow the trouble, and don't let trouble follow you."

If wisdom is a dimension of healing, the good news is that many incarcerated teenagers already possess this experiential knowledge.

85

"I Am Enough. This Is Enough"

DURING MY WRITER'S RESIDENCY, Carol, a licensed therapist, graciously offered to facilitate the mindfulness group in my absence. Like me, Carol is White. Unlike me, she has professional training in working with trauma survivors. Knowing the group would be in such capable, compassionate hands was a huge relief. Still, I knew I'd miss the residents, and so we planned that I would make the two-and-a-half-hour trek to visit the group once a month.

On my first trip back, Carol started the group with a two-minute meditation using a mantra. Breathing in, she encouraged us to silently say to ourselves: "I am enough." Breathing out: "This is enough." She explained that this mantra runs counter to pervasive cultural messages that tell us we're not "good enough" and that we can't be happy until _____ (fill in the blank) happens.

That afternoon, just the word "enough" was enough to trigger a lump in my throat. I'd been struggling with self-doubt and depression. Several facets of my life felt impossibly hard. Against this backdrop of anxious sadness and yearning, even two minutes of practicing the counternarrative that both my life and I were *already* "enough" brought temporary relief.

When we'd finished the mantra meditation, Carol invited everyone to share our experience of this practice. Lamar said repeating the mantra felt "calming." Adrian described the practice as "chillin'" (relaxing). I expressed appreciation for the reminder that I'm "enough" because I'm always thinking I have to do more to feel okay or prove my worth. Then Nikan said: "It's hard for me to believe that 'this is enough' . . . because . . . basically, I'm in jail. And how can that be enough?"

"Yes, you're in jail," Carol's replied, "and you're also in a treatment program that's designed to help you develop the skills you need so you don't have to spend the rest of your life in prison. So maybe that's enough for now. Maybe, just for today, that is enough."

As Nikan contemplated Carol's response, I noticed my own internal resistance to it. I knew what she said was true, but this truth felt unsatisfying—ironically, *not enough*. The fact that Nikan was "in jail" in the first place seemed wrong because whatever he did that got him locked up was undoubtedly a desperate effort to deal with suffering caused by a society that had failed him. Moreover, the phrases "enough for now" and "just for today" sounded tentative and incomplete. I wanted more triumphant and permanent solutions: a happy ending, a redemption story, a ten-step salvation plan with a money-back guarantee. I wanted the promise of the world I envisioned at the end of this book's Preface: "a world where no child will be inclined to manage their suffering by passing it onto others."

This world continues to be my North Star. But the youth in the mindfulness group are teaching me that healing is a holy/wholly unpredictable odyssey, not something I get to control, and that this pilgrimage starts in the present, in whatever situation we inhabit *right now*.

Reflecting on her life as a social justice activist, Alice Walker says that the world is both easier and harder to change than we realize, "Because the change begins with each one of us saying to ourselves, and meaning it: I will not harm anyone or anything in this moment."[1] She likens this minute-by-minute spiritual practice to the daunting and courageous commitment a recovering addict must make to relinquish the destructive urges of addiction. Recovery unfolds a minute at a time, which becomes an hour at a time, then a week at a time, then a year at a time, and, with dedicated practice, even longer. This moment-by-moment effort to stop the cycle of harm and start the process of healing ourselves and our society is not only enough. It's all we ever really have.

The moment is ripe for Americans to admit that our addiction to punishment hasn't worked. Like any other harmful habit, an eye-for-an-eye approach to justice exacerbates the hurt we hope to alleviate because it doesn't address the roots of harming behavior: unhealed pain.

Hurting kids are prone to harming others. The more deeply we understand this dynamic, the more inclined we'll be to support the kind of youth justice that prioritizes healing. Our understanding may also prompt us to turn toward, grapple with, and grow through our own unresolved hurt. Once we see—and *feel*—the connection between our own suffering

---

1. A. Walker, *Anything We Love*, 214.

and that of others, something will shift. The walls protecting our hearts will feel less solid—and less necessary. Released from the prison of our own self-preoccupation, we can experience our connection with the divine humanity of others, including the teenagers our society condemns.

Incarcerated or not, we all need liberation. The struggles and pains of people with privilege are both immeasurably different than and inescapably connected to the challenges and suffering of the kids you've met in this book. The sooner we recognize both those differences and connections, the sooner we can work together to create the kind of justice—systemic, compassionate, accountable, and healing—that hurting kids, and all of us, deserve.

Conclusion: "LOVE ME"

IN HER MANIFESTO ON love, the renowned author, activist, and professor bell hooks says, "There can be no love without justice."[1] For hooks, "love" entails nurturing the well-being and growth of self and others, and justice means freedom from oppression. hooks's claim that there is "no love without justice"—rings true to me. Is the reverse equally true? Can there be justice without love?

If this question sounds corny, maybe it's because of how we've been conditioned to think about "love" and "justice." Whereas love is often synonymous with sentimental affection or romantic attraction, justice is associated with punishment for breaking the rules. Given these popular definitions, the suggestion that love might be an integral part of justice sounds not just "soft," but a little weird.

Yet if we embrace the kind of love hooks advocates—a robust commitment to care deeply about and actively support the well-being and growth of self and others—the connection between love and justice makes sense. Because, despite their diversity, every resident who has ever shown up to the mindfulness group has one thing in common: each wears an invisible sign hanging around their neck that says: "LOVE ME."[2] Some kids' signs are harder to see than others'. But if you look carefully, they're always there.

Seeing these invisible signs, it's hard not to conclude that love is integral to the kind of justice incarcerated youth need. What other force is strong enough to enable any of us to be present with pain, to own and answer for our regrettable behavior, to turn toward the suffering we seek to transform in ourselves and in the world? To paraphrase Boyle, just love is

---

1. hooks, *All about Love*, 19, 4.

2. I've adapted the idea of an invisible "LOVE ME" sign from poet Anthony Abbott. Jacqueline Bussie describes Abbott's "LOVE ME" sign theory in the "Foreword" to his poetry collection (xiii).

the only non-delusional response to the hurting kids I've met in the mindfulness group.

Responding to a writing prompt that asked, "What would you like the outside world to know about you and your life?," Angelo wrote:

> I was only eleven years old. Nothing to eat. Nothing to buy clothes or water . . . I do bad stuff to benefit my needs. But deeply inside of me, I still have a heart and caring. But people judge us on what they see.

Bao responded:

> That I might be a bad person but inside I have a good heart that nobody sees. Only the outside they see. That's why people judge fast without knowing what I've been through.

And Lamar said:

> That not all people that go to juvie is bad, and that some of us regret what we did, like me. I regret the choices I made, the friends I was with. Because I know and the people that care about me know that I'm a good person, and loving. I been through a lot from the age of 13 to 16. Now I'm going to change my life around and make my mom and the people that died happy and proud of me. And I'm thankful that they are giving me another chance and I'm thankful for . . . letting me share this with the outsider.

Thank you for reading this book. I wrote it out of a sense of responsibility I feel to better understand the experiences and perspectives of teenagers in confinement, to examine the systems in which they are caught, to explore religion's role in shaping and challenging those systems, and to encourage ways of thinking about justice that promote equity, compassion, accountability, and healing for these kids—and for all of us. I pray that *Hurting Kids* does justice, so to speak, to the dignity, beauty, resilience, wisdom, and creative potential I've witnessed among the youth I visit, even as it illuminates the systemic injustices and traumatic backstories they have survived. I hope the many chapters leave you, the reader, with a better sense of the complicated but no less divine humanity of teenager "offenders." May this understanding motivate each of us to do our part to advocate for the kind of justice these hurting kids need and deserve.

Bibliography

Abram, Karen M., et al. "Suicidal Thoughts and Behaviors among Detained Youth." *Juvenile Justice Bulletin* (July 2014) 1–12. https://ojjdp.ojp.gov/sites/g/files/xyckuh176/files/pubs/243891.pdf.

Abrams, Laura S. "Juvenile Justice at a Crossroads: Science, Evidence, and Twenty-First Century Reform." *Social Service Review* 87 (2013) 725–52.

Alcoff, Linda. "The Problem of Speaking for Others." *Cultural Critique* 20 (1991–92) 5–32.

Alexander, Michelle. *The New Jim Crow: Mass Incarceration in the Age of Colorblindness*. New York: New, 2010.

Allen, Greg. "Parkland Survivors and Victim Family Members Unleash Anger at Shooter." NPR, Nov. 1, 2022. https://www.npr.org/2022/11/01/1133378511/parkland-survivors-and-victim-family-members-unleash-anger-at-the-shooter.

Allen, Summer. "The Science of Gratitude." Templeton, May 2018. https://www.templeton.org/wp-content/uploads/2018/05/GGSC-JTF-White-Paper-Gratitude-FINAL.pdf.

Annie E. Casey Foundation, The. "What Is Diversion in Juvenile Justice?" Annie E. Casey Foundation, Oct. 22, 2020. https://www.aecf.org/blog/what-is-juvenile-diversion.

Armenta, Christina N., et al. "Satisfied Yet Striving: Gratitude Fosters Life Satisfaction and Improvement Motivation in Youth." *Emotion* 22 (2022) 1004–16.

Armstrong, Karen. *Twelve Steps to a Compassionate Life*. New York: Knopf, 2010.

Atiba Goff, Philip. "Changing Behavior, Not Beliefs." Interviewed by Shankur Vedanta. *Hidden Brain*. Podcast audio. June 16, 2020. https://hiddenbrain.org/podcast/changing-behavior-not-beliefs/.

Azab, Marwa. "Gut Bacteria Can Influence Your Mood, Thoughts, and Brain." *Psychology Today*, Aug. 7, 2019. https://www.psychologytoday.com/us/blog/neuroscience-in-everyday-life/201908/gut-bacteria-can-influence-your-mood-thoughts-and-brain.

Baglivio, Michael, et al. "The Prevalence of Adverse Childhood Experiences (ACE) in the Lives of Juvenile Offenders." *Journal of Juvenile Justice* 3 (2014) 1–17.

Banks, Adelle M. "Evangelical Leaders Push for Criminal Justice Reform." *Religion News Service*, June 20, 2017. https://religionnews.com/2017/06/20/evangelical-leaders-push-for-criminal-justice-reform/.

Barna Group. "A Survey of Christian Perceptions on Incarceration & Justice Reform." Prison Fellowship, Oct. 2019. https://www.prisonfellowship.org/wp-content/uploads/2020/01/Prison-Fellowship-Christian-Barna-Polling-Results-2019.pdf.

Barnert, Elizabeth, et al. "Child Incarceration and Long-Term Adult Health Outcomes: A Longitudinal Study." *International Journal of Prisoner Health* 14 (2018) 26–33.

Baumgarten, April. "Slain Moorhead Taxi Driver's Family Says Shooter's Sentence Is Too Short." *Inform*, Nov. 7, 2022. https://www.inforum.com/news/moorhead/moorhead-man-gets-12-1-2-years-for-killing-taxi-driver-for-rent-money.

Baxter, Emily. *We Are All Criminals*. St. Paul, MN: We Are All Criminals, 2017.

Belden, N., and J. Russonello. "Existing Survey Research on American's Attitudes Regarding Juvenile Justice." NCJRS Virtual Library, 1996. NCJRS 166180. https://www.ojp.gov/ncjrs/virtual-library/abstracts/existing-survey-research-americans-attitudes-regarding-juvenile.

Bernstein, Nell. *Burning Down the House: The End of Juvenile Prison*. New York: The New Press, 2014.

Betts, Reginald Dwayne. *A Question of Freedom: A Memoir of Learning, Survival, and Coming of Age in Prison*. New York: Avery, 2010.

Birman, Daniel H., dir. *Murder to Mercy: The Cyntoia Brown Story*. New York: Netflix, 2020.

Blizzard, Robert. "National Poll Results." Public Opinion Strategies, Jan. 25, 2018. https://www.politico.com/f/?id=00000161-2ccc-da2c-a963-efff82be0001.

Blumstein, Alfred, and Joel Wallman, eds. *The Crime Drop in America*. Cambridge Studies in Criminology. Cambridge: Cambridge University Press, 2000.

Bolin, Riane, et al. "Americans' Opinions on Juvenile Justice: Preferred Aims, Beliefs about Juveniles, and Blended Sentencing." *Crime and Delinquency* 67 (Nov. 2019) 1–25.

Bolz-Weber, Nadia. *Shameless: A Case for Not Feeling Bad about Feeling Good*. Colorado Springs: Convergent, 2020.

Borg, Marcus. *The Heart of Christianity: Rediscovering A Life of Faith*. Minneapolis: Fortress, 2003.

———. *Jesus: Uncovering the Life, Teachings, and Relevance of a Religious Revolutionary*. New York: HarperSanFrancisco, 2006.

Boyle, Gregory. "Can You Really Conquer Hatred through Love?" Interviewed by Dan Harris. *Ten Percent Happier*. Podcast audio. Aug. 22, 2022. https://www.tenpercent.com/tph/podcast-episode/father-gregory-boyle-489.

———. *Tattoos on the Heart: The Power of Boundless Compassion*. New York: The Free Press, 2011.

Britannica, The Editors of *Encyclopaedia*. "Seven Deadly Sins." *Britannica*, Jan. 21, 2010; last updated Mar. 28, 2024. https://www.britannica.com/topic/seven-deadly-sins.

———. "Seven Virtues." *Britannica*, Apr. 13, 2023; last updated Oct. 10, 2023. https://www.britannica.com/topic/seven-virtues.

Brock, Rita Nakashima. *Journeys by Heart: A Christology of Erotic Power*. Eugene, OR: Wipf & Stock, 2008.

Brock, Rita Nakashima, and Gabriella Lettini. *Soul Repair: Recovering from Moral Injury after War*. Boston: Beacon, 2012.

Brock, Rita Nakashima, and Rebecca Anne Parker. *Proverbs of Ashes: Violence, Redemptive Suffering, and the Search for What Saves Us*. Boston: Beacon, 2002.

———. *Saving Paradise: How Christianity Traded Love of This World for Crucifixion and Empire*. Boston: Beacon, 2009.
Brown, Brené. *Atlas of the Heart*. New York: Random House, 2021.
———. *Braving the Wilderness: The Quest for True Belonging and the Courage to Stand Alone*. New York: Random House, 2017.
———. "Shame and Accountability." Brené Brown. Podcast audio. July 1, 2020. https://brenebrown.com/podcast/brene-on-shame-and-accountability/.
Brown, Stuart. "Play, Spirit, and Character." Interviewed by Krista Tippett. *On Being*. Podcast audio. June 19, 2014. https://onbeing.org/programs/stuart-brown-play-spirit-and-character/.
Brown, Stuart, and Christopher Vaughan. *Play: How It Shapes the Brain, Opens the Imagination, and Invigorates the Soul*. New York: Avery, 2010.
Burke Harris, Nadine. *The Deepest Well: Healing the Long-Term Effects of Childhood Adversity*. New York: Mariner, 2018.
Busch, Fredric N. "Anger and Depression." *Advances in Psychiatric Treatment* 15 (2009) 271–78.
Bussie, Jacqueline. "Foreword." In *Dark Side of North*, by Anthony S. Abbott, xi–xiv. Winston-Salem, NC: Press 53, 2021.
———. *Love without Limits: Jesus' Radical Vision for Love with No Exceptions*. Minneapolis: Broadleaf, 2022.
Campaign for Youth Justice. "Blended Sentencing." Campaign for Youth Justice, last updated Dec. 10, 2018. http://www.campaignforyouthjustice.org/images/factsheets/Blended_Sentencing_FINAL.pdf.
———. "Key Facts: Youth in the Justice System." Campaign for Youth Justice, last updated Feb. 22, 2018. http://www.campaignforyouthjustice.org/images/factsheets/KeyYouthCrimeFactsFeb222018Revised.pdf.
Chamberlin, Christine. "Not Kids Anymore: A Need for Punishment and Deterrence in the Juvenile Justice System." *Boston College Law Review* 42 (2001) 391–419.
Chödrön, Pema. *Welcoming the Unwelcome: Wholehearted Living in a Brokenhearted World*. Boulder, CO: Shambala, 2019.
Chu, Jane. "Dangerous Minds." *Slate*, Dec. 27, 2022. https://slate.com/technology/2022/12/teen-brains-neuroscience-justice-law-supreme-court.html.
Coates, Ta-Nehisi. *Between the World and Me*. New York: Spiegel and Grau, 2015.
Coleman, Monica A. *Bipolar Faith: A Black Woman's Journey with Depression and Faith*. St. Paul, MN: Broadleaf, 2016.
———. *The Dinah Project: A Handbook for Congregational Response to Sexual Violence*. Repr., Eugene, OR: Wipf and Stock, 2010.
Cone, James H. *Black Theology & Black Power*. Maryknoll, NY: Orbis, 1969.
———. *The Cross and the Lynching Tree*. Maryknoll, NY: Orbis, 2011.
Contreras-Byrd, Melinda. "Black Christians and the Problem of Black Anger." In *Toward a Theology of Holy Black Rage*, edited by Melinda Contreras-Byrd, 9–33. Trenton, NJ: Africa World, 2022.
———. "Introduction." In *Toward a Theology of Holy Black Rage*, edited by Melinda Contreras-Byrd, 1–8. Trenton, NJ: Africa World, 2022.
———, ed. *Toward a Theology of Holy Black Rage*. Trenton, NJ: Africa World, 2022.
Corliss, Julie. "Staying Positive during Difficult Times." Harvard Medical School, Oct. 1, 2020. https://www.health.harvard.edu/blog/staying-positive-during-difficult-times-2020100121047.

Davies, Benjamin R., and Nicholas B. Allen. "Trauma and Homelessness in Youth: Psychopathology and Intervention." *Clinical Psychology Review* 54 (2017) 17–28.

Davis, Fania. *The Little Book of Race and Restorative Justice: Black Lives, Healing, and US Social Transformation*. New York: Good Books, 2019.

Descartes, René. *Discourse on Method*. Translated by Laurence J. Lafleur. Upper Saddle River, NJ: Prentice Hall, 1956.

Desmond, Matthew. *Poverty, by America*. New York: Random House, 2023.

Development Services Group. "Alternatives to Detention and Confinement." OJJDP, last updated Aug. 2014. https://ojjdp.ojp.gov/model-programs-guide/literature-reviews/alternatives_to_detection_and_confinement.pdf.

———. "Arts-Based Programs and Arts Therapies for At-Risk, Justice-Involved, and Traumatized Youths." OJJDP, last updated May 2016. https://ojjdp.ojp.gov/mpg/literature-review/arts-based-programs-for-youth.pdf.

———. "Diversion from Formal Juvenile Court Processing." OJJDP, last updated Feb. 2017. https://ojjdp.ojp.gov/model-programs-guide/literature-reviews/diversion_from_formal_juvenile_court_processing.pdf.

———. "Juvenile Residential Programs." OJJDP, last updated Mar. 2019. https://ojjdp.ojp.gov/model-programs-guide/literature-reviews/juvenile_residential_programs.pdf.

DiAngelo, Robin. *What Does It Mean to Be White: Developing White Racial Literacy*. New York: Peter Lang, 2016.

———. "White Fragility." *International Journal of Critical Pedagogy* 3 (2001) 54–70.

Dorrien, Gary. "Cannon, Williams, and Womanist Survival." *Harvard Divinity Bulletin* (Autumn/Winter 2022) 15–21. https://bulletin.hds.harvard.edu/cannon-williams-and-womanist-survival/.

Dressinger, Baz. *Incarceration Nations: A Journey to Justice in Prisons around the World*. New York: Other Press, 2016.

Drinan, Cara H. *The War on Kids: How American Juvenile Justice Lost Its Way*. New York: Oxford University Press, 2018.

Dubler, Joshua, and Vincent W. Lloyd. *Break Every Yoke: Religion, Justice, and the Abolition of Prisons*. New York: Oxford University Press, 2020.

Dukes, Donna. "Let's Address the Needs of Critically At-Risk Youth." YouTube, Apr. 6, 2016. TEDx Talks. https://www.youtube.com/watch?v=T1_DJh10Mgs.

Dunbar, Paul Laurence. "We Wear the Mask." Poetry Foundation, n.d. https://www.poetryfoundation.org/poems/44203/we-wear-the-mask.

DuVernay, Ava, dir. *13th*. New York: Netflix, 2016.

———. *When They See Us*. New York: Netflix, 2019.

Edwards, Jonathan. "Sinners in the Hands of an Angry God: A Sermon Preached at Enfield, July 8th, 1741." Edited by Reiner Smolinski. *Electronic Texts in American Studies* 54. https://digitalcommons.unl.edu/cgi/viewcontent.cgi?article=1053&context=etas.

Ehrman, Bart. *Heaven and Hell: A History of the Afterlife*. New York: Simon & Schuster, 2021.

Epstein, Rebecca, et al. *Girlhood Interrupted: The Erasure of Black Girls' Childhood*. Center on Poverty and Inequality, June 2020. https://genderjusticeandopportunity.georgetown.edu/wp-content/uploads/2020/06/girlhood-interrupted.pdf.

Bibliography

Equal Justice Initiative. *Lynching in America: Confronting the Legacy of Racial Terror.* EJI, 2017. 3rd ed. https://eji.org/wp-content/uploads/2005/11/lynching-in-america-3d-ed-110121.pdf.

———. "The Superpredator Myth, 25 Years Later." EJI, Apr. 7, 2014. https://eji.org/news/superpredator-myth-20-years-later/.

Fatherree, Dwayne. "Criminal Injustice: States Unfairly Prosecute Children as Adults." Southern Poverty Law Center, Jan. 21, 2022. https://www.splcenter.org/news/2022/01/21/criminal-injustice-states-unfairly-prosecute-children-adults.

Fazal, Shaena M. *Safely Home.* Youth Advocacy Programs. June 2014. https://www.yapinc.org/portals/0/Docs/safelyhome.pdf.

Felsman, Peter. "How Improv Makes You More Confident and Less Anxious." Interview with Keltner, Dacher. *Science of Happiness.* Audio podcast. Aug. 23, 2023. https://www.podcasts-online.org/the-science-of-happiness-1340505607.

Fondacaro, Mark. "The Injustice of Retribution: Toward a Multisystemic Risk Management Model of Juvenile Justice." *Journal of Law & Policy* 20 (2011) 145–65.

Foucault, Michel. *Discipline and Punish: The Birth of the Prison.* Translated by Alan Sheridan. New York: Vintage, 1977.

Fox 9 Staff. "Pope County Deputy Killed." Fox 9, updated Apr. 16, 2023. https://www.fox9.com/news/pope-county-deputy-killed-in-western-minnesota-shooting-deputy-officer-also-hurt.

Frankl, Viktor E. *Man's Search for Meaning: An Introduction to Logotherapy.* New York: Pocket, 1963.

Gebhard, Amanda, et al., eds. *White Benevolence: Racism and Colonial Violence in the Helping Professions.* Black Point, NS: Fernwood, 2022.

Geertz, Clifford. *The Interpretation of Cultures: Selected Essays.* New York: Basic Books, 1973.

Gilliard, Dominique DuBois. *Rethinking Incarceration: Advocating for Justice.* Downers Grove, IL: IVP, 2018.

Ginsburg, Kenneth R., et al. "The Importance of Play in Promoting Healthy Child Development and Maintaining Strong Parent-Child Bonds." *Pediatrics* 119 (2007) 182–91.

Glassman, Bernie. *Bearing Witness: A Zen Master's Lessons in Peace Making.* New York: Bell Tower, 1999.

Glaude, Eddie S., Jr. *Democracy in Black: How Race Still Enslaves the American Soul.* New York: Crown, 2017.

Godsoe, Cynthia. "The Victim/Offender Overlap and Criminal System Reform." *Brooklyn Law Review* 87 (2022) 1318–50.

Graber, Jennifer. *The Furnace of Affliction: Prisons & Religion in Antebellum America.* Chapel Hill: University of North Carolina Press, 2014.

Graham, Billy. "Juvenile Delinquency and It's [sic] Cure." Billy Graham Evangelical Association, Sept. 16, 1954. https://billygraham.org./audio/juvenile-delinquency-and-its-cure/.

Greater Good Science Center at UC Berkeley. "Gratitude." John Templeton Foundation, May 2018. https://www.templeton.org/discoveries/science-of-gratitude.

Griffith, Aaron. *God's Law and Order: The Politics of Punishment in Evangelical America.* Cambridge: Harvard University Press, 2020.

Grossman, Andrew, and Charles Stimson. *Adult Time for Adult Crimes: Life without Parole for Juvenile Killers and Violent Teens.* Heritage Foundation, Aug. 17, 2009.

https://www.heritage.org/crime-and-justice/report/adult-time-adult-crimes-life-without-parole-juvenile-killers-and-violent.

Hadro, Matt. "We Must Speak, Act More on Criminal Justice Reform, Christian Leaders Insist." *Catholic News Agency*, June 21, 2017. https://www.catholicnewsagency.com/news/we-must-speak-act-more-on-criminal-justice-reform-christian-leaders-insist-73633.

Halperin, David M. *Saint Foucault: Towards a Gay Hagiography*. New York: Oxford University Press, 1997.

Hampton, Henry, prod. "The Time Has Come (1964–66)." Episode 7 of *Eyes on the Prize: America's Civil Rights Movement*. Aired Apr. 4, 2021, on PBS. https://www.pbs.org/wgbh/americanexperience/films/eyesontheprize/#cast_and_crew.

Hanh, Thich Nhat. *Living Buddha, Living Christ*. New York: Riverhead, 1995.

———. *Love in Action: Writings on Nonviolent Social Change*. Berkeley: Parallax, 1993.

Harvard Divinity School. "Christianity, Race, and Mass Incarceration." *Harvard News Archive*, Oct. 13, 2017. https://news-archive.hds.harvard.edu/news/2017/10/13/christianity-race-and-mass-incarceration.

Harvard Library. "Scientific Racism." Harvard Library, n.d. https://library.harvard.edu/confronting-anti-black-racism/scientific-racism.

Heller de Leon, Brian. "Study: Long-Term Juvenile Incarceration Fails to Decrease Reoffending Rates." CJCJ, May 3, 2012. http://www.cjcj.org/news/5476.

Henning, Kristen. *Rage of Innocence: How America Criminalizes Black Youth*. New York: Pantheon, 2021.

Hersey, Tricia. *Rest Is Resistance: A Manifesto*. New York: Little, Brown Spark, 2022.

Heschel, Abraham Joshua. *The Insecurity of Freedom: Essays on Human Existence*. New York: Schocken, 1966.

———. "The Reasons for My Involvement in the Peace Movement." *Journal of Social Philosophy* 4 (Jan. 1973) 7–8.

Hill Fletcher, Jeannine. *The Sin of White Supremacy: Christianity, Racism, and Religious Diversity in America*. Maryknoll, NY: Orbis, 2017.

Holman, Barry, and Jason Ziedenberg. *The Dangers of Detention: The Impact of Incarcerating Youth in Detention and Other Secure Facilities*. Justice Policy Institute, Feb. 2022. https://justicepolicy.org/wp-content/uploads/2022/02/06-11_rep_dangersofdetention_jj.pdf.

Holmes, Megan. "Juvenile Records: Misconceptions, Stigma, and Principles of Juvenile Record Protection." Coalition for Juvenile Justice, June 28, 2021. https://www.juvjustice.org/juvenile-records-stigma-misconceptions#.

hooks, bell. *All about Love*. New York: HarperCollins, 2001.

Howell, James, et al. "Young Offenders: What Happens and What Should Happen." National Institute of Justice, Feb. 2014. NCJ 242653. OJJDP Justice Research Series. https://nij.ojp.gov/library/publications/young-offenders-what-happens-and-what-should-happen.

Hull, John. *The Tactile Heart: Blindness and Faith*. London: SMC, 2013.

Human Rights Watch. "Children behind Bars: The Global Overuse of Detention of Children." Human Rights Watch, 2016. https://www.hrw.org/world-report/2016/country-chapters/africa-americas-asia-europe/central-asia-middle-east/north#a1dbdc.

Jackson, Regina, and Saira Rao. *White Women: Everything You Already Know about Your Own Racism and How to Do Better*. New York: Penguin, 2022.

Jakobsen, Janet R., and Anne Pellegrini. *Love the Sin: Religious Regulation and the Limits of Religious Tolerance*. Boston: Beacon, 2004.

Joseph, Frederick. *Patriarchy Blues: Reflections on Manhood*. New York: Harper Perennial, 2022.

Jouet, Mugambi. "Foucault, Prison, and Human Rights: A Dialectic of Theory and Criminal Justice Reform." *Theoretical Criminology* 26 (2022) 202–23.

Justice Policy Institute. *Sticker Shock 2020: The Cost of Youth Incarceration*. Justice Policy Institute, 2020. https://justicepolicy.org/wp-content/uploads/2022/02/Sticker_Shock_2020.pdf.

Juvenile Law Center. "Juvenile Life without Parole (JLWOP)." Juvenile Law Center, n.d. https://jlc.org/issues/juvenile-life-without-parole

Kaba, Mariame. *We Do This 'til We Free Us: Abolitionist Organizing and Transforming Justice*. Edited by Tamara K. Nopper. Abolitionist Papers. Chicago: Haymarket, 2021.

Kaplan, Tatyana, et al. "Individual Differences Relate to Juvenile Offender Stereotypes." *Applied Psychology in Criminal Justice* 13 (2017) 125–41.

Kelly, Erin I. *The Limits of Blame: Rethinking Punishment and Responsibility*. Cambridge: Harvard University Press, 2018.

Kendi, Ibram X. "How to Be an Antiracist." Aspen Ideas, 2019. https://www.aspenideas.org/sessions/how-to-be-an-antiracist.

———. *How to Be an Antiracist*. New York: One World, 2019.

———. *Stamped from the Beginning: The Definitive History of Racist Ideas in America*. New York: Bold Type, 2017.

Kimmerer, Robin Wall. *Braiding Sweetgrass: Indigenous Wisdom, Scientific Knowledge and the Teachings of the Plants*. Minneapolis: Milkweed, 2015.

King, Martin Luther, Jr. "Letter from a Birmingham Jail." African Studies Center—University of Pennsylvania, Apr. 16, 1963. https://www.africa.upenn.edu/Articles_Gen/Letter_Birmingham.html.

———. *Strength to Love*. Philadelphia: Fortress, 1963.

King, Ruth. *Mindful of Race: Healing Racism from the Inside Out*. Boulder, CO: Sounds True, 2018.

Knowles, Alissa, et al. "Risky Sexual Behavior among Arrested Adolescent Males: The Role of Future Expectations and Impulse Control." *Journal of Research on Adolescence* 30 (2019) 562–79.

Kornfield, Jack. "A Life of Greatness with Sarah Grynberg." *Heart Wisdom*. Podcast audio. Apr. 6, 2023. https://jackkornfield.com/heart-wisdom-ep-182-a-life-of-greatness-with-sarah-grynberg/.

Kraut, Michael E. "Community Based Alternatives." Child Crime Prevention & Safety Center, n.d. https://childsafety.losangelescriminallawyer.pro/community-based-alternatives.html.

Lahey, Jessica. "The Steep Costs of Keeping Juveniles in Adult Prisons." *Atlantic*, Jan. 8, 2016. https://www.theatlantic.com/education/archive/2016/01/the-cost-of-keeping-juveniles-in-adult-prisons/423201/.

Lakshmin, Pooja. *Real Self-Care: A Transformative Program for Redefining Wellness (Crystals, Cleanses, and Bubble Baths Not Included)*. New York: Penguin, 2023.

Lelwica, Michelle Mary. "The Power of Proximity: Embodying Anti-Racist Learning." *Liberal Education* 108 (2022) 34–41.

———. *Shameful Bodies: Religion and the Culture of Physical Improvement.* New York: Bloomsbury, 2017.

León, Concepción de. "Jason Reynolds Is on a Mission." *New York Times*, Oct. 28, 2019. https://www.nytimes.com/2019/10/28/books/jason-reynolds-look-both-ways.html.

Leonard, Nora. "Racial and Ethnic Disparities in the Youth Justice System." Coalition for Juvenile Justice, Mar. 2, 2023. https://www.juvjustice.org/blog/1436.

Linskey, Annie, and Marianna Sotomayor. "Worries over crime haunt democrats ahead of the midterm elections." *Washington Post*, June 8, 2022. https://www.washingtonpost.com/politics/2022/06/08/crime-midterms-democrats/.

Lipscomb, Ashley Y. "Abolitionist Theology Can Help Us Reimagine Schooling." *Harvard Divinity Bulletin* 22 (2022) 6–11. https://bulletin.hds.harvard.edu/abolitionist-theology-can-help-us-reimagine-schooling/.

Listenbee, Robert L., Jr., et al. *Report of the Attorney General's National Task Force on Children Exposed to Violence.* Office of the Juvenile Justice and Delinquency Prevention, Dec. 12, 2012. https://www.justice.gov/defendingchildhood/cev-rpt-full.pdf.

Lomax, Louis E. "A Summing Up: Louis Lomax Interviews Malcolm X." Teaching American History, 1963. https://teachingamericanhistory.org/document/a-summing-up-louis-lomax-interviews-malcolm-x/.

Males, Mike. "Age, Poverty, Homicide, and Gun Homicide: Is Young Age or Poverty Level the Key Issue?" *SAGE Open*, Mar. 5, 2015. https://journals.sagepub.com/doi/full/10.1177/2158244015573359.

Marx, Karl. "Critique of Hegel's *Philosophy of Right*." In *The Marx and Engels Reader*, edited by Robert Tucker, 53–65. 2nd ed. New York: Norton & Co., 1978.

McBride, Hillary L. *The Wisdom of Your Body: Finding Healing, Wholeness, and Connection through Embodied Living.* Grand Rapids: Brazos, 2021.

McCarthy, Patrick, et al. "The Future of Youth Justice: A Community-Based Alternative to the Youth Prison Model." *New Thinking in Community Corrections* 2 (2016) 1–36. https://www.ojp.gov/pdffiles1/nij/250142.pdf.

McDaniels, Johnnie. "Why Changing Juvenile Corrections Is Critical to American Criminal Justice." YouTube, Mar. 7, 2019. From PBS *NewsHour*. https://www.youtube.com/watch?v=IRKPLzrJvNE.

Meade, Sheena. "How 'Second Chance' Laws Could Transform the U.S. Justice System." TED, Apr. 2023. https://www.ted.com/talks/sheena_meade_how_second_chance_laws_could_transform_the_us_justice_system/c?language=en.

Medina, John. *Brain Rules: 12 Principles for Surviving and Thriving at Work, Home, and School.* Seattle: Pear, 2008.

Menakem, Resmaa. *My Grandmother's Hands: Racialized Trauma and the Pathway to Mending our Hearts and Bodies.* Las Vegas: Central Recovery, 2017.

Mendel, Richard. *No Place for Kids: The Case for Reducing Juvenile Incarceration.* Annie E. Casey Foundation, 2011. https://assets.aecf.org/m/resourcedoc/aecf-NoPlaceForKidsFullReport-2011.pdf.

———. "Protect and Redirect: America's Growing Movement to Divert Youth Out of the Justice System." Sentencing Project, Mar. 20, 2024. https://www.sentencingproject.org/publications/protect-and-redirect-americas-growing-movement-to-divert-youth-out-of-the-justice-system/.

---. *Why Youth Incarceration Fails: An Updated Review of the Evidence.* Sentencing Project, Dec. 2022. https://www.sentencingproject.org/app/uploads/2023/03/Why-Youth-Incarceration-Fails.pdf.

Messina-Dysert, Gina. *Rape Culture and Spiritual Violence: Religion, Testimony, and Visions of Healing.* Religion and Violence. New York: Routledge, 2014.

Miller, Kerri. "Talking Volumes: A Conversation with Reginald Dwayne Betts." Minnesota Public Radio, Mar. 12, 2021. https://www.mprnews.org/episode/2021/03/12/talking-volumes-a-conversation-with-reginald-dwayne-betts.

Mineo, Liz. "Good Genes Are Nice, but Joy Is Better." *Harvard Gazette*, Apr. 11, 2017. https://news.harvard.edu/gazette/story/2017/04/over-nearly-80-years-harvard-study-has-been-showing-how-to-live-a-healthy-and-happy-life/.

Minton, Todd D., et al. "Correctional Populations in the United States, 2019—Statistical Tables." Bureau of Justice Statistics, July 2021. https://bjs.ojp.gov/library/publications/correctional-populations-united-states-2019-statistical-tables.

Mok, Pearl L. H., et al. "Family Income Inequalities and Trajectories through Childhood and Self-Harm and Violence in Young Adults: A Population-Based, Nested Case-Control Study." *Lancet* 3 (2018) 498–507.

Morris, Monique W. *Pushout: The Criminalization of Black Girls in Schools.* New York: The New Press, 2018.

---. "Why Black Girls Are Targeted for Punishment at School—and How to Change That." TED, Nov. 2018. https://www.ted.com/talks/monique_w_morris_why_black_girls_are_targeted_for_punishment_at_school_and_how_to_change_that.

Murphy, Caryle. "Most Americans Believe in Heaven . . . and Hell." Pew Research Center, Nov. 10, 2015. https://www.pewresearch.org/fact-tank/2015/11/10/most-americans-believe-in-heaven-and-hell/.

NAACP. "Criminal Justice Fact Sheet." NAACP, 2021. https://naacp.org/resources/criminal-justice-fact-sheet.

---. "The Origins of Modern Day Policing." NAACP, n.d. https://naacp.org/find-resources/history-explained/origins-modern-day-policing.

National Center for Child Traumatic Stress Network. *Complex Trauma: In Juvenile Justice System-Involved Youth.* National Center for Child Traumatic Stress Network, Mar. 2017. https://www.nctsn.org/sites/default/files/resources//complex_trauma_in_juvenile_justice_system_involved_youth.pdf.

National Center for Injury Prevention and Control, Division of Violence Prevention. "About the CDC-Kaiser ACE Study." CDC, last reviewed Apr. 6, 2021. https://www.cdc.gov/violenceprevention/aces/about.html.

National Coalition against Domestic Violence. "Statistics." NCADV, n.d. https://ncadv.org/STATISTICS.

National Conference of State Legislatures. "Admissions and Access for Incarcerated Individuals." NCSL, Jan. 2023. https://documents.ncsl.org/wwwncsl/Education/Admissions-and-Access.pdf.

National Institute for Mental Health. "The Teen Brain: 7 Things to Know." NIMH, revised 2023. NIH Publication 23-MH-8078. https://www.nimh.nih.gov/health/publications/the-teen-brain-7-things-to-know.

National Juvenile Justice Network. "Keep Youth at Home." National Juvenile Justice Network, 2012. From Youth Transition Funders Group, *Juvenile Justice Reform:*

A Blueprint. https://www.njjn.org/about-us/create-a-range-of-community-based-programs.

———. "Polling on Public Attitudes: Treatment of Youth in Trouble with the Law." NJJN, Oct. 2016. https://www.njjn.org/uploads/njjn-publications/Polling-Oct2016.pdf?phpMyAdmin=14730ab3483c51c94ca868bccffa06ef.

———. "Raising the Minimum Age for Prosecuting Children." NJJN, Oct. 2022; partially updated Feb. 2024. https://www.njjn.org/our-work/raising-the-minimum-age-for-prosecuting-children.

National Research Council. *The Growth of Incarceration in the United States: Exploring Causes and Consequences.* Washington, DC: National Academies Press, 2014.

Neff, Kristin. *Fierce Self-Compassion: How Women Can Harness Kindness to Speak Up, Claim Their Power, and Thrive.* New York: Harper Wave, 2021.

———. *Self-Compassion: The Proven Power of Being Kind to Yourself.* New York: Morrow, 2011.

Nijhof, Sanne L., et al. "Healthy Play, Better Coping: The Importance of Play for the Development of Children in Health and Disease." *Neuroscience & Biobehavioral Reviews* 95 (2018) 421–29.

Nortey, Justin, et al. "Few Americans Blame God or Say Faith Has Been Shaken amid Pandemic, Other Tragedies." Pew Research Center, Nov. 23, 2021. https://www.pewresearch.org/wp-content/uploads/sites/20/2021/11/PF_23.11.21_problem_of_evil.pdf.

Office of Juvenile Justice and Delinquency Prevention. "Research Central: Measuring What Works in Juvenile Reentry." *OJJDP News @ a Glance* (Nov./Dec. 2020). https://ojjdp.ojp.gov/newsletter/ojjdp-news-glance-novemberdecember-2020/research-central-measuring-what-works-juvenile-reentry.

Orendain, Natalia, et al. "Juvenile Confinement Exacerbates Adversity Burden: A Neurobiological Impetus for Decarceration." *Frontiers in Neuroscience* 30 (2022) 1–9. DOI: 10.3389/fnins.2022.1004335.

Pennebaker, James W. *Writing to Heal: A Guided Journal for Recovering from Trauma and Emotional Upheaval.* Wheat Bridge, CO: Center for Journal Therapy, 2004.

Peterson, Bruce. "'The Judge'—Points to Heart—'Is in Here Now.'" *Star Tribune*, Apr. 6, 2023. https://www.startribune.com/the-judge-points-to-heart-is-in-here-now/600265169/?refresh=true.

Pew Charitable Trusts. *Public Opinion on Juvenile Justice in America.* Pew Charitable Trusts, Nov. 2014. https://www.pewtrusts.org/-/media/assets/2015/08/pspp_juvenile_poll_web.pdf.

Pew Research Center. "Global Survey of Evangelical Protestant Leaders." Pew Research Center, June 22, 2011. https://www.pewresearch.org/religion/2011/06/22/global-survey-beliefs/.

———. "In Their Own Words, How Americans Explain Why Bad Things Happen." Pew Research Center, Nov. 19, 2021. https://www.pewresearch.org/interactives/in-their-own-words-how-americans-explain-why-bad-things-happen/.

———. "Most Americans Favor the Death Penalty despite Concerns about Its Administration." Pew Research Center, June 2, 2021. https://www.pewresearch.org/politics/2021/06/02/most-americans-favor-the-death-penalty-despite-concerns-about-its-administration/.

———. "When Americans Say They Believe in God, What Do They Mean?" Pew Research Center, Apr. 25, 2018. https://www.pewresearch.org/religion/2018/04/25/when-americans-say-they-believe-in-god-what-do-they-mean/.

Pickett, Robert S. *House of Refuge: Origins of Juvenile Reform in New York State, 1815–1857*. Syracuse: Syracuse University Press, 1969.

Pilnik, L., and M. Mistrett. *If Not the Adult System, Then Where? Alternatives to Adult Incarceration for Youth Certified as Adults*. Campaign for Youth Justice, 2019. http://www.campaignforyouthjustice.org/images/ALT_INCARCERATION__FINAL.pdf.

Pogin, Kathryn. "Conceptualizing the Atonement." In *Voices from the Edge: Centering Marginalized Perspectives in Analytic Theology*, edited by Michelle Panchuk and Michael Rea, 166–84. Oxford Studies in Analytic Theology. New York: Oxford University Press, 2020.

Porges, Stephen. "The Neuroscience & Power of Safe Relationships." Interviewed by Jayson Gaddis. *Relationship School*. Podcast audio. Jan. 3, 2023. https://podcasts.apple.com/us/podcast/relationship-school-podcast/id997215878?i=1000592067194.

Price, Michelle L., and Jesse Bedayn. "GOP Steps Up Crime Message in Midterm's Final Stretch." *AP News*, Oct. 7, 2022. https://apnews.com/article/2022-midterm-elections-gun-violence-new-york-race-and-ethnicity-campaigns-dfba652ac7409c64311efcd7c908ed08.

Puzzanchera, Charles, et al. *Youth and the Juvenile Justice System: 2022 National Report*. OJJDP, Dec. 1, 2022. NCJ 305721. https://ojjdp.ojp.gov/library/publications/youth-and-juvenile-justice-system-2022-national-report.

Raine, Adrian, et al. "Omega-3 Supplementation in Young Offenders: A Randomized, Stratified, Double-Blind, Placebo-Controlled, Parallel-Group Trial." *Journal of Experimental Criminology* 16 (2020) 389–405. DOI: 10.1007/s11292-019-09394-x.

Rapanut, Kimberly, et al. "Patchwork Education System in Juvenile Centers Often Falls Short." *News 21*, Aug. 21, 2020. https://kidsimprisoned.news21.com/education-juvenile-detention/.

Reséndez, Grecia, and Maureen Washburn. "Crisis before Closure: Dangerous Conditions Define the Final Months of California's Division of Juvenile Justice. Center on Juvenile and Criminal Justice, Feb. 23, 2023. https://www.cjcj.org/reports-publications/report/crisis-before-closure-dangerous-conditions-define-the-final-months-of-californias-division-of-juvenile-justice.

Reynolds, Jason. "Fortifying Imagination." Interviewed by Krista Tippett. *On Being*. Podcast audio. June 25, 2020; last updated July 1, 2021. https://onbeing.org/programs/jason-reynolds-fortifying-imagination/.

Rips, Eve. "A Fresh Start: The Evolving Use of Juvenile Records in College Admissions." *University of Michigan Journal of Law Reform* 54 (2020) 217–82.

Robert, Nikia S. "Penitence, Plantation and the Penitentiary: A Liberation for Lockdown America." *Graduate Journal of Harvard Divinity School* 12 (2017) 41–69.

Rohr, Richard. *A Spring within Us: A Book of Daily Meditations*. Sheridan, WY: CAC, 2016.

Rossing, Barbara R. *The Rapture Exposed: The Message of Hope in the Book of Revelation*. New York: Basic Books, 2005.

Rovner, Joshua. "Youth Justice by the Numbers." Sentencing Project, May 16, 2023. https://www.sentencingproject.org/policy-brief/youth-justice-by-the-numbers/.

Ruether, Rosemary Radford. *Women and Redemption: A Theological History*. Minneapolis: Fortress, 1998.

Rumi, Jalal al-Din. *The Essential Rumi*. Translated by Coleman Barks. New York: HarperOne, 2004.

Ruttenberg, Dayna. *On Repentance and Repair: Making Amends in an Unapologetic World*. Boston: Beacon, 2022.

Saada Saar, Malika, et al. *The Sexual Abuse to Prison Pipeline: The Girls' Story*. Center on Poverty and Inequality, June 2020. https://genderjusticeandopportunity.georgetown.edu/wp-content/uploads/2020/06/The-Sexual-Abuse-To-Prison-Pipeline-The-Girls'-Story.pdf.

Sahu, Anamika, et al. "Depression Is More Than Just Sadness: A Case of Excessive Anger and Its Management in Depression." *Indian Journal of Psychological Medicine* 36 (2014) 77–79.

Sawyer, Wendy. "Youth Confinement: The Whole Pie 2019." Prison Policy Initiative, Dec. 19, 2019. https://www.prisonpolicy.org/reports/youth2019.html.

Sawyer, Wendy, and Peter Wagner. "Mass Incarceration: The Whole Pie 2023." Prison Policy Initiative, Mar. 14, 2023. https://www.prisonpolicy.org/reports/pie2023.html#smallerslices.

Saxon, Shani. "U.S. Has World's Highest Child Incarceration Rates." *Colorlines*, Nov. 19, 2019. https://www.colorlines.com/articles/us-has-worlds-highest-child-incarceration-rates.

Scott-Clayton, Judith. "Thinking 'beyond the Box': The Use of Criminal Records in College Admissions." Brookings Institution, Sept. 28, 2017. https://www.brookings.edu/research/thinking-beyond-the-box-the-use-of-criminal-records-in-college-admissions/#footnote-8.

Sered, Danielle. *Until We Reckon: Violence, Mass Incarceration, and the Road to Repair*. New York: The New Press, 2021.

Serres, Chris, and Liz Sawyer. "Minnesota Lawmakers OK 'Transformative' Juvenile Justice Package." *Star Tribune*, May 15, 2023. https://www.startribune.com/minnesota-colorado-juvenile-justice-crime-youth-restorative-probation-legislature-prison-justice/600275115/.

Shay, Jonathan. "Moral Injury." *Psychoanalytic Psychology* 31 (2014) 182–91.

Sherman, Francine T., and Annie Balck. *Gender Injustice: System-Level Juvenile Justice Reforms for Girls*. Portland, OR: National Crittenton Foundation, 2015. https://njjn.org/uploads/digital-library/Gender_Injustice_Report_Sept-2015.pdf.

Shotwell, Alexis. *Against Purity: Living Ethically in Compromised Times*. Minneapolis: University of Minnesota Press, 2016.

Smith, Ali, et al. *Let Your Light Shine: How Mindfulness Can Empower Children and Rebuild Communities*. New York: Penguin Audio, 2022.

Snyder, T. Richard. *The Protestant Ethic and the Spirit of Punishment*. Grand Rapids: Eerdmans, 2000.

Solzhenitsyn, Alexander. *The Gulag Archipelago, Part 1*. New York: Collins, 1974.

Spelman, William. "The Limited Importance of Prison Expansion." In *The Crime Drop in America*, edited by Alfred Blumstein and Joel Wallman, 97–129. Cambridge Studies in Criminology. Cambridge: Cambridge University Press, 2000.

Stanford Medicine. "Understanding the Teen Brain." Stanford Medicine, n.d. https://www.stanfordchildrens.org/en/topic/default?id=understanding-the-teen-brain-1-3051.

Steindl-Rast, David. *Essential Writings*. Edited by Clare Hallward. Modern Spiritual Masters. Maryknoll, NY: Orbis, 2010.

Stevenson, Bryan. "Finding the Courage for What's Redemptive." Interviewed by Krista Tippett. *On Being*. Podcast audio. Dec. 3, 2020; last updated Nov. 4, 2021. https://onbeing.org/programs/bryan-stevenson-finding-the-courage-for-whats-redemptive/.

———. *Just Mercy: A Story of Justice and Redemption*. New York: One World, 2015.

Stuart-Smith, Sue. *The Well-Gardened Mind: The Restorative Power of Nature*. New York: Scribner, 2020.

Sullivan, Becky. "Kyle Rittenhouse Is Acquitted of All Charges in the Trial over Killing 2 in Kenosha." NPR, updated Nov. 19, 2021. https://www.npr.org/2021/11/19/1057288807/kyle-rittenhouse-acquitted-all-charges-verdict.

Teigen, Anne. "Juvenile Age of Jurisdiction and Transfer to Adult Court Laws." NCSL, updated Apr. 8, 2021. https://www.ncsl.org/civil-and-criminal-justice/juvenile-age-of-jurisdiction-and-transfer-to-adult-court-laws.

Teske, Steven C. "A Study of Zero Tolerance Policies in Schools: A Multi-Integrated Systems Approach to Improve Outcomes for Adolescents." *Journal of Child and Adolescent Psychiatric Nursing* 24 (2011) 88–97.

Titova, Milla, and Kennon Sheldon. "Happiness Comes from Trying to Make Others Feel Good, Rather than Oneself." *Journal of Positive Psychology* 17 (2021) 1–15.

Treleavan, David A. *Trauma-Sensitive Mindfulness: Practices for Safe and Transformative Healing*. New York: Norton & Company, 2018.

Troutman, Brooke. "A More Just System of Juvenile Justice: Creating a New Standard of Accountability for Juveniles in Illinois." *Journal of Criminal Law & Criminology* 108 (2018) 197–221.

Turner, K. B., et al. "Ignoring the Past: Coverage of Slavery and Slave Patrols in Criminal Justice Texts." *Journal of Criminal Justice Education* 17 (2006) 181–95. DOI: 10.1080/10511250500335627.

Van der Kolk, Bessel. *The Body Keeps the Score: Brain, Mind, and Body in the Healing of Trauma*. New York: Penguin, 2014.

Van der Weij, Rebecca. "Play Is the Natural Expression of Learning, Growing, and Healing." Trauma Research Foundation, Aug. 22, 2022. https://traumaresearchfoundation.org/play-is-the-natural-expression-of-learning-growing-and-healing/.

Virginia Sexual and Domestic Violence Action Alliance. "Punishment Is Not Accountability." VSDV Alliance, Nov. 15, 2020. https://vsdvalliance.org/press_release/punishment-is-not-accountability/.

Wagner, Peter, and Wanda Bertram. "What Percent of the U.S. Is Incarcerated?" Prison Policy Initiative, Jan. 16, 2020. https://www.prisonpolicy.org/blog/2020/01/16/percent-incarcerated/.

Walker, Alice. *Anything We Love Can Be Saved: A Writer's Activism*. New York: Ballantine, 1998.

Walker, Taylor. "New Poll Shows Most Americans Believe Goal of Criminal Justice Systems Should Be Rehabilitation, Not Punishment." *WitnessLA*, Jan. 26, 2018. https://witnessla.com/new-poll-shows-most-americans-believe-goal-of-criminal-justice-system-should-be-rehabilitation-not-punishment/.

Wallace, Jeff. "An Insider's Plan for Rehabilitating the Juvenile Justice System." YouTube, Jan. 7, 2016. https://www.youtube.com/watch?v=TOxpjjzP6lM.

Weaver, Vesla. "Frontlash: Race and the Development of Punitive Crime Policy." *Studies in American Political Development* 21 (2007) 230–65.

Whitaker, Amir, et al. *Cops and No Counselors: How the Lack of School Mental Health Staff Is Harming Students*. ACLU, Mar. 4, 2019. https://www.aclu.org/report/cops-and-no-counselors.

White House, The. "Fact Sheet: Department of Justice Review of Solitary Confinement." Obama White House, Jan. 25, 2016. https://obamawhitehouse.archives.gov/the-press-office/2016/01/25/fact-sheet-department-justice-review-solitary-confinement?utm_source=youth.gov&utm_medium=federal-links&utm_campaign=reports-and-resources.

Whyte, David. *Consolations: The Solace, Nourishment, and Underlying Meaning of Everyday Words*. Langley, WA: Many Rivers, 2015.

Wright, Jeremiah A. "The Time for Pious Words Is Over." In *Toward a Theology of Holy Black Rage*, edited by Melinda Contreras-Byrd, 55–66. Trenton, NJ: Africa World, 2022.

Yehuda, Rachel. "How Trauma and Resilience Cross Generations." Interviewed by Krista Tippett. *On Being*. Podcast audio. July 30, 2014; last updated Nov. 9, 2017. https://onbeing.org/programs/rachel-yehuda-how-trauma-and-resilience-cross-generations-nov2017/.

Yoder, Klaus C. "Prison Theology." *Harvard Divinity Bulletin* (Autumn/Winter 2022) 70–76.

Zehr, Howard. *The Little Book of Restorative Justice*. Rev. ed. New York: Good Books, 2015.

www.ingramcontent.com/pod-product-compliance
Lightning Source LLC
Chambersburg PA
CBHW022028240426
43667CB00042B/1314